Fifty Years of Indian Archaeology

(1960-2010)

Journey of a Foot Soldier

Fifty Years of Indian Archaeology

(1960-2010)

Journey of a Foot Soldier

Dilip K. Chakrabarti

Aryan Books International
New Delhi

FIFTY YEARS OF INDIAN ARCHAEOLOGY (1960-2010)
Journey of a Foot Soldier

ISBN: 978-81-7305-429-7

Published in **2012** by
ARYAN BOOKS INTERNATIONAL
Pooja Apartments, 4B, Ansari Road, New Delhi-110 002 (India)
Tel.: 23287589, 23255799; Fax: 91-11-23270385
E-mail: aryanbooks@gmail.com
www.aryanbooks.co.in

Printed in India at Mudrak, Delhi-110091

For

Siv-ji (Abhigyan), my grandson, and his parents — Nayana (Sonai), my daughter and only child, and Arindam, my son-in-law

Preface

This book is a professional chronicle of a student of Indian archaeology for the last fifty years. It was in 1960 that archaeology was introduced as an MA subject in a handful of Indian universities.

In this professional chronicle of mine, I offer the history of the subject for this period with my own experience and work as its main point of reference. I do so in the hope that that this will throw light on the personal histories of Indian archaeology when Indian archaeologists eventually get interested in them. At present, this interest is marginal. Apart from H.D. Sankalia's *Born for Archaeology—An Autobiography* (1978), S.R. Rao's *Reminiscences of an Archaeologist* (2008), and B.B. Lal's *Piecing Together: Memoirs of an Archaeologist* (2011), there has been no personal history of Indian archaeology.

There is very little outside my professional life here. The impermanence of all things personal is graphically expressed in the form of a couplet by my friend Kailas Nath Dikshit, a former Joint Director General of the Archaeological Survey of India and currently the Secretary of the Indian Archaeological

Society: *Gujre samay ki kahaniyan apne aap hi dafan ho jati hai, Hum hum na rahe wo wo na rahe* ('the stories of the bygone times get buried on their own. We did not remain what we were and neither did they').

Contents

By the Same Author

AUTHORED BOOKS

1. *The Antiquities of Kangra* (with S.J. Hasan): Delhi 1984: Munshiram Manoharlal
2. *A History of Indian Archaeology from the Beginning to 1947*. Delhi 1988: Munshiram Manoharlal
3. *Theoretical Issues in Indian Archaeology*. Delhi 1988: Munshiram Manoharlal
4. *The External Trade of the Indus Civilization*. Delhi 1990: Munshiram Manoharlal
5. *Ancient Bangladesh, a Study of the Archaeological Sources*. Delhi 1992: OUP
6. *The Early Use of Iron in India*. Delhi 1992: OUP
7. *Archaeology of Eastern India: Chhotanagpur Plateau and West Bengal*. Delhi 1993: Munshiram Manoharlal
8. *The Archaeology of Ancient Indian Cities*. Delhi 1995: OUP
9. *Copper and Its Alloys in Ancient India* (with Nayanjot Lahiri). Delhi 1996: Munshiram Manoharlal

10. *Colonial Indology: Sociopolitics of the Ancient Indian Past*. Delhi 1997: Munshiram Manoharlal
11. *The Issues in East Indian Archaeology*. Delhi 1998: Munshiram Manoharlal
12. *Bharatvarsher Pragitihas* (in Bengali). Kolkata 1999: Ananda Publishers
13. *India—An Archaeological History*. Delhi 1999: OUP
14. *Archaeological Geography of the Ganga Plain: The Lower and the Middle Ganga*. Delhi 2001: Permanent Black
15. *Archaeology in the Third World: A History of Indian Archaeology since 1947*. Delhi 2003: Munshiram Manoharlal
16. *The Archaeology of European Expansion in India, Gujarat, c. 16th-18th Centuries*. Delhi 2003: Aryan Books
17. *The Archaeology of the Deccan Routes, the Routes which Linked the Ganga Plain with the Deccan*: Delhi 2005: Munshiram Manoharlal
18. *The Oxford Companion to Indian Archaeology*. Delhi 2006: OUP
19. *Archaeological Geography of the Ganga Plain: Upper Ganga (Oudh, Rohilkhand and the Doab)*. Delhi 2007: Munshiram Manoharlal
20. *The Battle for Ancient India: An Essay in the Socio-Politics of Indian Archaeology*. Delhi 2008: Aryan Books
21. *Globalization and Indian Archaeology, and Other Essays*. Banaras 2009: Banaras Hindu University
22. *The Problem of the Sarasvati River and Notes on the Archaeological Geography of Haryana and Indian Panjab* (with Sukhdev Saini). Delhi 2009: Aryan Books
23. *The Ancient Routes of the Deccan and the Southern Peninsula*. Delhi 2010: Aryan Books
24. *The Geopolitical Orbits of Ancient India, the Geographical Frames of the Ancient Indian Dynasties*. Delhi 2010: OUP

25. Royal Messages by the Wayside: Historical Geography of the Asokan Edicts. Delhi, 2011: Aryan Books

EDITED BOOKS

1. *Essays in Indian Protohistory* (coeditor D.P. Agrawal). Delhi 1979: B.R. Publishing
2. *A Source-Book of Indian Archaeology* (co-editor F.R. Allchin), 3 volumes (Delhi 1979, 1997, 2003): Munshiram Manoharlal
3. *Indus Civilization Sites in India: New Discoveries*. Mumbai 2004: Marg Publications

1

The Background, 1941-62

THE FIRST ELEVEN YEARS

Although I left Halichhera Tea Estate of the Moulavibazar sub-division of the British Indian district of Sylhet in 1952 at the age of eleven and have not been back there except for a few hours in 1990, its outlines are still fresh in my memory—two clusters of workers' and others' houses, some open space for the garden office and 'factory', and patches of forest in an otherwise uninterrupted spread of tea-bushes shaded by trees. A Public Works Department road surfaced with small rounded pebbles linked the nearest railway station, Kulaura, with the sub-divisional headquarter of Moulavibazar and had tea-gardens on either side—Lungla, the first one on the Kulaura side, Halichhera where I was born, Luyauni, where I spent some early years, and Sunatala. The whole area was dotted with such gardens. In the British Indian tea-garden literature, they fell under the category of "Surma valley gardens", although the Surma flowed through the Sylhet town, more than an hour's ride away by train. Some of these gardens were managed by British managers but many of them were small Bengali-owned establishments. The two adjacent gardens of Halichhera and Luyauni were owned by two brothers who were related to us. Their ancestral village, which is also my ancestral village, was Baribari in the Kishoreganj sub-division of the undivided district of Mymensingh. These two brothers made enough money as "weaving masters" of a cotton mill at Rajnandgaon in the bordering area of Chhattisgarh and the easternmost part of Maharashtra to purchase two tea-gardens in lower Assam and bring in some of their relatives, of which my father was one, as garden employees. My father, a surveyor by training, used to work in the coal mines of Parasia in the Chhindwara district of Madhya Pradesh before being inducted to the tea-gardens sometime in the 1930s.

I visited my ancestral village Baribari for the first time in 1990. Lying at the foot of the Garo hills in Meghalaya or the Shillong plateau, this area forms a kind of bowl which stores monsoonal water for about 3 to 4 months in a year before this water passes on to the course of the Meghna river. All the villages of the area become islands during these months, with only boats of different shapes and sizes as their sole means of communication. The natural shape of the land can be seen only when the flood water moves away. A river called the 'Dhanu' flows on one side of our village, and from what I have heard of this river from my grandmother, I can make out that this is very much like the river Titash described in Advaita Mallavarman's celebrated Bengali novel, *Titash Ekti Nadir Nam* ("Titash is the name of a river"). The Titash belongs to the Brahmanbaria area which straddles the upper reaches of the Meghna. The bond between such rivers and the life of the people—men, women and children—living on their banks is very close and in fact, all-encompassing. In my grandmother's time, the Dhanu had, among other things, crocodiles which occasionally chased village ladies. Fishermen caught more fish in it than they could sell, and in winter wandering herdsmen settled with their herds on its grassy banks and could supply more milk and milk-products than the villagers needed. The only claim to fame of these obscure 'marsh villages' of Kishoreganj is the corpus of lyrical stories and ballads, which they have contributed to the Bengali literature as *Maimansingha Gitikavali* or 'ballads of Mymensingh'. In late autumn, when the household courtyards were full of unprocessed paddy and when people had to keep on working through the night to process and store them, these stories were told and the ballads sung. My grandmother used to call them 'Parastabs' ('Prastabs' – 'proposals'), although I do not know why. She was kind enough to treat her eldest grandchild to such stories, including snatches of songs in her narrative.

Halichhera lay at the edge of the Lungla hills, the blue of the hills being visible in the horizon. Once it yielded to a hunter's bullet, a large *Sambar* deer whose meat was reputedly distributed among no less than seventy-five people. The ordinary variety of deer--*chital*—was more common. Pythons were known. Once an eleven-feet-long python was captured and skinned. Wild hogs, including the pigmy variety, used to come close to human habitations. Almost every evening one could see wild dogs in a particular clump of trees. Wild fowls were less common but had wonderfully colourful wings. There was an apparent abundance of leopards whose roar was frequently heard at dusk. They were generally quiet but occasionally killed cattle. The eldest son of one of the owners of the garden had a habit of turning up at night with a dead leopard spread across the bonnet of his jeep. Migrant ducks were also known. Among the varieties of trees which shaded the tree-bushes and reputedly contributed nitrogen to the soil, there was a variety known locally as *Koroi*. They grew tall and had light seed-pods which, when dry in early summer, used to get separated from the leaves and float around in hot gusty winds. A variety of wild grass known as *San*, which was used in thatching roofs, used to be cut at this time of the year. The sight of *Koroi* seed-pods floating in the air in the hot early summer afternoons and the smell of *San* grass are inseparable from my boyhood memories.

The pre-monsoonal thunder showers did something to the fishes in the garden's swamps or *Jhils*. Three varieties of fish known in Bengali as *Koi*, *Magur* and *Singhi* made beelines for the adjacent fields and were caught and stored in small cemented tanks in the employees' houses. These fields also produced paddy which used to be separated from the sheafs by making the cattle walk in circles over them. One also remembers the fruit trees, mostly mango, jackfruit, and various kinds of wild or domesticated berries, which offered great incentive to the boys to be expert climbers of trees and stealers of fruits. Migrant ducks came in winter but they were comparatively rare. The topography was dominated by what was locally called *Tilas*, small grass-covered hillocks with smooth slopes. One could glide down these slopes in some style and speed. The forests contained large groves of bamboo, a particular variety of which attracted large herds of monkeys for some reason. The way they clung to the swinging bamboos and made noise has not gone out of memory in all these years. In places there were dry *nalas* with a canopy of plants. One could comfortably walk along them. It was in a patch of forest in Luyauni that a leopard took a swipe at Shafi, a Pathan watchman who somehow survived, although with a part of his face permanently damaged. Poor people from the villages outside the garden boundary generally collected wood from the garden forests, which was not encouraged by the garden authorities. Usually, the garden watchmen confiscated their cutting tools and I remember one such villager, very thin with his ribs showing, crying on our verandah to get his *Dao* (a chopper with its blade curved at the top) back. That was my earliest introduction to the misery of man. Many years later, in a winter evening, a similarly clothed and equally thin man, holding a hand of his bare-bodied young son, tried to stop the rented vehicle I was travelling by for a lift to Purulia. By the time I realized what he expected, we had travelled too far to turn back, but somehow it has been difficult to forget the thin, stooping figure in the evening shadow as it has been difficult to forget the figure crying on a tea-garden verandah.

The only other place that I was closely familiar with during this period was Bamai, a village in the Lakhai police station of the Habiganj subdivision of Sylhet. That was my mother's place to which she made periodical visits with her children. The village could be approached only by boat during the monsoon, and the few hours of boat-ride from Habiganj to Bamai had for me always a sense of wonder and excitement. The image of the red disc of the sun sinking down rapidly behind the shadowy outlines of trees at the edge of a vast watery expanse still lingers in memory. Early in 1990, I took the same route with my wife, daughter and a young kinsman named Suman, but this time we travelled in an auto-rickshaw along the top of a high embankment serving as an all-weather road.

The ancestral house of my mother's family, which was set in many acres of land with its appendage of tanks, gardens and some waste land, lay at the edge of the village and looked across a large swathe of fields with a huge banyan tree in the middle distance. The nucleus of the house comprised a few bamboo-and-tin buildings around an inner courtyard which was open to the sky. The outer courtyard had a similarly constructed structure to receive visitors and also a mud-and-bamboo pavilion to house the family deity and for the autumnal worship of the goddess Durga. Plucking flowers for the deity very early in the morning and putting them in bell-metal caskets called *Saji* was one of the pleasant boyhood tasks.

There were dense bushes of cane at the edge of one of the tanks. They yielded a kind of edible berries and supplied cane for cane furniture but more importantly, they harboured some wild cats which fed on household pigeons and ducks. One could collect in winter mornings eggs from holes where turtles had laid their eggs at night. There was plenty of fish all around. One could go out at night in boats with a large burning torch in hand and spear large fishes which used to be drawn to the light of the torches. Large boats with a whole lot of goods for sale berthed at the edge of the village in the monsoon months.

The family was by no means rich, but the annual worship of the goddess Durga was an elaborate affair and nobody in the neighbouring villages had to go hungry during the three main days of the *Puja*. Hundreds of people were welcome to eat their fill of a simple lunch of rice and fish served on banana leaves in the outer courtyard. People usually sat in rows on long trunks of palm trees. On the second day of the *Puja*, or, as it is called, *Mahastami day*, the family used to sacrifice a buffalo at noon to the goddess. The sight of my maternal grandfather sitting with folded hands and bent knees before the image of the goddess and loudly invoking her to accept the sacrifice is still fresh in memory. As winter mist settled in the fields, there was a fresh round of festivities, including the day of winter solstice (*Paush Sankranti*), when we took dips in tanks before sunrise, warmed ourselves standing before bonfires and spent the rest of the day eating various delicacies made from rice and cocoanut. It was in winter again that flocks of migrant birds settled for a few nights on the village trees and fields on their way to the areas further afield and were killed in their dozens by simple bows and arrows and pellet bows. Pellet bows can be very effective in expert hands. I can still recall the sound which came from the wings of these birds as they tried to settle in for the night on the trees.

There was *Puja* in Halichhera too. The image took about a month to complete from its straw-and-bamboo base to the clay-modelled and coloured form with eyes. For me, the highlight of the *Puja* in Halichhera was the white carpet of *Sephalika* (*Harsingar* in Hindi) flowers that one could find around that time every morning below a particular *Sephalika* tree. Kripa Shankar Saraswat, formerly of the Birbal Sahni Institute of Palaeobotany in Lucknow, has identified *Harsingar* in the Indus context putting *Harsingar*-lovers like me eternally in his debt.

AGARTALA

I first went to school in 1952 in Agartala, the capital of Tripura State in India, to which we migrated in the same year before the introduction of the passport system between India and Pakistan. In 1947, Halichhera along with the district of Sylhet fell to the lot of Pakistan. Things got difficult in 1950-51, and when there was talk of introducing passports for travel between the two countries, the family decided to migrate to India, joining the vast hordes of people trying to move across the border before the movement got severely restricted. There was a great exodus of people from one side to the other during this period. They were leaving behind everything they had known or possessed and throwing themselves on the mercy of the government and the people on the other side. It was a very murky, insecure and wretched phase of life for all concerned.

The former princely state of Tripura was ruled by a succession of benevolent, enlightened and liberal kings, and Agartala in 1952 was a small pleasant town. Parts of it were beautiful. Rows of *Mayflower* trees gave elegance to the wide roads of lateritic gravels in the government areas. Somebody shot a large tusker in the forest at the edge of the hill, which contained the local undergraduate college named after a king. Tales of elephants blocking human movements in the hills at night were common. There were also tales about single-tusked elephants or *Ganesh Hathis* which were deemed sacred and auspicious. Viewed from a hilly stretch outside the town, the dome of the *Kunjaban* palace had a fairytale quality about it.

Streams of people were then moving from East Pakistan to Agartala everyday. There was a cholera epidemic and on most of the days there were long rows of dead bodies outside the government hospital.

There is no special memory of the Agartala school Umakanta Academy except that it had a large red building with a playing field and a hostel for the students from the interior attached to it. I was a member of the school scouts for a brief period and that ensured a spell in a camp in the rather remote town of Udaipur famous for its royal lakes and an old temple in the adjacent hills. A small tank at the foot of this temple contained very large and old tortoises and the neighbouring hill-slopes were full of *Bel* or wood-apple trees with plenty of wood-apples lying on the ground. It is worth recording that Tripura had then a rich supply of wild fruits of various kinds, mostly jackfruits, oranges, pineapples and mangoes. In a time when regular meals were difficult to come by, many people survived on these fruits.

In Agartala I missed the quiet of the tea-bushes. Mercifully, there were tea-gardens within a couple of hours of walking distance from the town. I began to skip school and roamed in those gardens. One day, during a spell of heavy rain, I took shelter in a small empty hut made of jute stalks and was soon joined by a pair of bird-catchers of roughly my age. They were carrying a bamboo cage with a partridge inside which would be used to ensnare wild partridges. The thought of walking out with them certainly crossed my mind. Many years later, I saw a tall and blanket-wrapped partridge-catcher walking through a patch of waste-land in the mist of a wintry Delhi morning.

CHAKDAHA

In 1954 we moved to Chakdaha, a small town-cum-village about an hour-and-a half's journey by steam locomotives to the north from Kolkata. About 2 to 3 kilometres to the east of the Bhagirathi or Ganga, the Chakdaha town comprised a railway station, a market, a post office, a public library and two or three schools, one of which was meant for the girls. The school I went to was Ramlal Academy which was established early in the twentieth century and had the reputation of being more academic than its local rivals. Beyond its core, Chakdaha petered away into a number of 'colonies' which were named after the East Pakistan districts from which the settlers of these 'colonies' came. The people from Mymensingh had a colony of their own, and we settled in a village close by. This village used to be known as Pumlia. Chakdaha had a lot of vegetational cover in 1954. It was one of the reputed old villages on the bank of the Bhagirathi and people from the outlying villages used to bring regularly their dead for cremation on the bank of the river. A lot of jute used to be grown in the countryside, and Chakdaha was a centre where this produce was collected by the agents of the jute mills near Kolkata. The farmers used to bring their raw jute in long convoys of bullock carts and cook for themselves by the side of these carts after the day's chores were over. There were still some large and old mango groves in the area. Somebody shot a leopard in one such grove which lay by the side of the road which went to the sub-divisional town of Ranaghat. Till the 1950s leopards were reasonably familiar animals in the Bengal countryside. In the early 1960s when we went to excavate at Chhiruti in Murshidabad, we were told that till several years ago, a leopard used to take a walk in the fields near the mound every evening. There were wild boars too. I also heard leopard tales in the Jahangirnagar university campus near Dhaka. People used to see leopards in the well-wooded landscape of the campus in the early 1970s.

Chakdaha is in the Nadia district of West Bengal. The beauty of this part of the Bengal countryside was very different from the beauty of the tea-bushes. The birthplace of one of the most famous Bengali writers, Bibhuti Bhushan Bandopadhyay, was in the area of modern Kalyani, only a little to the north of Chakdaha. The beauty of this landscape and its human types are celebrated in his writings. The lushness of vegetation during the monsoon can be overpowering, but in winter the environment is more open and in the soft glow of the sun in the afternoon, there is a sense of peace and hope in the air. Paddy is reaped in late autumn with the vegetables taking their place in winter. In the early morning or late afternoon dew, the large patches of vegetables possess a charm of their own and there is always the pleasure of munching sweet peas as one walks across the fields.

Alexander Cunningham's assistant, the Armenian J.D. Beglar (1845-1907), who was an engineer from the Bengal College of Engineering at Shibpur, Howrah, and designed the railway bridge over the Bhagirathi between Hooghly and Naihati, built a large house at Chakdaha. I found it in a semi-ruinous state but the compound had a large Pala period Buddha image which he supposedly brought from Nalanda. In later years, this image was shifted to the Ashutosh Museum of Calcutta University. I later came to know that Beglar's daughter, an old lady by then, used to visit the house from time to time. According to his inscribed tombstone in the Armenian cemetery in Chinsurah, Beglar was 'late Executive Engineer, PWD and Archaeological Surveyor of Bengal'. Mrs. Beglar, according to the same source, died at Chakdaha in 1911. Not far from the ruins of Beglar's house was a brick temple richly embellished with terracotta plaques on the front. It was – and possibly still is – a 'protected' monument under the care of the Archaeological Survey of India. I know nothing of the history of this temple but the locality in which it is located, the Palpara locality, was a prosperous place in the seventeenth or eighteenth century, the traces of which could be seen in a large but derelict brick-built residence with high boundary walls. Locally it was known as the *Kazibari* or 'the house of *Qazi*', and I remember having read somewhere that a person of eminence from this house visited England in the late eighteenth century or earlier. The Palpara temple was located in a compound with one or two *Jamun* trees which yielded good quality *Jamun*. When I visited the temple after many years, I found it in the care of a mendicant who converted it into a living temple with or without the connivance of the Archaeological Survey of India. The peace of the place was disturbed and there was also no sign of the *Jamun* trees.

I soon struck roots in Chakdaha. There was nothing unpleasant about the school. Some teachers, in fact, tried to impart a love for learning to the students, most of whom came from a hopelessly shaky economic background. Very few of them wore shoes to the classes. The teachers of English and Sanskrit were among the inspirational teachers. The Headmaster, a strict disciplinarian, cared for the academic reputation of the school. There were also a few bright students. Nani Gopal Chakrabarti (no relation), who later stood first in the School Final examination in the whole of the Nadia district and lived, like many of us, in a thatched mud-and-bamboo house surrounded by a few banana plants, used to write excellent idiomatic English. Suniti, my cousin who recently retired as a consulting paediatrician of Staffordshire National Health Service was as bright then as he is now. We took long walks across the freshly cultivated fields and we clambered up the date-palm trees to drink straight, with the help of a straw, from the earthen pots which were tied to the top of these trees to collect their morning sap. There were also books to be borrowed from the small public library. We read mostly Bengali novels, and even the 'foreign works' could be read only in Bengali translations. I remember having read the translations of Andre Malreaux's *Storm in Shanghai* (1934) and Pearl Buck's *The Good Earth* (1931).

I crossed the hurdle of the school final examination in 1956. That was the year when excavations began at Chandraketugarh under the Ashutosh Museum of Calcutta University and I remember the excitement I felt on reading its reports in the Bengali newspapers. I suppose I had developed an idea of what archaeology was by that time and found it, in an immature way, very romantic. The point is that my mind was slowly getting focussed on historical things and I became more or less certain that studying history and archaeology would be rather an exciting thing to do, provided there was chance at all for further studies. Nobody, especially my father, brushed it aside as a luxury which somebody from our economic background could not afford, and I opted for the Humanities stream in the Intermediate course which in my case lasted from 1956 to 1958.

It is difficult to think clearly of how I was drawn to the historical studies. There was a small hand-composing press (*Udayan* press) near the railway station at Chakdaha, which fell on our way to school. The man who used to supervise its work was named Sunil Mitra, a young man who had drifted to Chakdaha after serving a spell in *Searchlight*, an English daily newspaper of Patna. He was a good source of stories of distant lands and an ardent reader of history books including Stuart Piggott's *Prehistoric India*. He was also a Marxist of some kind and led a small group of people made up of fellow-thinkers. I came to know some of them, all of whom were very decent and kind men. At that age I did not understand politics but occasionally I accompanied them in their day-tours of the neighbouring villages. I may add as a footnote that many years later I met *Sunil-da*, as we used to call Sunil Mitra, in the company of his wife and daughter in a late night flight from Mumbai to Kolkata. I recognized him but there was no flicker of recognition in his eyes, and there was no conversation.

In retrospect, I find it amazing how deep was the hold of books written by Gordon Childe, Stuart Piggott, Grahame Clark and other writers of Penguin and similarly priced volumes on the minds of the generally educated public in various parts of the Third World including West Bengal. Gordon Childe was the most favoured of them all. His Communist connection gave him a special kind of aura among the people I had then known. I find it somewhat curious that in the many analyses of Childe's work in the First World archaeology, there is not even a whiff of perception of the level of his popularity in the Third World. I also find it natural in a way because the First World is simply not interested in the Third World archaeology unless the work there is conducted by the First World archaeologists, i.e., Euro-American archaeologists. Later, I learnt that Childe was friendly with Rajani Palme Dutt, a prominent theoretician of the British Communist movement and son of a Bengali doctor in Cambridge. Dutt, a Classics graduate with a first from Balliol (Oxford) and a lifelong hardliner/Stalinist, wrote, among other things, *India Today* (1940), a compelling study of modern Indian history. One of the reasons why modern First World archaeologists, whatever their reputation, cannot even think of coming anywhere close to Gordon Childe's and to some extent Grahame Clark's level of acceptance in the Third World may be their essentially non-humanistic and non-historical approach. Besides, with the increasing polarisation between the First World and the Third World archaeologies, a situation where the First World archaeologists are not simply interested in knowing beyond what their Euro-American colleagues are doing in those parts of the world, Archaeology in the First World has become basically insular in outlook. The last time there was a single-authored publication on *World Prehistory* from Cambridge was in 1961, with two later editions. That was authored by Grahame Clark.

CHINSURAH

I went to study Intermediate Arts in Hooghly Mohsin College of Chinsurah, the district town of Hooghly located on the right bank of the Bhagirathi. The two neighbouring towns of Hooghly and Chinsurah formed a single urban complex. There was a late Mughal period Imambara in Hooghly as well as a church with Portuguese ancestry, the latter popularly known as Bandel church. Chinsurah had Dutch ruins, the Dutch having a settlement there between c.1650 and c.1825. The college, established in the 1830s lay in a palatial building inside a large walled compound on the bank of the Bhagirathi, the water of which swirled round its foundation pillars. It was the house of the French general Perron who witnessed service under the Marathas and later settled in this Dutch colony. The college bears the name of Haji Mohammad Mohsin (1732-1812), a rich trader who spent his wealth in charity, an example of which was the establishment of the college. Two *Krishnachura* trees flanked its main gate and in summer their red flowers and the occasional parrots screeching and sitting on the wooden window shutters lent an aura of beauty and excitement to the college campus. The college compound also had a *Nag Kesar* tree (*Mesua ferrea*) which was a rarity in West Bengal. Many years later, it was a great delight to find rows of these trees in the Jahangirnagar university campus. The classrooms had high ceilings and equally high windows. A large balcony, occasionally used as a classroom, directly overlooked the river. The college library, which was an appealing place to go to, had a lot of old books. The students' hostel where I stayed lay at the edge of a vast open field and was a short walking distance away from the main gate of the college.

My two years in the Hooghly Mohsin College made me aware of many things of which I was unaware before. Mainly, I became aware of the world of academic books. At least three of the teachers were inspirational. The principal of the college, A.W. Mahmood, reputedly more of a tennis player than a History teacher, taught us ancient Greek history making us feel that it was desperately important to know what the Greeks did. He was a B.Litt from Oxford and I recall him as one of the finest teachers I have had. Another B.Litt from Oxford, Raghubir Chakrabarti taught us political studies and went to inordinate lengths to introduce us to the major social and political thinkers. Bhavani Mukhopadhyay, an orthodox Brahmin who usually wore only *Dhoti* and *Uttariya* in summer, taught us Sanskrit and opened the door of the Sanskrit literature for us.

I became determined by this time to pursue historical studies including archaeology as my career option. This was the period when Will Durant's multi-volume work on the story of civilization came my way along with Childe's *What Happened in History* and *Man Makes Himself*, and Grahame Clark's *From Savagery to Civilization*. If I remember correctly, Raghubir

Chakrabarti also gave me Childe's *Progress and Archaeology* and *Society and Knowledge* to read, although I am afraid I did not understand much of the latter. He specialized in international law and political science but was an avid reader and buyer of books in many subjects. He died a sad man. He did not get the professorship of political science in the newly established university at Burdwan ('Barddhaman') near Kolkata, although he was certainly one of the best persons around for the job. I gratefully recall his kindness to me.

For some reason, I read Kalidasa's *Malavikagnimitram* and wrote on that basis an essay entitled 'Ancient India in Kalidasa's *Malavikagnimitram*'. This was published in the Hooghly Mohsin college magazine of 1957. Regretfully, I do not possess any copy of the first 'publication' of mine. One of the important Bengali books that I read during this period was *Lokayata Darsan* ('philosophy sprung out of people's life') by Debi Prasad Chattopadhyay. Its English version came out later (1959) as *Lokayata, a Study in Ancient Indian Materialism*. Modelled somewhat on George Thomson's *Studies in Ancient Greek Society*, this book tried to underpin a recurring element of primitivism in Indian philosophy and culture. Chattopadhyay was associated with the Communist movement in India in the 1950s (and possibly later) and wrote a large number of historical and philosophical books in Bengali. He had an associate named Ramakrishna Maitra and they set up a press in Chattopadhyay's house in Bhavanipur, Kolkata, and began to publish an academic journal called *Indian Studies Past and Present*. Among the books popular during those days in Kolkata's 'left' circle were Thomson's *Marxism and Poetry* and Robert Briffault's three-volume study, *The Mothers, a Study of the Origins of Sentiments and Institutions* (1927). The abridged edition of J.G. Fraser's *The Golden Bough* was also easily available in Kolkata of this period. The Hooghly Mohsin College library had a complete set of *The Golden Bough* (3rd edition of 12 volumes), and my friend Narendra Nath Bhattacharya based himself on the theoretical ideas and examples of these books and others like them (cf. Jane Harrison's *Prolegomena to the Study of Ancient Greek Religion*) and did his own studies of Indian mother-goddess, Indian puberty rites and ancient Indian rituals. He was a resident of Chinsurah and taught in a school in the neighbouring Chandannagar, a former French colony. He supplemented his income during this period by writing columns in various newspapers and magazines. One of these columns on the popular literature of different parts of the world was later published as a major Bengali book on world literature. The material for his study came mostly from the Hooghly Mohsin College library. He later joined the Department of Ancient Indian History and Culture of Calcutta University and went on doing research and publishing regularly till his death a few years ago. Tall, thin, *Dhoti*-clad and pipe-smoking, he was a remarkable conversationalist because of his wide learning. I learnt much from him.

The fact that the Hooghly Mohsin College had a good library (at least in 1956-58) has been worth emphasizing because libraries do not now figure high in the Indian academic agenda. Most of the undergraduate college libraries are dismal affairs with little more than a haphazard collection of text books in regional languages. The condition of many university libraries is no better. There is no lack of 'research institutes' and other professional bodies in modern India. Regrettably, these supposedly academic places are not bothered by the necessity of building a decent library. Among the libraries of the various professional bodies, that of the Archaeological Survey of India offers a convenient example. This library was once an intrinsic part of the Survey headquarters on Janpath, Delhi. The Survey officers could easily spend their spare hours in the library. Soon, the library was shifted out, and its present location behind the National Archives is not easy of access and in any case far removed from the Survey office. During my last visit to this library, I found it a dusty and dismal place headed by people with least concern for research or study of any kind. Many of the old books were missing and one doubted if the 'stock verification' had taken place in many years. The purchase of books was primarily dependent on what the Delhi booksellers decided to supply. One also hears nowadays that the booksellers offer commissions to the concerned people to get their books accepted and paid for. This last bit of rumour is not merely about the Archaeological Survey of India library but also about all other Delhi libraries including the Delhi university libraries.

OPTING FOR THE STUDY OF HISTORY AND ARCHAEOLOGY

In 1958, I passed the Intermediate Arts examination and joined the History Honours course of Presidency College and the Sanskrit pass course of Sanskrit College in Kolkata. Gourinath Sastri, who taught us Sanskrit, was an impressive teacher. In Presidency College two of its history teachers were equally impressive: Amalesh Tripathi and Dilip Kumar Biswas. Tripathi was a specialist in the early economic history of British India but gave a wonderful series of lectures on the Italian renaissance, taking us to Jacob Burckhardt's *The Civilization of the Renaissance in Italy* (1860). Biswas, a specialist in the history of Brahmo Samaj and life and thought of its founder Rammohan Ray, taught us ancient Greek and Indian history. He had an enviable collection of books including a complete set of the *Loeb Classical Library* series and many Sanskrit works. There was a distinct social division in Presidency College between the urban sophisticates and the country bumpkins like me, but there was a good library and there were also some gifted teachers and students. The College magazine of 1959 was edited by Gayatri Chakravarty who was possibly a final year undergraduate student of English then. This contained an article by me on the Belgian historian Henry Pirenne, the author of *Mohammed and Charlegmane*. Gayatri Chakravarty later became Gayatri Chakravarty-Spivac and made an outstanding name for herself as a semiologist. The Pirenne thesis regarding the decline of antiquity was later applied in a rather juvenile fashion to the study of ancient India by Ram Sharan Sharma who became the chairman of the Indian Council of Historical Research and was a leading member of the Indian History establishment for many years. Hirendra Nath Gohain was one of my neighbours in Hindu Hostel and had a voracious appetite for reading books beyond his own subject English. It was Hiren who introduced me to the charms of the books in the Penguin Classics series. Later, he did his Ph.D. in English from Cambridge and retired as a professor of English literature at Guwahati University. He also turned out to be a notable figure of the modern Assamese literature. Vachaspati Upadhyay, originally from Sultanpur, never failed to turn up in the Sanskrit College library early in the morning. He became the vice-chancellor of a Sanskrit university in north India at a young age.

Kolkata of the day was a good place to look for second-hand books. The Penguin books used to be priced 'two shillings and six pence' during that period and some selected areas of the Kolkata footpath were full of many of these volumes on sale. For a rupee or two one could pick up second-hand publications by Childe, Stuart Piggott and others. My collection of Rudyard Kipling's books or those by T.E. Lawrence came invariably from the footpath. The books found their way to the footpath in Kolkata from the sale of various small or large private collections. The supply seems to have dried out these days and what one finds in the footpath these days is mostly school and college text books. This truly reflects the current Bengali intellectual situation. Old books could then be had mostly in three localities: College Street, Wellington Square and New Market.

The teaching of History in the Indian universities, schools and colleges has seldom been an exciting affair. As most of the teachers are not researchers in their own rights, they refer students only to other people's opinions, without any clear or critical formulations of their own. Further, the syllabi are heavily loaded in favour of the modern periods, both European and Indian. Archival research in these fields is beyond the grip of many of them. Things could have been better in the case of ancient and mediaeval India but here the teachers' general inability to read the relevant languages such as Sanskrit, Arabic and Farsi does not allow them to critically evaluate the sources. Moreover, the job-market in history is almost monopolised in India by the students of 'modern India', which means that very few motivated or bright students opt for ancient or mediaeval India. This is a pan-Indian situation. Teachers teach mostly on the basis of the various 'note books' and the students follow the notes provided by the teachers. There is a large and old all-India professional body of Indian historians, Indian History Congress, and there is also a separate and powerful funding body called Indian Council of Historical Research. However, the existence of these organizations has not prevented the teaching of history in India from being a singularly wasteful and puerile activity. History is reputedly a popular subject, or has been so, among the candidates for the competitive examinations for the Indian Administrative Service and other related federal and provincial examinations.

The effect of a rather wasteful history teaching runs wide and deep in the country. For instance, this teaching is still far from generating any serious interest in the history of the country among the generally educated people. The kinds of objective and illustrated books on the material life of different periods that even the school children get in Britain are simply unthinkable in India. Most of the research projects funded by the Indian Council of Historical Research have been fairly useless and they also remain unpublished. In fact, when scrutinised closely and objectively, the list of various chairmen and 'members of the council' who have been associated with this Government of India organization since its inception will amply highlight what is professionally wrong with the historians and historical research in the country. Most of them gave up active archival or field-research long before they were inducted to this organization with political or network support of various kinds. Incidentally, an outstanding piece of historical documentation that I have read in recent years—*Beseiged: Voices from Delhi 1857* by Mahmood Farooqui—is way outside the Indian Council of Historical Research network. So are the thoroughly researched books on Indian Ocean trade and related issues by another Indian, Sanjay Subrahmanyam.

In 1960, I completed my BA History Honours course and joined the newly established Department of Archaeology in Calcutta University as an MA student. The course lasted till 1962, and the examination results came out in March 1963. Independent and separate departments of Archaeology were established in 1960 in several Indian universities including Kolkata, Pune, Chennai and Lucknow. The funding came from University Grants Commission and had provisions for building and related infrastructure, teaching and support posts including those of a draftsman-cum-surveyor and a photographer, surveying, photographic and camping equipment and recurrent annual grants for explorations, excavations and various contingencies.

The context of this UGC funding of archaeology is not known to me. Since R.E.M. Wheeler's stewardship of the Archaeological Survey of India (1944-48), there had been a general awareness of the importance of introducing archaeology teaching and field-research in Indian universities. The exact steps leading to the implementation of this idea would need research in the UGC and the relevant university archives, provided such archives exist.

Another important development took place in the 1950s and 1960s. That was the creation of 'State'-level archaeology departments in the various 'States' on the model of the central government's Archaeological Survey of India. In a sense, these 'State' departments were the new versions of the archaeology departments of the old princely states such as Baroda, Gwalior, Kashmir and Hyderabad. An analysis of the Kashmir situation is already available in Mridu Rai's commendable article, 'To 'tear the mask off the face of the past', archaeology and politics in Jammu and Kashmir in *The Indian Economic and Social History Review* (vol. 46, pp. 401-426, 2009) but factual surveys of these 'princely state' archaeology departments are missing in all cases. It is not true that these departments were limited only to Gwalior, Baroda, Kashmir and Hyderabad. Travancore and Cochin. Mysore, Pudukottai and Khiching also had their archaeology establishments, if one remembers correctly. There may be more examples, and it is important that the history of archaeology departments of the Indian princely states is researched and integrated into the framework of the general history of archaeology in India. However, the creation of new State departments or directorates of archaeology and museums was a major institutional impetus to archaeological research in the country.

Another important point regarding the development of archaeology in India in the 1950s and 1960s was the inauguration of a 'School of Archaeology' as a wing of the Archaeological Survey of India. This was basically intended to provide in-service training to those appointed by the Archaeological Survey of India, but there was also provision for admitting a few students from the universities and neighbouring countries like Nepal. The system of recruiting bright students of Sanskrit, Arabic/Farsi and History from the Indian universities by the Survey as 'scholars' had been in place since John Marshall's time. The system seems to have continued up to the 1950s, and one gathers that Debala Mitra, who retired as the Survey's Director General in the 1980s and N.R. Banerjee, who had excavated Ujjayini in the 1950s as a 'Superintendent', were both recruited as 'scholars'. The major advantage of this system was that the bright students from the universities were given a chance to look forward to a career in the Survey.

The first trainees of the Survey 'school' graduated in 1960. It was initially a twenty-month course. The main strength of the 'school' lay in the rigorous field-training it provided—about six months of excavation work in addition to many exploratory spells. In the class-rooms there was an attempt to introduce the students to the detailed academic context of Indian archaeology from prehistory to numismatics. Students were further involved in hands-on structural and chemical conservation work. As long as teaching and field-training were taken seriously, it was an excellent programme.

There are reasons to believe that in its early years the 'school' functioned splendidly well. At the same time, it had a few in-built snags. First, the Survey jobs this training led to were Class III jobs in the category of Technical Assistants who had to wait for many years for promotion to the executive level. The bright students of the universities usually expected to be inducted to Class I positions. The Geological Survey of India, for instance, recruited geologists by holding competitive written examinations and appointing the successful candidates to its Class I jobs. The Archaeological Survey of India failed to recruit bright students through their system. Secondly, no safeguard was taken to ensure that the quality of teaching and training remained constantly at a high level in the 'school'. Regrettably, this quality has sharply deteriorated in recent years. Thirdly, no importance was ever laid on publishing field-results. On the other hand, a great 'mystery' was created about archaeological publications. In contrast to the run-of-the-mill and yet objective field-publications of the Geological Survey of India, which are printed on the normal quality paper and contained all the necessary illustrative materials, the Archaeological Survey of India publications were expected to be much glossier in appearance and thus more time was needed to print them. The senior Survey officers of the time were not noted for timely publications and thus did not set good precedents when the setting of such precedents was necessary.

The newly established Department of Archaeology of Calcutta University began its MA classes sometime in November, 1960, in the room 19B of the Ashutosh Building located at the crossing of the Mirzapur and College streets. The ground-floor rooms facing College Street were rented out to a few shops in those days. In fact, before Ashutosh Building was constructed, the space was occupied by a market known as Madhab Babu's Bazaar, a name which outlived the actual physical existence of the bazaar. When I arrived at Sealdah Station from Chakdaha to go to Hindu Hostel on Peary Sarkar Street in 1958, the *Tangawala* or the driver of the horse-drawn cart I approached asked me if I had wanted to go to 'Madhab Babu's Bazaar'. Still, the College Street campus with its neo-

Classical Senate House (1862) and rows of Sago-palms leading from College Street entrance to Darbhanga Building at the rear was a beautiful and imposing place. However, in 1960/61, the University took the decision of pulling down this building and erect a multi-storied match-box-like structure in its place. Throughout the MA session in 1960-62, we saw Senate House being pulled down bit by bit, and if I have to point out a period when the University had given up all hopes of rejuvenation and came to be exclusively dominated by unimaginative people refusing to look beyond their own interests, I would categorically point out this period, 1960-62.

There were three students beside me on the inaugural day of the Department: Samir Kumar Mukhopadhyay who became professor of Museology, Calcutta University, Bijon Bihari Dey who became professor of Ancient Indian History and Culture, Calcutta University, and died before he retired, and Pran Gopal Paul who, having obtained a Ph.D. from Amsterdam, decided to continue to live in that city.

This new Department of Archaeology was an offshoot of the University's much older Department of Ancient Indian History and Culture which held its MA examination first in 1918 or 1919 and was the first Indian university to set up such a specialised department on the MA level. By this time archaeological research had made considerable headway in India, leading to the discovery and publication of a lot of ancient historical material including inscriptions, coins and architectural and sculptural remains. There was also a spirit of nationalism at this time and it was natural that people would like to have the study of ancient India incorporated in the universities. Besides, the city of Kolkata had a long institutional record of research in this field in the shape of the Asiatic Society, which was joined in the second half of the nineteenth century by some scholarly Indians.

THE ANCIENT HISTORICAL RESEARCH TRADITION AMONG THE BENGALIS AND IN CALCUTTA UNIVERSITY

The intellectual tradition of ancient historical research in Kolkata was certainly deep-rooted, based almost exclusively on the researchers' ability to handle various types of primary sources, and not confined to any particular geographical area or regional cultural tradition. How far this affected the research tradition of Calcutta University is a different matter. Some of the most formidable names in this field did not teach at the University. Rajendralal Mitra, Haraprasad Shastri, R.D. Banerji, R.P. Chanda, N.G. Majumdar and many others were not even associated with the university in any significant way. Haraprasad Shastri remained a teacher of Sanskrit in a college (Sanskrit College) throughout his working career. However, the university research tradition was not completely separate from the research tradition of the Asiatic Society, and anybody studying ancient India in Kolkata had to remain aware of the early pioneers, beginning with Rajendralal Mitra (1824-1891), who was appointed the Librarian and Assistant Secretary of the Asiatic Society in 1846 and rose to become the President in 1885. He also served as the Secretary (1857, 1865) and the Vice-President (1861-65, 1870-84). His no doubt is an illustrious name in the history of ancient Indian studies in the second half of the nineteenth century. Mitra edited 14 texts in the Asiatic Society's *Bibliotheca Indica* series, publishing *Sanskrit Buddhist Literature of Nepal* in 1882. His contribution to the study of archaeology in Orissa and at Bodhgaya was immense: *The Antiquities of Orissa* and *Buddhagaya, the Hermitage of Sakya Muni*. Mitra became the subject of a vicious racist and personal attack by James Fergusson who argued in his book *Archaeology in India, with Especial Reference to the Works of Babu Rajendralal Mitra* that Indians, of whom Rajendralal Mitra was a highly educated example, could not be trusted to sit in judgement over the

Europeans. This was in the context of the Ilbert Bill (1884), which empowered the Indian magistrates precisely to do that. Fergusson, an early historian of Indian architecture, was upset with Mitra mainly because the latter supported the opinion of an independent beginning of stone architecture in India. It is worthy of notice that this did not prevent Mitra from becoming the President of the Asiatic Society in 1885 at the height of the British empire, and incidentally, recognition and honour of this kind are simply unthinkable in the 'colour-coded' atmosphere of the current set-up of ancient Indian and archaeological studies in Euro-America.

One of Mitra's major publications was *Indo-Aryans: Contributions towards the Elucidation of their Ancient and Mediaeval History*. The individual chapters of this book ('origins of Indian architecture, principles of Indian temple architecture, Indian sculpture, dress and ornament in ancient India, furniture, domestic utensils, instruments, arms, horses and cars in ancient India, beef in ancient India, spirituous drinks in ancient India, a picnic in ancient India) contain much that is still academically valuable, showing a detailed concern with the material basis of life in ancient India. By the 1880s, the notion of the Aryan invasion of India was securely in its place, with many contemporary Indian scholars (cf. Ramesh Chandra Dutt) falling ardently for it. Mitra's links with the formative stage of Indian nationalism is clear. He was the president of the British-India association for many years and an important functionary of the second session of the Indian National Congress in Calcutta in 1886.

A later contemporary of Mitra, Haraprasad Shastri (1853-1931) was his assistant at the Asiatic Society and continued his task of looking for ancient Sanskrit manuscripts in India and Nepal, publishing eventually a catalogue of ten thousand such manuscripts. In 1907, he discovered the earliest evidence of Bengali literature in the *Charyapada* manuscripts (c.8th-12th centuries AD) in the royal library of Nepal. Shastri was a professor of Sanskrit in the Sanskrit College, Calcuta, and later its principal. He also served a spell as the professor of Bengali and Sanskrit literature at Dhaka University. Like Mitra before him, Shastri served in various capacities at the Asiatic Society, but the fact that he was the president of the *Vangiya Sahitya Parishad*, a society established at the turn of the twentieth century to investigate the literature, history and culture of Bengal shows his close links with local and regional history writings. He wrote extensively in Bengali, including a delightful commentary on Kalidasa's *Meghadutam* and a historical novel (*Bener Meye* or 'the merchant's daughter'), the latter evocative of Bengal's trade with southeast Asia.

Rajendralal Mitra and Haraprasad Shastri represent between themselves the Sanskritic tradition of Bengali historical scholarship. The tradition later expanded into Pali and Prakrit scholarship, of which a leading example was B.M. Barua (1888-1948), who taught Pali and ancient Indian history at Calcutta University for many years. He specialised in the history of Indian philosophy and Buddhism, one of his famous books in the field being *A History of Pre-Buddhist Indian Philosophy, a Prolegomena to the History of Buddhist Philosophy*. He also specialised in the inscriptions of the early sites of Bharhut, Bodhgaya and Udayagiri-Khandagiri and later summed up his Buddhist literary knowledge and epigraphic understanding in *Asoka and His Inscriptions*. Another leading scholar in this field was B.C. Law, who is primarily known for his encyclopaedic *Historical Geography of Ancient India* which represents the culmination of his lifelong studies in Buddhist literature from the various geographical points of view.

Inscriptions have long been an important component of the Kolkata tradition of scholarship on ancient India. Even

Rajendralal Mitra edited Sanskrit inscriptions in the pages of the *Journal of the Asiatic Society of Bengal*. In 1912, Akshay Kumar Maitra published a corpus of inscriptions found in Bengal with their translations in Bengali, *Gaudalekhamala*. In comparatively recent times, R.G. Basak with his knowledge of Sanskrit wrote extensively on the history as reconstructed from both texts and inscriptions, *Asokan Inscriptions* and the earlier *History of North-Eastern India: Extending from the Foundation of the Gupta Empire to the Rise of the Pala Dynasty of Bengal, c.320-760 AD* being two representative examples of his writings. Scholars like R.D. Banerji and N.G. Majumdar were good epigraphers, having a good number of publications on inscriptions in *Epigraphia Indica*. The historical aspects of the pre-Muslim inscriptions from Bengal were analysed by B.C. Sen (1942). The tradition found its best expression in D.C. Sircar who, besides being the Chief Epigraphist of the Archaeological Survey of India, taught for many years in Calcutta University. Numismatics figured equally importantly with epigraphy. Most of the scholars were concerned as much with numismatics as with epigraphy. Scholars who pioneered the study of the political dynasties had focussed on both as the major source-materials. Issues related to the history of sculpture, painting and architecture, including detailed analysis of various iconographies, drew early attention from the Bengali scholars, notably in the writings of J.N. Banerjee (cf. *The Development of Hindu Iconography*, 1st ed. 1924), H.C. Raychaudhuri (cf. *Materials for the Study of the Early History of the Vaishnava Sect*, 1920), N.K. Bhattasali (cf. *Iconography of Buddhist and Brahmanical Images in the Dacca Museum*, 1929), Benaytosh Bhattacharya (cf. *The Indian Buddhist Iconography*, 1924), Brindavan Chandra Bhattacharya (cf. *Jaina Iconography*, 1939) and others. R.P. Chanda's *The Beginning of Art in Eastern India* (1927) was a pioneering analytical work on the history of ancient Indian art with reference to the relevant sculptures in Indian Museum. The mainstay of the studies in the political history of India was a combination of inscriptions and numismatics, and a major example of this tradition was H.C. Raychaudhuri's *Political History of Ancient India* (5th edition, 1950), which in its different editions covered the ground up to the end of the Gupta period. For the early mediaeval context, H.C. Ray's *The Dynastic History of Northern India* (2 volumes, 1931, 1936) was an important study.

Archaeological investigations figured only sporadically among Bengal's research interests in ancient India. In 1910, R.P. Chanda, Akshay Kumar Maitra and Sarat Kumar Roy (of the Dighapatiya State, a major princely landholding of the northern Bengal) set up *Varendra Anusandhan Samiti* or a 'society for investigations in Varendra land', and although occasional archaeological field-investigations were conducted under its auspicies, nothing much was achieved apart from the establishment of an archaeological museum at Rajsahi, the heartland of the Varendra area. Calcutta University's excavations at Paharpur lasted only for a year, and even the University's later excavations at Bangarh, although the first Indian university work of this kind, did not lead to an unbroken tradition of archaeological investigations at the University. Three major Bengali scholars were associated with the Archaeological Survey of India: Rama Prasad Chanda who, in addition to his Archaeological Survey of India memoir on the beginning of art in eastern India, wrote three more 'memoirs' in this series, two examining the possible relationship between the Indus civilization and the Vedic literature and one on the exploration of Orissa. Chanda also wrote on the dating of the votive inscriptions of Sanchi. R.D. Banerji/Rakhal Das Bandopadhyay, although primarily known for being the first excavator of Mohenjodaro, was a formidable scholar in virtually everything related to ancient India—political history, epigraphy, numismatics, iconography and also ground investigations of archaeological ruins. He wrote three *Memoirs* for the Survey—one on the Siva temple of Bhumara, another on the Haihaya kings of Tripuri and their monuments, and the third one on the bas-reliefs of Badami. He was also a major writer of historical novels in Bengali. His *Pashaner Kotha*, which basically narrates the history as seen by a piece of stone in the Bharhut stupa, has continued to inspire the imagination of his young readers. The impact of this book and other Bengali novels by Rakhal Das Bandopadhyay on me was immense. A senior officer of the Archaeological Survey of India, he could not adjust himself well to the framework of governmental rules and regulations and had in fact acquired a bad name for himself for his various acts of indiscipline including drunkenness, but all that one has to do to forget his 'sins' is to read, among others, his historical novels, archaeological reports, and above all, his groundbreaking and insightful works on the imperial Guptas and the books on the history of Bengal and Orissa. I do not think he understood much of what he found at Mohenjodaro, but he certainly was a virtuoso in the field of ancient Indian historical research. N.G. Majumdar/Nani Gopal Majumdar made his name in the explorations for protohistoric sites in Sind but he also studied the inscriptions of Sanchi for the monograph on Sanchi by John Marshall and wrote a catalogue of sculptures in the Indian Museum, Kolkata.

R.D. Banerji was an applicant for the post of the first Carmichael Professor of Ancient Indian Indian History and Culture in Calcutta University, but the post went to D.R. Bhandarkar of the Archaeological Survey of India, who made a name for himself at the university by his lectures on ancient Indian numismatics and the reign of Asoka. He also lectured on the ancient history of India from c.650 BC to c.325 BC, i.e., pre-Mauryan history. The foundations of ancient Indian art historical studies were laid at the University by Stella Kramrisch who taught at the University from 1923 to 1950 when she went to the United States. Her *Indian Sculpture* (1932) and *The Hindu Temple* (1946) are, among others, examples of her inspired scholarship.

It is not that ancient Indian historical scholarship in Calcutta University lay confined only to its traditional venues of epigraphic, literary, numismatic and art history. Social institutions and political ideas were the subjects of investigation by many scholars including Binoy Sarkar (cf. *Hindu Achievements in Exact* Science, 1920) and U.N. Ghoshal (cf. *A History of Indian Political Ideas: the Ancient Period and the Period of Transition to the Middle Ages*, 1959, with earlier editions going back to 1923), two outstanding and original scholars of the period.

In retrospect, I shall point out only two aspects of Bengali scholarship in the field of ancient India. First, it was thoroughly based on the ability to critically appraise and analyse the relevant sources, and secondly, the coverage was by and large pan-Indian. No part of the country was quite alien to them, and they almost considered it a duty to understand what was going on in all parts of the country in their chosen fields of study. There was, of course, a strong regional research tradition based on Bengal, which found a representative expression in the first volume of the Dhaka University project on the history of Bengal, but the celebrated editor of that volume, Ramesh Chandra Majumdar, also did not hesitate to edit perhaps the most ambitious and authoritative series so far on the history of India, *The History and Culture of the Indian People* under the auspicies of the *Bharatiya Vidya Bhavan.* Majumdar could also edit inscriptions, write on 'corporate life in ancient India' and greatly expand the research on India's influence on and interaction with, different parts of southeast

Asia. A good number of Majumdar's associates in the Bharatiya Vidya Bhavan enterprise were Bengali scholars and these volumes in a sense underline the pan-Indian scholarly grip of these scholars trained and/or teaching in Bengal. Majumdar's study of southeast Asia was in a sense paralleled by P.C. Bagchi's study of ancient Indian contacts with China.

In 1960, when I went to study archaeology and ancient history at the University of Calcutta, this scholarship had lost its edge. The subject itself had lost its importance in post-Independence India, giving its place rather rapidly to the study of 'modern India' and European history in the universities. The subject was never taken seriously at the BA level and this led to the formal debarment of the MAs in Ancient Indian History and Culture from the teaching of BA students in the 'affiliated' colleges of Calcutta University. I am told that this 'debarment' has recently been withdrawn by the University, but as long as the study of ancient India is not a significant part of BA history syllabus, it is unlikely to draw bright students. Secondly, many scholars and teachers of the earlier generation had lost their urge or enthusiasm to do or inspire good quality research by the 1960s. There must be a whole lot of factors—the Bengal famine of 1943 (about 3 million people dead, many on the streets of Calcutta), the Great Calcutta Killing of August 1946 (more than 10000 people butchered and many more wounded between 16 and 20 August, 1946), and the Partition of Bengal in 1947 (large-scale genocide and the uprooting of millions of people)—in the background but the degeneration the city itself began to face because of the ever-increasing local political unrest and the population pressure due to the influx of the post-Partition refugees must have taken its toll. The University leadership was hardly willing to seek funds from the federal government for the development of the university in the face of strong competition from many smaller and previously unknown places. A fair amount of responsibility has also to be shared by individual teachers who more or less kept resting on their laurels and did not guide their students in new directions.

There was a chance to rejuvenate things in the field of ancient India in Kolkata after the UGC put in money, sometime in the 1960s, to set up an Advanced Centre of research in Ancient Indian History and Culture at the university. This led to the recruitment of a large number of Senior and Junior research fellows, the regular holding of national-level and other seminars and the publications of their proceedings, and finally, the publication of a journal entitled *Journal of Ancient Indian History*. D.C. Sircar headed this Centre for many years. Regrettably, his interest in ancient India did not extend beyond the technicalities of coins and inscriptions, but he took good care of his duties as the Director and was ably assisted by young teachers like Samaresh Bandopadhyay who was also interested primarily in coins and inscriptions. Some good publications resulted (cf. J.N. Banarjea, *Pauranic and Tantric Religion*, 1966; R.S. Sharma, *Indian Feudalism*, 1965) but one of the formal research projects, the one on the ancient geography of India died a natural death because the whole objective was to compile only a dictionary. Some of the appointed research fellows found teaching positions in the Department and some simply drifted into oblivion. The fate of one of them, Mr. Ramprasad Majumdar, is worth mentioning because this highlights more than anything else the academic status to which the study of ancient India had sunk by that time. Although not a personal friend of mine, he was well-known to Dr. Sarjug Prasad Singh of Gaya, who was a friend of mine. I do remember him because he used to attend the seminars of the Centre regularly. What I write about him here is based on what Dr. Singh told me. Mr. Majumdar was a tenured lecturer in

Sanskrit in an affiliated undergraduate college in Ranigunge, a Colliery town of West Bengal. When the 'Advanced Centre' was established in the Department of Ancient Indian History and Culture of Calcutta University, he resigned his college position and applied for a junior research fellowship in the Centre to work for Ph.D. on some aspects of the traditional political history of India on the lines of F.E. Pargiter and A.D. Pusalker. Nobody, in fact, guided his studies, and the Director, D.C. Sircar, was indifferent to his fate. So, a stage came when he had no Ph.D. and no 'fellowship' and no prospect to go back to his Ranigunge college job. He simply dropped out of the scene. One day, Dr. Sarjug Prasad Singh told me that he was dead and had died basically of starvation. Mercifully, as we say in such situations in Bengal, he had no family to support. If I remember correctly, Mr. Ramprasad Majumdar contributed a note or two to the *Journal of the Asiatic Society of Bengal* and regularly read papers in the weekly seminars of the Centre.

The Indian university system can be chillingly cruel, and unless one is a conformist and knows how to move in the shadow of the important people, one is less likely to survive in it or move up the academic hierarchy. The fate of Dr. Madhu Mangal Singh, a friend of mine from Chhapra, Bihar, is also a case in point. He was an exceptionally bright student, standing first in first class in both Political Science and Law in Calcutta University. He became a lecturer and then successfully submitted a thesis on the Indian constitution for his D.Litt., the highest academic degree of the University. However, he did not quite feel happy in the university system or strictly, the intra-departmental atmosphere of his Department. We drifted apart, and after some years I heard that he had committed suicide. I could never know the reason but sometimes I wonder what could be there in the Calcutta University system, which led to the unfortunate death of such an academically bright person as Dr. Madhu Mangal Singh.

I was a part of this system for a long time and however insignificant I was, I can still offer an insider's view of the functioning of this place. In its day-to-day existence and operations, it was a kind of slum in comparison with many other less known Indian universities. The reason of this rather sordid state of affairs was the degeneration of the city which became less and less habitable as years rolled on, and partly this was due to the refusal of everybody concerned to set up a new campus where things would be better organized.

The university system in Bengal began to deteriorate rapidly in the 1960s, for which the irresponsible leftist agitations or 'student movements' have to be considered largely responsible. In 1967, I had the misfortune to be an invigilator in one of the MA examination centres of the university, and the open and arrogant 'copying' that I saw practised on a large scale by boys and girls of normal middle class households was a traumatic experience.

The downward flow of the Kolkata academic life continues unabated. A Kolkata doctor-scientist, Subhas Mukhopadhyay, was an early pioneer of 'test tube baby' research and under his supervision such a baby was born on October 3, 1978, less than three months after the birth of the first baby of this kind on 25 July, 1978 under the tutelage of Robert Edwards in Britain. Dr. Mukhopadhyay earned implacable hostility from his professional colleagues. Regrettably, he could not continue to cope with the insult to which he had also been subjected by the left government of the day and committed suicide sometime in 1981. The point I am making is that by the time I came to Calcutta University, it was long past its academic prime. Two senior students who deserve mention in this context in the field of ancient India are Bratindra Nath Mukhopadhyay (better known as B.N. Mukherjee) and Pratapaditya Pal. Mukherjee did his Ph.D. later in London and became well-known for his specialisation in Kushan history, on which he has a number of major publications. Some of his ideas regarding the early history of Bengal are not acceptable but there has never been any doubt regarding his gentlemanly qualities and commitment to learning. He retired as a professor of ancient Indian history from the university. Pratapaditya Pal who retired from a senior post at the Los Angeles County museum several years ago taught us as a research scholar when we were MA students. He did two successive Ph.Ds. (one from Calcutta and the other from Cambridge) on ancient Nepalese sculpture and architecture and went on to become the most distinguished art historian of his generation in the field of Indian and southeast Asian art. His long series of publications on virtually all aspects of Himalayan, and orthodox Indian and southeast Asiatic art is a singular tribute to his academic commitment, vision and capability and serves as an example to be followed by students of ancient India of the Kolkata tradition. It may be noted that Pal failed to receive a suitable appointment at the University on his return from Cambridge with a second Ph.D.

THE MA SYLLABUS IN ARCHAEOLOGY IN CALCUTTA UNIVERSITY

There was nothing wrong with the syllabus that we were expected to follow as MA students in archaeology. It was divided into eight full papers, each comprising 100 marks. The full papers were divided into two sections comprising 50 marks each. The full range was the following: Paper I—ethnology, and ancient geography of India; Paper II—history and theories of archaeology, and field-methods of archaeology; Paper III—prehistory and protohistory of India; Paper IV—palaeography and epigraphy; Paper V—numismatics and iconography; Paper VI—sculpture, painting, and architecture; Paper VII—

Mesopotamian history and archaeology; Paper VIII—principles of conservation and viva voce examination on the field-work done as a compulsory part of the course. The statutory requirement was a 12-week spell of excavations and explorations work. Paper I was taught entirely by S.R. Das, with some inputs from S.S. Sarkar of Department of Anthropology and K.G. Bagchi of Department of Geography. In the ethnology section he dealt with the various racial classificatory systems of India and the results of the studies of different excavated skeletons, the latter also tied to the racial framework. This made us familiar with the general range of physical anthropological literature on India in the 1950s and earlier. In the ancient geography section, Das depended on Hsuang-Tsang's account and its archaeological corroboration by Alexander Cunningham. We were introduced to the problems of identifications of many archaeological sites. Equally importantly, from my point of view, I was introduced to the first edition of O.H.K. Spate's *India and Pakistan: A Regional Geography* which, with its terse and sardonic prose and coverage of many things human, made Indian geography exciting to read. It is a volume to which I have turned again and again. For archaeological theories, Grahame Clark's *Archaeology and Society* and Gordon Childe's *Piecing Together the Past* provided the basic framework and for field-methods we read R.E.M. Wheeler's *Archaeology from the Earth* and R.J.C. Atkinson's *Field Archaeology*. For history of archaeology, it was Glyn Daniel's *Hundred Years of Archaeology*, supplemented by A.W. Ceram's *Gods, Graves and Scholars*. It is interesting to reflect that I acquired a copy of Daniel's *Hundred Years* along with a copy of *The Old Stone Age* by Miles Burkitt, another Cambridge person, from a departmental store called *Kamalalay*. This store, once located on the Dharmatala street, has long ceased to exist, but it is unlikely that books of this kind by

Cambridge archaeologists will ever be found in such obscure places as this. Archaeology no doubt has progressed but without its historical content it has allowed itself to be merely an anthropological and 'scientific' academic exercise without firm intellectual roots.

For the history of Indian archaeology, it was basically the couple of relevant articles in *Ancient India* 9 (1953). Das, who taught us the archaeology papers, was trained in the Taxila school under Wheeler, and scrupulously made us face the rigour and discipline of that school. I am glad that he did that, and even now I would find it difficult to go through a non-productive day in the field. Prehistory was taught us by D. Sen of the Department of Anthropology, who participated in the Soan valley expedition led by H. de Terra and T.T. Paterson and co-authored with N.K. Bose a monograph on the prehistory of Mayurbhanj. V.D. Krishnaswami's article on Stone Age in *Ancient India* 3 (1947) served as the basic text and was supported by his article in *Ancient India* 9 (1953). The prehistory articles, which were rather important during those days, included the review of the Indian prehistoric material in *Studies in the Ice Age of Kashmir* by de Terra and Paterson, which dealt, besides their main work in the northwest, with the Narmada valley and the Madras (Chennai) area as well. B.B. Lal's study of the Kangra prehistoric situation was adapted from the terrace sequence of the Soan but the regional situations were noticed more closely by K. Soundara Rajan and others in the context of the Singrauli basin of Uttar Pradesh and Giddalur in the Kurnool area of Andhra. The prehistory of the Sabarmati valley of Gujarat received a geomorphological treatment from F.E. Zeuner, among others and the *Teri* microlithic industry of the fossil sand dunes near modern Tuticorin was studied by Zeuner and Bridget Allchin. Microliths at Birbhanpur in West Bengal were put in their stratigraphic and typological contexts by B.B. Lal. If all these writings lacked anything, it was clarity and a generally integrated picture of Indian Stone Age stratigraphy and technology. The Deccan College under H.D. Sankalia had already begun its prehistoric ventures, especially at Langhnaj in north Gujarat and at Nevasa on the Pravara in Maharashtra. It was also around this time that A.P. Khatri, then a research student at the Deccan College, argued for a pebble-tool horizon on the model of the Oldowan, but the significance of this claim was more or less ignored by his colleagues. In fact, the genuineness of his finds was doubted. The Archaeological Survey organized an international seminar in 1961 to mark its centenary but, as far as I know, Calcutta University archaeology was not represented there and the seminar proceedings, although I remember to have come across one or two volumes of abstracts of the papers presented in the seminar, the proceedings were never published. There is a notice in *Indian Archaeology - A Review, 1961-62* to the effect that there was in that 'international seminar on Asian archaeology' a committee to "consider the problem of the terminology of Indian prehistory" with F.R. Allchin, R.J. Braidwood, R.V. Joshi, V.D. Krishnaswami, B.B. Lal, H.D. Sankalia, B. Subbarao and F.E. Zeuner as members. With dissent from Braidwood who preferred cultural-historical terms, the committee recommended the use of the terms Early, Middle and Late Stone Ages in preference to the nomenclature of Series I, Series II and Series III tools. There were isolated publications on the finds of prehistoric tools in many parts of the country, and whatever prehistoric studies were made from the 1940s to the very beginning of the 1960s was summarised by H.D. Sankalia in 1962 in his *Prehistory and Protohistory in India and Pakistan.*

One has a serious problem with this and other publications on prehistory dating from this period. They carry the impression that it was an utterly new phase of the study of Indian prehistory and that Robert Bruce Foote was the only early prehistorian worth mentioning. This was not the case. The stratigraphical and typological basis of the study of Indian prehistory was laid down in the second half of the nineteenth century by a number of geologists working in different parts of India. For instance, in a sense the discovery of a large number of microlith-bearing sites in the Belan valley and its adjacent regions was in a direct continuation of J. Cockburn's and A.C.L. Carlleyle's work in the same general region and that there were both Mesolithic and Neolithic phases in the adjoining part of the Ganga plain was highlighted by Carlleyle's excavations at Jahuraganj between Banaras and Ghazipur.

Protohistory was taught by Das and possibly by A.C. Pal, who had joined the Department of Archaeology of Calcutta University after successfully going through the course of the School of Archaeology of the Archaeological Survey of India. As a part of their training, they had excavated at Gilund under B.B. Lal. The results of this excavation remained unpublished. In any case, Pal had first-hand familiarity with the prehistoric material found at many newly excavated sites in the country. The basic frame of teaching the paper was partly provided by Lal's article on 'progress in protohistory' in *Ancient India* 9, but otherwise the volumes on the Indus civilization by Wheeler and Mackay were among the compulsory readings. The Baluchistan discoveries figured in W.A. Fairservis' publications on the Quetta valley, especially his Quetta and Zhob reports published by the American Natural History Society, but for the other Baluchistan areas we depended primarily on Stuart Piggott's *Prehistoric India* (1950) and his papers in *Ancient India*. Childe's *New Light on the Most Ancient East* was not ignored in the case of the Indus civilization, although it was read along with Wheeler's now-famous report on the Harappa excavations in 1946 (published in 1947). We took a long time to know about F.A. Khan's excavations at Kot Diji and J-M Casal's work at Amri, but the information eventually came in, and we became aware of the slowly expanding image of the antecedence of the Indus civilization.

There was by now a slow accumulation of the protohistoric material from different parts of India, mainly Navdatoli in central India, Nasik-Jorwe and Nevasa in Maharashtra, Sanganakallu, Piklihal and Utnur in the south, Painted Grey Ware profile at Hastinapur, Ochre-Coloured Pottery and Copper Hoards of the upper Ganga valley, and so on. A beginning of protohistoric research was made by this time in West Bengal as well under its Director of State Archaeology, P.C. Dasgupta, at Pandu Rajar Dhibi, but the University establishment did not take kindly to his work and so there was no interaction between the new prehistoric and protohistoric discoveries in West Bengal and Calcutta University's Department of Archaeology. Sankalia's 1962 volume, cited earlier, summed up the pan-Indian protohistoric situation till that date.

For palaeography, J.G. Buhler's book on Indian palaeography and its accompanying chart, which were reprinted around this time in D.P. Chattopadhyay's *Indian Studies: Past and Present*, were our life-line. The first volume of D.C. Sircar's *Select Inscriptions* served our needs for epigraphy. For numismatics, our primary source was J. Allan's catalogue of early Indian coins in the British Museum and we followed this up with a few secondary sources. J.N. Banerjee's *The Development of Hindu Iconography* had to be read rather closely for the paper on iconography. For sculpture, painting and architecture, we closely followed the chapters on sculpture and painting by N.R. Ray in the relevant volumes of the *History and Culture of Indian People* series and for architecture we followed S.K. Saraswati's chapters in the same volumes. The teaching of these papers in the hands of Amita Ray and Pratapaditya Pal was good, and we were interested enough to lay our hands on the different volumes by A.K. Coomaraswamy, L. Bachofer, Stella Kramrisch and Percy Brown, whether we understood them fully at that stage or not.

Stella Kramrisch (1896-1993), as I have noticed before, taught at the University from about 1923 to 1950. She came to Calcutta University from Santiniketan to which she was invited by Rabindranath Tagore after she finished studying art history under Joseph Strzygowski in Vienna. Her basic work on the diverse aspects of the history of Indian art both at the elite and the village level was done while she was in Calcutta. The different strands in the development of an art historical school in Calcutta owe a lot to her. Her metaphysical approach has generally kept her away from the mainstream of archaeological concern with Indian art objects, but books like *Indian Sculpture* (1932) are products of both mundane scholarship and wonderful flashes of metaphysical insight. A comprehensive analysis of her writings, placing her in the broad context of the development of the study of ancient Indian art, does not seem to have been attempted. On the other hand, N.R. Ray's *Maurya and Sunga Art* (1944), supposedly an iconic publication of the time, was, in retrospect, a disappointment. It was a straightjacketed Maurya versus Sunga approach where no continuity or link has been envisaged between the two art styles. The emphasis on Maurya art as exclusively an imperial and courtly art did not consider the possible multiplicity of Mauryan art traditions, nor could it throw any new light on the origins of this art beyond repeating the theories advocated by B. Spooner and others.

On Mesopotamian history and archaeology, there was only reading of one or two secondary books such as Leonard

Woolley's *Ur of the Chaldees* and Seton Lloyd's *Foundations in the Dust*. The Mesopotamian history paper was taught by Pradyot C. Mukherji whose speciality was central European history which he studied in London. He was very kind to me and used to tell me stories of his boyhood when he used to run away from home and occasionally find himself in remote areas such as the land of the Hazaras in the northwest. We obtained mostly 'notes' from teachers on conservation, but that a general idea of the basic principles and techniques of both structural and chemical conservation was rammed down our throats subsequently stood us in good stead.

THE FIELD-WORK COMPONENT OF THE MA SYLLABUS, 1960-62

As I have already noticed, there was no interaction between the University department of archaeology and the West Bengal government department of archaeology in Kolkata, with the university people consciously trying to pull down the significance of the discoveries made by the government department. It was unfortunate because that was the period when under P.C. Dasgupta, the government department of archaeology went on making a long series of discoveries in the field of Bengal prehistory and protohistory. Dasgupta was Assistant Curator of Ashutosh Museum of Art, Calcutta University. Before that he was a lecturer in an undergraduate college at the famous archaeological site of Tamluk where he picked up from the surface and wherever the earth was dug in the area, a large collection of early historic terracottas. The abundance of such terracottas available in Tamluk in the 1950s can be guessed from Dasgupta's rather cheerful claim that occasionally he collected terracottas from the cliffs and the beds of the ponds where he used to take his mid-day bath. The terracottas seem to have been the principal collecting interest of Ashutosh Museum then. This museum, which was set up by D.P. Ghosh in 1937 with only a handful of objects, had grown by then into a respectable collection of antiquities and folk-art from different parts of Bengal and Orissa. Places which yielded historical antiquities along the old course of the Bhagirathi south of Calcutta came to be slowly recognized in the academic circles mainly due to the efforts of local antiquarians like Kalidas Datta. Ghosh had good contacts with Datta and others, and many of the antiquities collected by them were donated to his museum. Although not a field-person himself, Ghosh did not hesitate to involve the museum in the excavations at the early historic site of Bangarh in north Bengal in 1937-41 and then in Chandraketugarh (also called Berachampa) in 1956 and later. On both these occasions, the field responsibility was given to K.G. Goswami, a teacher of Sanskrit at the University and trained at Mohenjodaro under the Archaeological Survey of India. Goswami was recruited as a 'scholar' to the Survey but was subsequently retrenched due to the economic drive initiated by the government. His *Pragaitihasik Mohenjodaro* (in Bengali) is a fine personal memoir of his experience in the Survey. I am not sure if Dasgupta was trained in archaeology anywhere except in the Chandraketugarh/Berachampa excavations of the museum, but he became a great enthusiast for roaming around in the field and picking up antiquities, especially after he became Director of the West Bengal State Department/Directorate of Archaeology, which was formally established in 1958. Within a few years of his taking charge, he built up a dependable academic framework of prehistory and protohistory in West Bengal, in addition to throwing light on many historical sites. He fully understood the significance of newspapers to make the work of his department familiar to the Bengali public. The Calcutta newspapers frequently published his hand-outs on his sites. He drew to himself an equally enthusiastic band of young assistants who were second to none in undergoing physical hardships to locate sites. In detail, their academic claims were fairly off-putting; in the case of Pandu Rajar Dhibi they invoked contacts with both Egypt and Crete. But overall, their contribution to Bengal archaeology under the leadership of Dasgupta was immense. They would know their sites and pass on some of their wild enthusiasm for them to others. The main problem of Dasgupta was that he left his collections and excavations virtually unpublished.

Dasgupta died a premature death and towards the end he was treated shabbily by the government. The following incident may give us a little idea of what type of a human being he was. On my first visit to Chandraketugarh in 1958, I ended up at Haroa, some miles away, and collected from the Vidyadhari cliff a pot which was possibly nothing more than a modern example of clay pots left behind at cremation grounds. I wanted to have my pot dated and so I went to meet him in the Ashutosh Museum, where he was then the Assistant Curator. He took a glance at the pot and then at me, and said that it dated from the second century BC. I was very thrilled but, as I realized later, his basic aim was to infect history students like me with the bug of archaeology.

I remember my first Chandraketugarh visit also for another reason. Chittaranjan Raychaudhuri was running the excavation camp at the site, and as I walked in, I found him returning from the waste land behind the camp with a complete terracotta mother goddess in one hand and a *lota* in another. While squatting in the field, he noticed a pile of loose earth dug possibly by jackals and noticed the mother goddess figurine sticking out of that earth. The figurine was identical with that of the famous Oxford figurine from Tamluk.

For its excavation programme, the University department could select one of the many protohistoric sites of the region, but it decided to excavate a Buddhist monastery, regarding whose identity there was some doubt. The monastery of *Raktamrittka*, associated with the capital city of the Gauda kingdom, Karnasuvarna, was visited by Hsuang-Tsang, but there was a discrepancy in its geographical bearings as given by Hsuang-Tsang and his ancient Chinese biographer. This led to various hypotheses regarding the identification of this place, although there was an attempt to identify it with the mound near Chhiruti in the district of Murshidabad. Before the excavations were undertaken at Chhiruti in April-June 1962, we went to Dulmi on the bank of the Subarnarekha to assess its archaeological potential. It drew more or less a blank. There was a dilapidated brick temple of c.10th/11th century on the top of a large gravelly upland, and the sculptures associated with the temple site were shifted years before to the palace compound of the kings of Ichhagarh in the Singhbhum district, formerly of Bihar but now of Jharkhand. I remember our Dulmi-Ichhagarh trip (1961) mainly because of the beauty of this part of the Suvarnarekha valley in winter and also because we visited a weekly market-place which was attended by many people from the forested interior. In those days, when there was plenty of food in the forests, people of the forests used to have statuesque physical proportions, and I still remember a scantily but beautifully dressed Kharia couple engrossed in themselves. A young woman was selling spirituous liquor straight from an earthen pot, and one had to kneel in front of her and shape one's hands like a cup to get a drink from her. I had been back to Ichhagarh sometime in the 1980s, but the area was by then largely deforested and the market-place we visited did not hold markets anymore.

In the autumn of 1960, I accompanied a friend of mine, Rameshwar Shaw, to his village home on the bank of the Ganga near Dumraon in Bihar. He later became the professor of

Bengali literature in Kalyani University and an eminent scholar of Bengali linguistics. Moving about among the long stalks of Sorghum millet by the side of the Ganga in autumn was a novel experience for a Bengali like me, and that was something which has remained with me since then. We also went then to Sasaram where I climbed the Chandan Shahid hill to see Asoka's Minor Rock Edict I. From Dumraon we also went to Buxar which was a small town then surrounded by mango and *lichi* orchards.

Chhiruti, a little away from the right bank of the Bhagirathi in Murshidabad, was an altogether different place. The meander of the old bed of the river was still there below the mound which also partly overlay the modern village of Jadupur. Through a vast stretch of paddy fields and intermittent pools of water, this old bed was linked on the west with the main course of the river and served as an area where fishermen caught fish during the rains and the cultivators reaped paddy in late autumn. There were the ruins of an old indigo plantation nearby, and from the top of the mound, one could see the last ripples of the Chhotanagpur uplands merging in the Bhagirathi plain. The neighbouring village of Rangamati-Chandpara was then known for bandits, some of whom decided to engage themselves in our dig. We camped not in the immediate neighbourhood of the mound but in the local school compound near the railway station. The school authorities gave us a couple of rooms to use in their building, but most of us pitched tents outside. We developed excellent friendly relationships with the villagers, and the friendship has lasted through all these years. The non-working days were spent mostly in wandering around in the countryside. In my case, this involved recognizing different kinds of birds, and the man (Arun Kumar Das of the village Madhupur) who taught me, among other things, how to distinguish between a *Chakravak* (in Sanskrit; *Chakha* in Bengali) duck and a duck of the ordinary variety, still remains a cherished friend. I still cherish the memory of the countryside of this part of Murshidabad.

The daily routine of the excavation was conducted fairly efficiently and with a lot of discipline. The students were put in different trenches, with the teachers and the draftsman and the photographer forming the supervisory staff. The people who wielded the pick-axes and carried the earth were villagers employed on daily wage, usually six to a trench. Three of them carried the excavated earth to the dump and three others remained inside the trench. The general level of economy of the area may be gauged from the fact that lunch for most of our workers did not extend beyond a few mouthfuls of puffed rice and fermented juice of palm trees or *toddy*. The strokes of the pick-axes became naturally difficult to control after lunch because of the inebriating effect of *toddy*.

As we went to Chhiruti year after year and as we were all young, we interacted well with those who worked with us in the trenches. Many of the names still come back to me. Some of them later served jail sentences for banditry and other violent crimes, but they treated us as friends or even brothers, and at no point was there any problem with them. Occasionally, of course, there were unexplored depths of the rural life to contend with. A young man barely in his teens, who used to work with me went in search of liquor to the house of a fellow-villager, but beat him up and took liberties with his sister when he refused to sell him drinks. In retaliation, the liquor-seller raised hue and cry and alleged that the young man had robbed him of money and other valuables. A criminal case was registered in the nearest town and the accused hid himself in the paddy fields for a few days, with his co-workers briefing me about his whereabouts every day.

The academic aspect of this excavation programme was, however, something very different, although we did not understand it at the time. The work began in 1962 (*Indian Archaeology—a Review*, 1962-63, p. 46) and continued with some annual gaps up to 1972-73. For seven seasons, the university put people in the field (*IAR*, 1962-63, p. 46; *IAR* 1963-64, pp. 62-63; *IAR* 1964-65, pp. 48-51; *IAR* 1966-67, pp. 46-47; *IAR* 1968-69, p. 43; *IAR* 1971-72, pp. 49-51; *IAR* 1972-73, pp. 37-38). The report of the first season was published by the Asiatic Society in 1968 (S.R. Das, *Rajbadidanga, 1962, (Chiruti Jadupur): An Interim Report on Excavations at Rajbadidanga and Terracotta Seals and Sealings*) and to this may be added *Archaeological Discoveries from Murshidabad District, West Bengal*, 1971, by the same author. Everybody else of the excavation team was kept out of the data-processing and data-reporting. The inscribed terracotta seals of the first season were read by D.C. Sircar and published, but the hundreds of such seals and sealings found subsequently are still awaiting publication. At one point, there was a mention of Roman names on seals (*IAR* 1968-69) and on another occasion, a seal supposedly contained the name *Tamraparni* or Sri Lanka (*IAR* 1972-73). The readings do not carry much weight because D.C. Sircar was no longer involved in them, and the whole lot of unpublished seals and sealings from this site will need careful reading, analysis and publications. As a part of the MA students' training, the Department of Archaeology, Calcutta University, has organized excavations, often for multiple seasons, at many sites since then—Mangalkot, Pakhanna/Pokharna, Dihar and Mughalmari. These excavations have been directed by various Head of the Departments after S.R. Das and all of them have distinguished themselves by not publishing any formal report. One considers oneself lucky if there are occasional papers by them on these sites.

The issue of publication notwithstanding, the site of Chhiruti was a good training ground for us. Basically, we learnt how to excavate brick structures and organize large excavations on day-to-day basis.

Another aspect of our field-training was a study-tour of a few major sites in south India and Orissa in the summer of 1961. In the south, we travelled from Chennai to Cape Comorin, and in addition to the major temple-sites and places such as Mahabalipuram, we explored Attirampakkam, Sawyerpuram and Adityanallur. Mahabalipuram had only a small Archaeological Survey of India guesthouse then and the site was otherwise deserted except for a small fishermen's village on the sea-shore near the Tiger Cave. We had Mahabalipuram more or less to ourselves, and the sight of the first sunlight of the day breaking on the face of the recumbent Vishnu in one of the caves is still vivid in my memory. A good collection of palaeoliths was made at Attirampakkam, and I can still recall the sight of a large cleaver below the rushing and sparkling water in the bed of a rivulet as I knelt down to have a drink. On the bank of the Tamraparni near Adityanallur, we recorded a few Vishnu images and collected one of them for the Calcutta University collection. In the large sand-dunes of Sawyerpuram, microliths could then be picked up in handfuls. A remarkable experience happened in the outer part of the painted cave at Sittanavasal near Pudukottai. I fell briefly asleep there at noon, and when I woke up I felt that I was in the middle of a lotus tank with blooming lotuses. The vibrancy of the colour of the paintings on the ceiling, which gave me this feeling, also speaks for the excellent stage of preservation those paintings had in 1961. I had been back to the cave in 2004 and found not even a faint trace of the paintings. Thanks to the 'care' taken by the chemical preservators of the Southern Circle of the Archaeological Survey of India, the Sittanavasal paintings have been destroyed.

The superintendent of the Southern Circle during that period was S. Chandra. Regrettably, I have never come across any publication by him, but he was a very nice person and extremely cooperative and helpful to our small group. Later on, I learnt that he was the son of G.C. Chandra who at some point conducted excavations at Nalanda.

In 1961 Bhuvaneswar was being built as the capital of Orissa. The caves of Udayagiri and Khandagiri then lay way outside the city limits and were surrounded by jungles. We found S.K. Mukherjee of the Archaeological Survey of India living alone in the local Inspection Bungalow and getting some clearance work done at the caves. We imposed ourselves on his hospitality, and the kindness with which he made all arrangements for us lives in the memory as an example of the friendliness with which archaeology people were then greeted in all parts of India by fellow-archaeologists. Mr. Sushanta Kumar Mukherjee was the principal assistant of Debala Mitra in the Ratnagiri excavations and held the same role in the excavations at Mahishdal by R.P. Das. Mahishdal was a lovely site just by side of the railway bridge over the Kopai at Santiniketan. It was a beautifully conducted excavation and I remember being buffeted by a strong January wind blowing across the site. Mr. Mukherjee later became a Class I officer of the Eastern Circle of the Survey. I am not sure if he ever published anything under his own name, but he lives in the memory as an example of archaeologists who lived mostly from camp to camp and was a model to many of us as an impeccable 'field-man'.

INDIAN ARCHAEOLOGICAL RESEARCH FROM 1947 TO THE EARLY 1960S

The details of the discoveries and major publications of this period have already been incorporated in the first chapter of my *Archaeology in the Third World: A History of Indian Archaeology Since 1947*, and I find no reason to repeat that discussion. However, certain general observations on the archaeological approach and attitude of that period may not be misplaced in the present context.

First, chronology was much muddled during this period. In prehistory that never went beyond purely wild speculations, limited to such broad time-spans as the middle or late Plestocene. Even in the case of the Holocene, nothing could be pinpointed to specific time-brackets. In the case of the newly discovered protohistoric contexts, things were slightly better but no less speculative. For example, in the case of the upper limit of the Navdatoli chalcolithic, it was opined (*IAR* 1957-58, p. 32) that it should be c.500 BC because the chalcolithic layers were sealed by those containing the NBP. However, "more positive dating evidence" was found in the supposed similarity between the Navdatoli channel-spouted vessels with the "distinctive channel-spouted cup and certain other pottery types" of Cemetery B at Sialk, Iran. This level of Sialk in the far-off Zagros mountain of Iran was hypothetically dated c.1000-c.800 BC and on the basis of this date and the thickness of the Navdatoli chalcolithic deposit including its floor-levels and 'three main conflagrations', the Navdatoli chalcolithic was placed between 1200 and 700 BC. It was a wild guess and the Sialk analogy was plainly uncalled for. The only thing which could be said on the basis of the occurrence of the NBP at the site is that its chalcolithic deposit was certainly pre-NBP and considering its thickness of 10 to 11 feet, its earliest phase possibly went back well into the second millennium BC.

B.K. Thapar in *Ancient India 14* (1957) dated Period I or the Chalcolithic period at Maski between sometime in the early first millennium BC and c.400 BC. Thapar wrote two years before the first set of radiocarbon dates from Navdatoli (5 dates) and

Nevasa (1 date) was published by the radiocarbon dating laboratory of the University of Pennsylvania and put their Chalcolithic phase securely early in the second millennium BC ('notes' in *Ancient India* 15, 1959). By this time, a date from Utnur, c.2000 BC, was also published by the British Museum.

The NBP, which occurred in the upper phase of the first period of occupation at Ujjain, gave the upper limit of the period around 500 BC, and Period I of the site was put as a whole between c.700 and c.500 BC. Considering that Period I represented 6 feet deposit, the allocation of merely 200 years to its total span was unduly conservative. What I gather from the reading of the literature of the period is that the chronological estimates were based in many cases on convoluted arguments and that they were unduly conservative on the whole.

Secondly, virtually no allowance was made for the continuity of occupations at sites. 'Breaks' were supposed to intervene between the Harappans and the Painted Grey Ware and between the central Indian chalcolithic and the succeeding iron-bearing deposit.

The Alamgirpur case in 1958-59 offers a ready example:

> The break between Periods I and II was demonstrated not merely by their respective cultural assemblages but also by a difference in the texture and composition of their layers. Thus, while the deposits of Period I were compact and brownish, those of Period II were loose and grey with frequent bands of burnt earth and ash. Further, the top-surface of Period I was hard and whitish, signifying a long exposure (*IAR* 1958-59, pp. 52-53).

One fails to understand how the differences in the composition of layers would signify breaks in stratigraphy and also how apparently a 'hard and whitish' top-surface would signify 'long exposure'. This idea of a break between the

Harappans and the PGW level at Alamgirpur was accepted by A. Ghosh in his introduction to this volume of *IAR*. It is apparent that the idea of breaks between the different early periods was, for some unknown reasons, almost axiomatic in the Indian archaeological writings of the period.

Thirdly, nobody was interested in fully exploring the possibilities of archaeological research in expanding the scope of Indian history and trying to generate a true people's history of India. The Aryans and the literary tradition occupied most of the archaeological minds. In 1952, Sankalia published a small volume (*Archaeology and Indian Universities*) where he emphasized the need for "University Departments of Archaeology" which should not replace government departments but "should serve as so many branches of one central organization, carrying on purely local or regional surveys or operating in Joint Expeditions as suits their needs and capacities." Not much attention was given to academic problems in this pamphlet, but there was a recurrent emphasis on such 'major problems' as "whether the Aryans are foreign or indigenous to India, whence and how did the Indus Civilization grow up, whether hundreds of kings and numerous dynasties mentioned in our Puranas are all mythical".

Lal's hypothesis of the Painted Grey Ware people being Aryans was more effective in consolidating the hypothesis of Aryan migration in Indian archaeology. There was a section on "painted and plain grey wares in western Asia and southern Europe" in Lal's Hastinapur report, and because the Painted Grey Ware was found to be associated with many of the sites mentioned in the *Mahabharata*, the idea of its Aryan affiliation gained more acceptance. Throughout the north Indian universities, the correlation between the Painted Grey Ware and the Aryans was seldom doubted, and this even got down to the level of school text-books. In his 'notes' to *Ancient India*,

10-11, which published Lal's Hastinapur report, A. Ghosh offered unstinted support to the Aryan theory and argued that the Painted Grey Ware, because it was 'unconnected' with the relics of any previous culture, was "reasonable to suppose that its authors did not spring out of the Indian soil".

Fourthly, the archaeologists of the period were not always aware of the geographical implications of some of the earlier research. The survey of the Ghaggar stretch in Rajasthan under A. Ghosh significantly expanded the Harappan area in post-1947 India as early as 1950. It may not be forgotten that the Ghaggar stretch as a whole was considered archaeologically significant for a very long time. J. Tod's *Annals and Antiquities of Rajasthan* makes clear reference to the archaeological significance of this zone in the early nineteenth century and yet Ghosh's exploration of the area had to wait for the persuasion of K.M. Panikkar who, apart from then being the Dewan of the Bikaner state, was also a principal historian of India (I owe this information to Nayanjot Lahiri). One is somewhat surprised by this because Tod's *Annals and Antiquities* is a famous book, the main source of the study of Rajasthan's princely history. Any reader of Tod's book should have been aware of the archaeological possibilities of the Ghaggar zone.

If one looks back at the developments of Indian archaeology between c.1947 and c.1962, one realizes that the archaeologists were not yet sure of the intellectual impact of the new prehistoric and proto-historic discoveries. Long occupational sequences were being discovered in different parts of India, giving each of them a history of occupation, regarding the length of which there was previously no idea at all. It was a classic case of finding through the microscopic gaze of archaeology many relics of occupation which were undetected before. Instead of being excited by this development and the prospect of enormously diversifying the scope of ancient Indian historical studies, all that the archaeologists could think of was to interpret the new discoveries in the light of the Puranic traditions and the idea of Aryan invasions. Even while announcing the first C-14 dates, all obtained from the foreign sources, A. Ghosh, the Director General, shows no sign of being thrilled by the discovery of an agricultural stage as early as 2000 BC in south Deccan or by the discovery of a rich chalcolithic profile in central India, Maharashtra and elsewhere (editorial notes in *Ancient India 15*). It is doubtful if the Indian archaeology leaders of the day realized the tremendous potential of the radiocarbon dating or were interested in setting up a laboratory for it under the aegis of the Archaeological Survey of India itself.

The main reason why such an intellectual apathy could develop was due to the fact that archaeology in India had, till the 1960s, been an exclusively government-controlled exercise. Whether things changed for the better in the succeeding decades remains to be seen.

2

Kolkata, 1963-77

PERSONAL NOTES

The result of our MA examination (1962 batch) was declared in March, 1963, and I became a departmental research fellow in archaeology in April. Sometime in 1964, I was awarded a Junior Research Fellowship of the Indian UGC, but there was no change in my departmental affiliation. In 1963 April itself, I was asked to contribute to the departmental teaching, and on November 11, 1965, I became a member of the teaching faculty in the same department, i.e., the department of archaeology of Calcutta University. I continued to work there till the end of February, 1977 with a break of three years when I was on 'study leave' from the University in 1973-76.

The reason of my leaving Calcutta University was my inability to get on well with the then Head of the Department, Dr. Mrs. Amita Ray, whose way of running the department and idea of archaeological field-research were disputable. I do not remember the details after so many years, but in Indian universities conflicts between teachers can take ugly turns, and I remember that I had then taken the precaution of watching over my shoulder while walking the streets. It is normal in Indian universities to involve the present and former students in the departmental conflicts of interests, which means that the teachers without students' support may have hired thugs set upon them. After D.C. Sircar retired from Carmaichael professorship sometime in the late 1960s, there was some conflict among the possible contenders for his job and I clearly remember how A.N. Lahiri, one of the claimants, was shouted at and harassed by the student supporters of another applicant, B.N. Mukherjee who eventually got the position. Sometime during this period, I sought an appointment with the Vice Chancellor, a soil scientist named S.R. Mukherjee. That was the first time that I met somebody so important in my *alma mater*. The Vice Chancellor, reputedly a decent man but then apparently under the influence of the Head of the Department Dr. Mrs. Ray, spoke of dire consequences if I had dared go off to a different university without a proper 'release order'. I decided to ignore this warning and soon joined Delhi University.

The responsibility of conducting archaeological field-work in Calcutta University's archaeology department rested exclusively with the Head of the department, who was involved with the digging of a Buddhist monastery site. Nothing else was considered worthwhile. Besides, the ordinary antiquities recovered from the annual departmental excavation of the concerned monastery site, such as pottery, iron nails, and so on, were never handed over to the departmental juniors for analysis and publications. The Department had no programme for explorations either. It is rather important that this aspect of the newly established Department of Archaeology of Calcutta University is duly noted, because right from the beginning, the Department cut itself off from any systematic programme of field-work outside its annual programme of excavations at the monastic site of Chhiruti, which, as we have already noticed, has remained basically unpublished except for the first season's work in 1962. The responsibility lay squarely on the shoulders of S.R. Das who personally was as good an excavator as one came across, but he sadly lacked academic vision and was incapable of building a dynamic university department. He trained his students well and was a good man—I certainly owed my teaching job in 1965 to his support—but the leadership of a university department also requires a person of some academic imagination and grit.

The organizational structure of fieldwork that I have outlined above is by and large true of most of the Indian universities having interest in archaeology. When the focus of fieldwork also incorporates regular explorations, the Head of the Department normally deputes research students and others to the field. The universities of Poona, Allahabad and Banaras did this regularly and thus these universities played a leading role in the development of archaeology of their respective regions. In Poona, i.e., the Deccan College, the scale of explorations by the research students was much larger than elsewhere. In Calcutta, this was avoided and thus its fieldwork was almost exclusively excavation-oriented and dependent entirely on the Head of the Department who kept all the data to himself.

It must also be noted that the Department did not try to develop a scientific wing for even elementary soil and other relevant analyses. If I remember correctly, Deccan College had such a section in the early 1960s. One teacher from geography (K.G. Bagchi) and two teachers from Anthropology (D. Sen, a prehistorian and S.S. Sarkar, a physical anthropologist) were inducted to teach us, but the problem was that there was no long-term collaboration with the geography, geology and anthropology departments of the university. A few pieces of wood from Chhiruti excavations were identified by a suitable person in the university's Botany department, but this was an isolated thing. Students of these science departments could be persuaded to do Ph.D. work on the various analyses of the Chhiruti excavated materials and the whole 'science' part of archaeology would have been properly organized in Calcutta University. The situation continues down to this day. Although there is now a large induction of B.Sc students of geology, geography, etc. to the MA archaeology programme and the students with science background are awarded M.Sc degree in Archaeology, no laboratory infrastructure has been built for these students and there is nothing called 'archaeological science' for them.

Before I got the job in Calcutta, I tried for jobs in three places—the Archaeological Survey of India (1964), Banaras Hindu University (1964) and Panjab University (Chandigarh)—and was unsuccessful everywhere. The Archaeological Survey job entailed an interview at the Union Public Service Commission, Shahajahan Road, Delhi. There, in the waiting hall attached to the interview chamber, I found interviewees from the Archaeological Survey of India congratulating the candidate who would be selected. They were apparently aware of the Board's decision even before the interview. In Banaras, as soon as I entered the room, I overheard the Vice-Chancellor muttering to the subject expert the following instruction: "Here is another show-piece; do not detain him for long." In Chandigarh, the chairman of the selection board, M.S. Randhawa, sounded a bit overpowering and I failed to impress him. Academic factors may play a role in the selection of teachers in the Indian universities but far more obvious is the role played by such non-academic factors as regionalism, casteism and affiliation to, and support of, the important political party/group of the day. In the affiliated colleges at least, money also has now begun, reputedly, to play a role. Sometime in the mid-1980s, I was interviewed for a professorship in Banaras and found, to my great amusement, that everybody present in the interview room as a selector belonged to a particular caste. The person who was eventually selected turned out to be a member of that caste.

In 1963, soon after the MA result was out, I went out in the company of M.A. Konishi, a Japanese who was then a MA student in our department, on a long study-tour of archaeological places including Ajanta, Ellora, Nevasa, Kanheri, Elephanta, Sanchi, etc. We spent a few days in Poona and went to the Deccan College to pay our respects to Professor Sankalia. He took us to the gravel deposits of the Mula and the Mutha, kindly interpreting for us the sections. What impressed us most was his total commitment to the cause of archaeology in the Deccan College which, by that time, bore every imprint of his archaeological planning. Among other things, the campus was spotlessly clean and so was the students' dormitory where we stayed. While staying in the students' hostel of the Deccan College, we met Vishnu Deo Sisodia who was then a student of the Deccan College but also well-known to D.D. Kosambi, who had a house in the Shivaji Nagar area of the city. At our request, Vishnu Deo made an appointment with him and asked us to come along. One of the first questions Professor Kosambi asked was why we were interested in meeting him, especially because we were attached to the Deccan College. There was apparently no love lost between Professor Kosambi and the Deccan College, and later, he wrote a most unkind review of Sankalia's *Prehistory and Protohistory in India and Pakistan* in the *Times of India* suggesting, among other things, that the book was of an inferior academic quality than the Piklihal and Utnur volumes of F.R. Allchin. However, as Sankalia writes in his autobiography, the relationship improved after Kosambi visited the Deccan College and became familiar with Sankalia's work at first-hand. In later life, I have noticed with some amusement that Professor Kosambi was a darling of a wide range of Western and Indian scholars, whether they knew anything of Indian archaeology and ancient history or not. I remember that A.L. Basham wrote a very adulatory review of his *An Introduction to the Study of Indian History* (1956) in the *Bulletin of the School of Oriental and African Studies.* Many of the details of Kosambi's historical and archaeological arguments were not correct. If I remember correctly, in his *Culture and Civilization of India in Historical Outline* (1965) he went to the extent of calling Painted Grey Ware 'Puru-Kuru ceramic', thus displaying a touching faith in the correlation between archaeology and Indian tradition, but within the limited boundary of an individual problem he was often brilliant, capable of marshalling his arguments from diverse points of view. He accused the editor and contributors of the Vidya Bhavan series of volumes on the history and culture of Indian people of having 'tunnel vision' but the fact remains that his own writings hardly led towards a multi-chanelled but unified vision of ancient Indian history. He was certainly brilliant in his own way—his *Exasperating Essays* shows the wide range of his literary sensibilities and other concerns and he must have been good in his chosen sphere of speciality, mathematics—but his fame as a historian rested possibly partly on his incisive, if not brusque, English prose, evidence of wide reading, some good analysis, and the general image of being a leftist intellectual. The fact of being a leftist certainly helped because in the 1960s and later, it is the leftists who were on the ascendant in the Indian historical world. He collaborated in his translation of an anthology of Sanskrit poetry with a Western scholar and was otherwise at home in Sanskrit literature. To historians like Basham, he must have been a world apart from the Indian students of ancient India he was used to interacting with in his own institution in London. However, spending about two hours in the presence of Professor Kosambi was a very exciting and educative experience. He never hesitated in laying down laws on archaeology and history, and I came away with the impression that he possibly typified the best of the Maharashtrian intellect.

Both Ajanta and Ellora were quiet places then, and the thing which I carry about Ajanta from that time was the extraordinary glow of its paintings—the glow generated by the sheer colour of the paintings. That glow has disappeared now, making modern Ajanta a poor shadow of what it was in 1963. We also went to Pitalkhora which was then somewhat difficult of access. I remember the Banjara village at the foot of the Pitalkhora hill. The Banjaras are supposed to represent the ancient *Vanijyakaras* or traders who conducted the trade between north India and the Deccan. The Banjara women were generally handsome and wore colourful Rajasthani dresses. The environs of Sanchi in 1963 were beautiful too, and one could spend hours lying below one of the gateways and looking at the narrative reliefs and lovely human figures above.

Somewhere around this time, although not on this occasion, I also went to Lothal, spending a couple of nights on the top of the mound and looking at the reflection of the moon in the accumulated rain-water of the dock-yard at the dead of night. My major encounter with the Harappans took place at Kalibangan where for three months in 1964 I was a trainee student in the Archaeological Survey excavations there. It was a large excavation camp full of people from various parts of India, and it is through camps like these that the archaeological tradition of the country gets passed down from one generation to another. It is also in camps like these that lifelong friendships with fellow archaeologists are built. In my case, friendship with B.M. Pande and Birendra Pratap Singh has lasted a lifetime. The aridity of the Rajasthan desert was noticeable right at the back of the camp but the arid landscapes have their charm too. The lush sugarcane fields of the actual bed of the Ghaggar contrasted strongly with the barrenness of its banks. I also took a short trip to the area of Nohar and Sothi. I believe I stayed at Nohar and took a camel-ride to Sothi. The charm of riding a camel in this sector lies in the fact that from the camel-back, one can see the scatters of potsherds easily, and perhaps more clearly.

What we call the 'Puja vacation' in Calcutta—a period of little more than a month in autumn—afforded good opportunities for moving about. One year I ended up at Lauriya Nandangarh and another year at Ujjayini. Sights and sounds of various parts of the country slowly began to get familiar, and Madhya Pradesh with its forests and comparatively sparse population seemed to have a special appeal of its own. One day, while sitting in a patch of jungle at the southern edge of Surguja, I tried to carry on a conversation with a local goat-herd who was not from that particular area but from a place on the other side of the hill which lay in front of us. When asked how he drifted to his present area, he replied that it was by following a river, adding, almost poetically, that his own village was located near a jungle pool where one could see animals drinking water at day-break. The river's name was 'Hasdo' and many years later we followed this route to cross over from Surguja to Bilaspur as a part of our study of the Deccan routes. At some point I also went to Amarkantak to see the source of the Narmada and the Son, travelling by bus from Pendra Road railway station on the Bilaspur-Katni line. In autumn, there were large stretches of yellow mustard flowers in the valleys. My friend and former student, Asit

Kumar Bandopadhyay, a retired officer of the Archaeological Survey of India, spent his early days at Shadol in this area, where his father used to work for the railways. I can gather from what he tells me that till the late 1950s, tigers used to appear occasionally in the area of the railway quarters. The area which begins with the Kaimurs and the scarp of the Vindhyas and continues right up to the Satpuras in west-central India must be considered one of the most beautiful stretches of the country.

The Department of Anthropology, Calcutta University, had a small section of prehistoric studies. P. Mitra of this department published a book titled *Prehistoric India, Its Place in the World Culture* as early as 1927. In 1929-30 Mitra was admitted to the Ph.D. degree in Anthropology at Yale for his dissertation on the history of American anthropology, which was later published as a book by Calcutta University (1933).

As a part of the M.Sc programme of the Department, the students were obliged to do fieldwork and the students opting for prehistory had to do prehistoric fieldwork. The main teacher of prehistory was D. Sen, who is known primarily for his work on Mayurbhanj prehistory in collaboration with N.K. Bose who was associated with the department. G.S. Ray was another teacher but his main interest was in the material studies such as potters' clay, etc. D. Sen had a Ph.D. student working on the Palaeolithic of the Singhbhum district. The student, A.K. Ghosh, was somewhat senior to me but soon became a good friend of mine. He was a meticulous field-worker, studying the sites of West Bengal, Singhbhum and partly Mayurbhanj. His Ph.D. thesis on Singhbhum was later published as a memoir of the American Philosophical Society, and he himself spent a year at Harvard as a Fullbright scholar under Hallam Movius. He decided to give up archaeological field-work soon after that and showed, like some of his contemporaries (cf V.N. Misra of Poona, G.C. Mohapatra of Chandigarh and D.P. Agrawal of Ahmedabad), a remarkable keenness and effort to attend international conferences. The Chhotanagpur plateau section of West Bengal, Bihar (now Jharkhand) and Orissa had been visited by many generations of students of the so-called 'field-subjects' like geology, anthropology, zoology, botany, etc. from Kolkata. It is still a beautiful forested area, only a night's journey away from Kolkata. The area has also a special place in Bengali literature, and gradually I began to dream of Chhotanagpur as my field-area too. But in the early 1960s that lay deep in the future.

FINDING AN ACADEMIC FOCUS: EARLY URBAN CENTRES IN INDIA, AN ARCHAEOLOGICAL PERSPECTIVE c. 2500 BC–c. AD 300

The topic I selected for my Ph.D. work was "The early urban centres in India: An archaeological perspective, c.2500 BC-c.300 AD". Considering that this covered the whole of the sub-continent over a vast time-period, this was not a particularly suitable topic for Ph.D. I am glad that I was then too inexperienced to realize this and that my Ph.D. supervisor, Professor Nihar Ranjan Ray, left me to my own devices. Ray was well beyond his academic prime by then but he had a good idea of the academic structure of an argument and never dissuaded a student from experimenting with ideas. In Bengal, Professor Ray is noted for his monumental book in Bengali, *Bangalir Itihas* ('History of the Bengalis') where he synthesized the various categories of evidence to weave, in inspired prose, a brilliant inter-related history of people living in the land which later became known as Bengal. It was not a book which tried to relate historical data, even the textual data, to the different strands of Bengali tradition. It was an honest attempt to understand and narrate the flow of historical events and its various dimensions in the context of Bengal's natural landscape. One of the unstated assumptions of this book is that the ancient human landscapes are not quite extinct yet, offering occasional glimpses through former descriptions in literature and one's own historical perceptions. The idea can be traced to the essays on history by R.N. Tagore at the turn of the twentieth century. Tagore's emphasis on the history of people as lived at the grassroots level has seldom been followed even in Bengal, but Ray, a well-known interpreter of Tagore's writings himself, tried to achieve some of that in his book on the history of the Bengalis. That early urban growth and the morphology of early urban centres deserved attention in the context of ancient India was something he was fond of mentioning while lecturing on ancient Indian sculpture, painting and architecture because some of it was certainly imbued with urban ethos, but this was not the only reason why I ventured to select this topic. The main reason was that the issue had already entered the limelight in archaeology.

As early as 1956-57 and later, there was a debate in *Antiquity* about the applicability of the term 'civilization' to Neolithic Jericho. The excavator of the site, Kathleen M. Kenyon, had no hesitation in using the term in the context of the pre-pottery Neolithic complex of the site dated by radiocarbon to the late 6th and early 7th millennia BC. The idea was strongly disputed by R.J. Braidwood who, apart from doubting the radiocarbon dates produced for the site by F.E. Zeuner, argued that the evidence implied "an incipient town in a somewhat marginal region". In reply, Kenyon pointed out that even an incipient town of 5000 BC, assuming that Zeuner's dating was lowered to 5000 BC, "would be a remarkable achievement". The same situation arose at Catal Huyuk which was described by its excavator James Mellaart as 'a neolithic city in Turkey'. No positive conclusion emerged from either case, but the complexity of such terms as 'city' and 'civilization' was highlighted.

In 1960, C.H. Kraeling and R.M. Adams edited a volume entitled *City Invincible, a Symposium on Urbanization and Cultural Development in the Ancient Near East, Held at the Oriental Institute of the University of Chicago, December 4-7, 1958*. About 49 American scholars including Near Eastern specialists and those in general and related fields, such as geography, history, anthropology, etc., participated in the seminar. H.L. Mumford, a noted historian of cities, was also involved. Regarding the developmental sequence, it was pointed out that each country had its own development with its own characteristics. As R.M. Adams wrote in the volume edited by Kraeling and Adams (p. 292):

> History is not a mathematical exercise in the application of 'laws', and the meaning of human experience is not be found by suppressing its rich variety in the search for common, implicitly deterministic, denominators.

The emphasis of the articles of the volume was on the development and not on the urban or political growth or sociological processes of urbanization. Mumford (Kraeling and Adams volume, p. 236) described the ancient cities in the following terms:

> Whatever else they were, they were above all containers of religious and royal power; and it was that central nucleus of power, itself contained in the palace and the temple, that called people from a distance and united them in tasks that men had never attempted before. Thus the city became the great reservoir of manpower, available for digging, building, trading, fighting, engaging in the specialized trades and professions, the arts and sciences, no longer needed for agricultural labour. The market is a by-product of this concentration and the

> surplus; but it is the drawing power of the city that brings the trader, not the trader who created the city.

Mumford's own *The City in History: Its Origins and Transformations* was published in 1961, and being at that point of time an avid reader of Mumford's writings, I soon became aware of the importance of knowing about the ancient Indian cities in detail.

In 1962, R.J. Braidwood and G.R. Wiley published the book edited by them, *Courses toward Urban Life: Archaeological Considerations of Some Cultural Alternates*. This volume was also the result of a symposium and considered the varieties of cultural build-ups leading to the thresholds of urban civilizations. It also contained an article by H.D. Sankalia on the stages of 'food-collection to urbanization' in India. The focus of the volume was primarily on the achievement and spread of agriculture.

That was a period when there was some excitement about the beginning of agriculture. The issue was already brought into focus by Braidwood in his *The Near East and the Foundations for Civilization* in 1952 but it was given an exciting shape in *Prehistoric Investigations in Iraqi Kurdistan* in 1960. By this time the existence of early village-farming communities was known in Baluchistan, especially after the Quetta and Zhob-Loralai valley investigations by Fairservis in1956 and1958 and the investigations in the Kalat plateau by B. de Cardi in1959. The impact of the new proto-historic village communities virtually all over the sub-continent was tremendous, highlighting the growth and spread of agriculture and their subsequent role in the development of Indian cities. J-M Casal elaborated the sequence at Amri in Sindh, substantiating its significance already postulated by N.G. Majumdar. Nobody entering the study of Indian archaeology at the research level in 1963 could quite ignore these and similar developments which were then taking place in the study of the background of the earliest cities. Glyn Daniel's *The First Civilizations: The Archaeology of Their Origins* (1968) is a reflection of these developments towards the end of the 1960s.

A debate which was paramount in this field in the 1950s took place around Gordon Childe's premise of technological innovations lying at the base of the growth of cities. The Bronze Age technological innovations led to the growth of the Bronze Age cities whereas the innovations associated with the new technology of iron led to the Iron Age cities. Childe developed this premise in a number of publications, notably *Man Makes Himself* and *What Happened in History* but most notably in his article on the 'urban revolution' in *Town Planning Review* in 1950. The idea was criticized primarily on two counts. First, scholars like Mumford thought that instead of being a 'revolution', the urban growth was an implosion, a process of coming together. Secondly, Childe's notion that it was technological developments which were the primary force behind the development of cities, was disputed by scholars of the American anthropological school like Braidwood who emphasized the primacy of the social-institutional factors.

In view of the foregoing developments both in the general field of archaeology and the more limited field of Indian archaeology, one might be excused for thinking in the early 1960s that going through the whole set of data relevant to the development and morphology of the ancient Indian cities would be an interesting exercise. It was, of course, understood that this would involve going through most of the details of the Indian geography and excavation reports before they could be synthesized to yield a pan-Indian picture of ancient urban centres and urbanism and that there was thus not much chance of completing the Ph.D. work in a hurry. Further, looking at the Indian situation one soon realized that there was no model to follow in this field and whatever had been written on the ancient Indian cities so far had been done basically on the basis of disjointed references in unsatisfactorily dated texts. A published work (1964) of this kind was near at hand in *Villages, Towns and Secular Buildings in Ancient India, c. 150* BC*-c. 350* by Amita Ray.

When I began my study of the early Indian urban centres, I was aware that I would not be able to excavate any ancient urban centre, nor would I be able to study many of these centres at the ground level. At the same time, I knew that if I could offer a sharp definition of the early Indian urban situation and make a clear and logical assessment of the current knowledge and the gaps in that knowledge, I could perhaps lay claim to some academic credit. The first requirement was a steady grip over all the relevant archaeological, historical and geographical data. That was easier said than done, and the memory of poring over one archaeological report after another may not in retrospect be particularly pleasant but was very necessary. Some effort also went into establishing an acceptable understanding of what could constitute a basic working definition of a preindustrial city. G. Sjoberg's book in 1960, *Preindustrial City*, was a very welcome publication in this context. This was also the beginning of my familiarity with the literature of Indian district gazetteers in my quest to get familiar with the geographical location of the ancient city sites. In the textual field, I recall with deep pleasure my first reading of the *Silappadikaram*, the story of Kannaki and Kovalan, in an English translation. The urban context of the time in Tamil Nadu was lovingly described, and suddenly one could go beyond the stereotyped descriptions of an ancient Indian city in Sanskrit literature and their equally stereotyped representation in early Indian art and call up the images of their tanks and gardens. The

Chaurapanchasika, a set of fifty verses written by Bilhana of Kashmir in the 11th century AD, does not mention cities but could not have been composed except in a warmly sensuous urban ambience.

The work became eventually complete in 1972, earning a Ph.D. (1973), although the book *The Archaeology of Ancient Indian Cities* was not published till 1995. Apart from the sections which needed updating, the book is substantially as it was as the Ph.D. dissertation. A summary of the general conclusions was published in *Puratattva* (no.6, 1972-73) and commented on by a number of scholars including A. Ghosh, who published his book *The City in Early Historic India* in 1973. A review of this book by me appeared in the 6th volume of *Journal of Ancient Indian History* (1972-73, pp. 315-319) published by the Department of Ancient Indian History and Culture, Calcutta University.

SOME THEORETICAL DIMENSIONS OF INDIAN ARCHAEOLOGY IN THE EARLY 1960S

The issues which I discuss below were not field-based. They were only concerned with how to interpret the emerging archaeological data and may, from this point of view, be considered a purely theoretical approach.

The first of these was the problem of India—West Asia relationships before the Achaemenids, which had also started taking shape during this period, beginning with Stuart Piggott's and others' studies based on the pottery and miscellaneous artifacts from Baluchistan and the adjacent regions. We have already noticed that scholars like Sankalia and Lal were thinking of west Asiatic parallels for the pottery they found in the Narmada valley and the upper Ganga plain and that in their attempts to look for parallels for Indian material in west and central Asia, they were joined by many other scholars, including D.H. Gordon and F.R. Allchin. The significance of this theme was also strengthened by a number of discoveries related to the Indus civilization. For instance, T.G. Bibby in *Antiquity* in 1958 reported seals of the ancient Indian type from Bahrein and in the same journal in 1963 S.R. Rao published a Persian Gulf seal from Lothal. It was also in *Antiquity* that George Dales in 1962 interpreted Sutkagendor as a Harappan port related to the Harappan trade with the Gulf. In his review of Wheeler's *The Indus Civilization* (1953) in *Antiquity* in 1955, Max Mallowan opined that Mesopotamia's links with the Indus were evident in Early Dynastic III, c.2600 BC. The significance of this argument was not seriously taken in the mid-1950s, but again brought one to the realization that the issue of Indus-Mesopotamia contact was important for a number of reasons, one of which was the problem of the Indus chronology. Alongside was Wheeler's idea that the idea of civilization came to the Indus from Mesopotamia. This idea was elaborated with the Indus contact with Mesopotamia in mind in 1952 by Wheeler. Mallowan, on the other hand, put emphasis on the 'Indian' character of the civilization, something that is missing elsewhere.

Secondly, the Aryan problem, sanctified first by Wheeler in his Harappa report and then mentioned in a whole host of publications including Piggott's *Prehistoric India,* kept on appearing in the background. Although B.B. Lal in his paper on protohistoric India in *Ancient India* no.9 (1953) pointed out there was a rubble deposit between the Harappan level and the succeeding Cemetery H level and thus the latter could not represent the invading Aryans, there were echoes of Wheeler's theory in T.G.E. Powell's *Antiquity* review of *Prehistoric India* in 1952. Powell modified the Wheeler-Piggott theory:

> It must suffice to say that the evidence embodied in Rana Ghundai IV, Shahi Tump, the Jhukar culture and Cemetery H

> at Harappa, points not to far-travelled Aryans, but to barbarous peoples from the periphery to the Indus civilization, who may have had a sprinkling of Aryan leaders (viz the shaft-hole axes), but who had become invaders on account of pressure in their own rear.

Mallowan in 1955 wrote of the possibility of the Aryans arriving before the end of the civilization and interacting with their people. The idea was not particularly new because R.P. Chanda in 1926 and 1929 argued elaborately in this vein long before Wheeler's excavations at Harappa. A recurrent theme of this welter of theories was the constant refrain of west Asiatic parallels of many objects found not merely in the Indus and Indus-related horizons but also in the proto-historic cultures of central India and the upper Ganga plain. By the early 1960s, it was absolutely essential to examine these ideas in some depth.

One of the first persons to try to do so cogently in the context of the non-Harappan chalcolithic was B.K. Thapar. His paper in the seminar volume *Indian Prehistory: 1964* (Misra and Mate 1965) was titled "relationship of the Indian chalcolithic cultures with west Asia". It was pointed out that many of the parallels in the field of Indian chalcolithic pottery forms and designs, which Sankalia and his associates suggested, were too general to be meaningful. However, Thapar failed to take a positive stand against Sankalia's one-sided views. Among the commentators of Thapar's paper, S.P. Gupta pointed out that in some cases, as in the case of Sialk channel-spouted bowls, Sankalia's Indian analogies were plainly wrong. He wanted "definite individualistic forms" "reinforced by other evidences of contacts" before thinking of any population movements from west Asia to India in the context of the Indian chalcolithic.

In retrospect, it is thus clear that three developments brought to the front the issue of India's relationship with west and central Asia before the Achaemenids in the early 1960s: the idea of the Indus civilization owing its idea of civilization to Mesopotamia; the series of writings by Sankalia on the so-called Iranian and west Asiatic parallels and thus of an assumed Aryan association of chalcolithic objects found at Navdatoli, Ahar and the sites in the Deccan; and finally, B.B. Lal's attempt to link the Painted Grey Ware with the miscellaneous grey wares of west Asia and the Mediterranean region and thus with the Aryans. One may also add to these the newly emerging problem of the Indus chronology in the light of the first available radiocarbon dates. The extent to which these science-based dates was supported by the existing archaeological evidence of Indus-Mesopotamia contact became important in 1964 when D.P. Agrawal, the Secretary of the Indian radiocarbon committee at the Physical Research Laboratory, Ahmedabad, published this laboratory's first crop of dated samples. One may further add that it was also in 1964 that George Dales published in *Expedition* his critique of Wheeler's idea of a massacre in the late level of Mohenjodaro. Again, the criticism was not a novel one, having been aired clearly by P.V. Kane in 1953. However, Dales' article brought once again the issue of Aryan-archaeology correlation in the case of India into limelight.

In a sense, A.H. Dani's synthesis of *Prehistory and Protohistory of Eastern India, with a Detailed Account of the Neolithic Cultures in Mainland South East Asia* (1960), although basically a typological analysis of the relevant stone tool types, conforms to the tradition elaborated in the case of west and central Asia. A detailed comparison of the Indian materials with the relevant or not-so-relevant assemblages outside India was almost a compulsory archaeological exercise in the early 1960s. The links between southeast Asia and eastern India were well understood in the historical context. Dani's book was the first systemisation of the earlier material from this point of view.

What lends interest to all these comparative exercises was their plain absurdity in many cases. For instance, there is no conceivable similarity between the channel-spouted vessels from the Iranian sites like Silak or Giyan and the Indian site of Navdatoli. Before travelling as far west as Thessaly in search of grey ware, as B.B. Lal did, assuming that grey ware anywhere denoted the same group of people, the concerned scholars could at least ask themselves if this kind of scholarship was necessary in the first place to explain the Indian material. To a great extent, this was the impact of the Aryan idea, but partly, it was also the Indian archaeologists' way to interpret the newly discovered material in terms of what they understood about Indian history. In the same vein, Mortimer Wheeler's constant reference to west Asia to explain most of the things Indian in the 1950s made them think of west and central Asia with far more importance than was necessary, suggesting in a way the basic intellectual subservience of the involved Indian archaeologists to what was being advocated by persons like Wheeler and Gordon.

The archaeologists who were keen to discover the traces of Aryans in the Indian protohistoric archaeological data forgot a number of simple points about them. First, the Aryans supposedly meant only a language group and if so, was there any acceptable methodology to identify an assemblage of archaeological material traits with a language? Secondly, although advanced in the guise of a language group, the term 'Aryan' has had too frequently a racial connotation and been subjected as such to various abuses in history. Why should this idea figure so prominently in Indian archaeology? Thirdly, the model of Aryan advent to India also meant their spread all over north India. How do archaeologists propose to prove this spread? It could never be an issue of holding up a particular archaeological item or culture and calling it 'Aryan'. It was linked to many wider issues. The ardent Aryanists of the time in Indian archaeology completely forgot these questions just as they forgot that in the name of archaeologically proving the advent of Aryans to India, they were putting forward only a motley of conflicting and methodologically unacceptable theories. They should also have realized that in the name of invoking the Aryans, they were detracting from the main task of archaeological field-research in India during that period, i.e., to lay down the basis of a detailed text-free people's history of India. In my study of the early Indian urban centres, I carefully avoided the Aryan trap, trying to understand if it was possible to understand a continuous history of India on the basis of the emerging archaeological data alone.

Another avenue of theoretical investigation opened in Indian archaeology in the 1960s. There was already an extensive body of literature on the history of iron in India, but in view of the excavations at Hastinapur, which showed the association of the Painted Grey Ware with iron, and also in view of Wheeler's idea in *Early India and Pakistan* (1959, pp. 24, 164) that the use of iron in India was due to the Achaemenid impact from Iran, there was a renewed interest to investigate what was the archaeological evidence of the Iron Age in India. N.R. Banerjee's analysis of the relevant data led him to conclude that the early Iron Age in India could be placed between c.800 BC and c.200 BC. More important than Banerjee's conclusion was the way he reached it.

> The foregoing discussion has sought to establish that it was the Aryan settlers in India, who also used the distinctive Painted Grey Ware ceramic, that were the first to use iron in ancient India around 800 BC or even earlier. Almost simultaneously or slightly later, the use of iron is

> testified among the people who buried fragmentary remains of their dead in cairns in the borders of Iran and Pakistan. It is possible that they obtained their knowledge of iron from Sialk VI in Iran even as the Aryans of the Ganga plains did. A little later iron comes into its own in west-central India in the post-Chalcolithic phase as also in the megaliths of south India. In both cases, the advent of iron is apparently later than its arrival in the Ganga plains, and possibly on that score, they, especially, the megaliths, owe not a little of its metallic inspiration to the northern plains. The possibility of a cultural influence direct from Iran (Sialk VI) being transmitted through the cairn-burials to the megaliths of south India, with substantial traces in the intermediate regions, cannot be ruled out. While Dravidian speakers appear to have taken special fancy to the megalithic mode of disposal of the dead, considerable numbers of bracycephalic people, akin to the Sialk VI folk, were present in their midst to accentuate the megalithic order of life.
>
> The relative superiority of the northerly Aryans in arms, more than in numbers, would possibly account for the ultimate confinement of the Dravidian speakers, who had earlier lived on the Indus plains, into Peninsular India, and would, by inference, confer on the Aryans the glories of being pioneers in a new metallurgical experience in the new land of their adoption. (Banerjee's paper in Misra and Mate 1965)

The whole emphasis of the foregoing discussion is on linking the early iron-bearing horizons with the possible archaeological traces of Aryan presence in India. The Aryans kept on providing the interpretative anchor-point of Indian archaeology.

Another anchor-point was Wheeler, whose opinions on virtually anything related to Indian archaeology were considered points of departure for any discussion by Indian archaeologists of the period. Closely involved with the Aryan issue was also the question of identifying various racial groups in the Indian archaeological record. The issue of the 'racial composition of these Iron Age peoples' was also within the academic purview of K.A.R. Kennedy at this stage. The first major critique of the attempts to locate various racial assemblages among the excavated human remains in Indian archaeology was made by D.K. Sen (*Ancient India 20-21,* 1964-65), and even then the concept of race did not actually go out of Indian archaeology. In the early 1960s, the Aryans, the Dravidians and various racial classificatory systems were the basic intellectual corner-stones of Indian archaeology. It is interesting to reflect that none of the commentators of Banerjee's paper tried to question any of these assumptions, although M.N. Deshpande (Misra and Mate 1965, p. 201) tried to introduce a cautionary note by saying that it was premature to identify the Aryans with the users of the Painted Grey Ware with any kind of certainty. A. Ghosh (Misra and Mate 1965, p. 203) also tried to argue that the interconnection between the existence of iron and the coming of the Aryans was 'far from established'. Banerjee's book contained a long and rather confused and messy excursion in the European literature on the Aryans. In my review of the book in *Journal of Ancient Indian History* (3, 1969-70, pp. 292-294), I raised questions about his dating of the iron-bearing level of central Indian sites like Nagda arguing that its date was likely to be above 1000 BC.

There were other major issues too in Indian archaeology in the early 1960s, for which the Misra and Mate volume is a fair guide. Whatever the archaeological community of the day understood of these issues may conveniently be found in the seminar volume edited by V.N. Misra and M.S. Mate (1965). In the case of the Palaeolithic, the focus was entirely on determining if the Soan pebble-tool industry could be interpreted as a separate culture. The debate was led by K.V. Soundara Rajan who thought that the Soan could be seen as an ethnic variant ('ethnic varia') in the Stone Age India. R.V. Joshi thought that the Soan was not 'independent and distinct culture'. Sankalia thought that this was indeed a 'culture' on its own. P.C. Pant argued, on the basis of his find of a 'true pebble-tool-industry' at Lahchura in the Dhasan valley, that the Soan was not limited only to the north-western subcontinent but also extended up to a part of central India. V.N. Misra reported that his exploration of the area reported by A.P. Khatri as bearing a pure pebble-based Oldowan culture in the Narmada valley failed to find such a tool-horizon. This discussion was a non-issue in the sense that one could not help finding pebble tools in areas which abounded in pebbles as raw materials. The most important paper in prehistory in this seminar volume was perhaps the stratigraphical and typological aspects of the Middle Stone Age tools in different parts of the sub-continent by H.D. Sankalia, although V.N. Misra seems to have preferred the term 'middle palaeolithic'. A.K. Ghosh used two terms—flake and flake-blade industries—putting the former in the middle Palaeolithic and the latter in the upper Palaeolithic. V.N. Misra submitted an overview of the Mesolithic in India, arguing that in certain areas like Gujarat, southern Tamil Nadu and West Bengal, their antiquity could go back to the early Holocene whereas in the areas like the 'jungle-clad country of central India' 'the use of microliths might have survived into well-nigh historical times'. Sankalia summed up the Mesolithic situation in India in the following fashion:

> There is no positive stratigraphic evidence about the Mesolithic stage of culture in India in the sense that it is available in Europe and Africa. But there is little doubt that we have got a cultural stage when man was emerging

> from the Old Stone Age period but was still a hunter-fisher and food-gatherer and carried out all his activities with small tools of stone (Misra and Mate 1965, p. 70).

An important part of the Mesolithic presentation in the Misra and Mate volume were the reports of their stratigraphic works at Baghai Khor and Morhana Pahar in Mirzapur by R.K. Varma and at Lekhahia, also in Mirzapur, by G.R. Sharma. They argued in this area an evolution of the Mesolithic assemblages from 'pre-pottery non-geometric' to 'geometric and diminutive tools with pottery' through the intermediate phases of 'geometric tools without pottery' and 'geometric tools with pottery'. Regarding the skeletal finds from Langhnaj K.A.R. Kennedy reported that a 'Mediterranean phenotypic complex' was present there, although' the identification of African racial elements' was not obvious to him. V.N. Misra clearly expressed his preference for the term 'mesolithic' in the Indian context without opting for such terms as 'Late Stone Age'. Two more papers of the Misra and Mate volume may be taken up for discussion here.

B.K. Thapar takes up a close study of the Neolithic problem, assuming that there could be models other than the model of the spread of the food-producing economy from the nuclear area of western Asia. Basically, he points out three Neolithic cultures in India—the northern Neolithic culture, the southern Neolithic culture and the eastern Neolithic culture. He keeps the Chalcolithic cultures of the rest of the sub-continent out of the scope of his discussion, for which he was criticised by several scholars on the ground that a limited use of copper does not make a culture any less 'neolithic' or 'metal-free' economically. The northern Neolithic culture, as typified in Kashmir, was linked to the northern belt of China and central Asia on the basis of the semi-lunar or rectangular knives or harvesters which occur in both the assemblages. The southern Neolithic "seems to have originated in the region itself", and from this point of view Thapar's opinion was different from the opinion of F.R. Allchin and others who tried to link it to a migration of grey-ware people such places as Shah Tepe in Iran. The east Indian Neolithic culture was supposedly "inspired by the Neolithic and later tradition in China and southeast Asia". Thapar's discussion clearly led to a multiplicity of Neolithic models for India.

A. Ghosh's paper on 'the Indus civilization; its origins, authors, extent and chronology', which was based both on his own work in the Ghaggar valley of Rajasthan and others' works elsewhere in India and Pakistan amply underlined 'a firm Sothi sub-stratum' in the 'make-up of Harappa'—"much firmer than that of the earlier cultures". In the context of the ongoing Kalibangan excavations, he stratigraphically assessed his earlier find of Sothi pottery in its 'pre-Harappan' context and argued, on the basis of various ceramic comparisons, that there was "every justification for regarding the Sothi as proto-Harappan". Eventually, he could not escape Wheeler's influence and accepted the notion of the borrowal of 'the idea of cities from the contemporary Sumerians'. His concept of the presence of a 'few genius-dictators' at the base of the transformation to the mature Harappan civilization was nothing but a rough attempt to combine Wheeler's idea of borrowal with the idea of an indigenous origin.

The writings which contain theoretical ideas of this period are not many. There was not much excitement about the rapidly expanding Indian archaeological world. There are routine references to possible west Asiatic analogues of the excavated pottery and other materials but the literature hardly shows any excitement at the prospect of the history of many areas going back by many centuries and the increasing details of the material remains of life, of which there was no earlier comprehension. By tying themselves to what Wheeler and others (cf. Sankalia, Lal, Gordon, Subbarao) wrote, Indian archaeology of the day showed a poverty of thought which it has been unable to overcome even today. It is just that Wheeler and his contemporaries have been replaced by some modern, mostly American, archaeologists.

EXPLORATIONS AND EXCAVATIONS IN THE 1960S AND THE 1970S

Explorations for prehistoric sites continued to be one of the most favourite items of India's archaeological agenda. Virtually, all the volumes of *Indian Archaeology—A Review* show an impressive list of the discovered prehistoric sites and their tools. In many cases, there are notes on their geological occurrence. Scholars who followed up their work and published the results of their explorations in some detail have acquired fame as prehistorians. For instance, V.N. Misra discovered a large number of prehistoric sites in the Banas, Gambhiri, and other river valleys of southeast Rajasthan in connection with hisDeccan College Ph.D. work on the prehistory and protohistory of this region. On the other hand, the extensive work on the prehistory of this region by S.R. Rao (cf. *IAR 1956-57, 1957-58*) has not been published outside *Indian Archaeology - A Review* and thus the work on the prehistory of the region seldom carries a reference to Rao's work. This is only one example. There can be many such instances all over India. It is rather important to draw attention to this feature of Indian Stone Age research because over the years the history of prehistoric research in post-Independence India has come to mean basically a check-list of the works carried out by the Deccan College. It is much more than that. Besides, this has led to the general impression that some archaeologists of India are only pre-historians. The fact is that the study of Indian prehistory has not yet reached that level of sophistication when it is necessary to have highly specialised knowledge (cf. sophisticated measurements on a large scale and statistical formulae to make sense of them) to handle prehistoric material.

The results of prehistoric explorations in India, which are mostly a catalogue of tool-types and the names of their geological contexts, are seldom exciting. Some finds, however, are of intrinsic academic interest. For instance, *IAR 1963-64* reports that M.L.K. Murty discovered at a site near Renigunta in Andhra "blade tools, resembling the typical Upper Palaeolithic of Europe". This was certainly a major step forward in Indian prehistoric studies. Further, it was noted in *IAR 1967-68* that the blade and burin industry was stratigraphically earlier than the Late Stone Age. In *IAR 1968-69*, there was a brief report on the excavations at Chirki Nala near Nevasa and the find of about 1700 artefacts in the rubble-gravel horizon of the Acheulian context. This strongly bolstered the claim of Chirki being a primary Acheulian site. *IAR 1962-63* contained the report on the work by R.K. Varma of Allahabad University on the Bhainsaur, Morana Pahar and Baghai Kor rock-shelters of Mirzapur and their sequence of microliths. The 1963-64 volume carried the report of the Banaras Hindu University work at the Lekhahia rock-shelter, also in Mirzapur. The 1962-63 volume is also noted for its report on the work on Kakoria and Banimilia (Chunar) megaliths by Banaras Hindu University. For the megalithic sites of Takalghat and Khapa near Nagpur, *IAR 1967-68* contains a report. The Rajasthani site of Bagor, noted for its Mesolithic phase and its subsequent association with copper, was reported in *IAR* 1967-68 and *IAR* 1968-69. The so-called Hoabinhian affinity of some tools from Selbalgiri in the Garo hills in Meghalaya was noted about this time. The Allahabad university work at Chopani Mando featured first in

IAR 1966-67 whereas the Guwahati university work at Daojali Hading in the Mikir and North Cachar hills, which showed neoliths in association with a large quantity of ill-fired pottery in a 45 cm thick stratum, was reported first in *IAR 1962-63*. The Allahabad University's work in the Allahabad-Banda-Mirzapur-Pratapgarh-Belan valley area and the area of the adjoining Vindhyas was apparently in full swing in 1969-70 (*IAR* 1969-70). Sarai Nahar Rai was first reported in *IAR* 1969-70. A number of rock-shelters and megaliths were also found in the Vindhyas along with various lithic assemblages. In Singhbhum, there was a single deposit of black soil containing Neolithic celts and pottery at Barudih (cf. *IAR 1963-64*). The same soil deposit later yielded an iron sickle as well. In Anantapur in Andhra, there were reports (*IAR 1965-66*) of 20 neolithic sites and 2 ash-mound sites, yielding in all about 1600 neolithic implements and 1000-odd associated microlithic tools. The ash-mound of Palavoy in Anantapur yielded a phase of patinated trap flakes and microliths, which was followed successively by Neolithic and post-neolithic iron-bearing levels (*IAR 1966-67*). The interesting part is the find of patinated flakes of trap and microliths in its phase 1, reflecting a situation comparable to the one at Sanganakallu near Bellary. Among the south Indian Neolithic sites excavated during this period are Tekkalakota (cf.*IAR 1963-*64), Hemmige (cf. *IAR 1963*-64), Hallur (cf. *IAR 1964-65*), Paiyampalli (cf. *IAR 1967-68*), T. Narsipur (cf.*IAR 1964-65*), Sanganakallu (cf. *IAR 1964-65*) and Kupgal (cf. *IAR 1964-65*). The Kashmir Neolithic level at Burzahom and the east Indian Neolithic level at Chirand also came to be excavated during this period (cf. *IAR 1963-64, 1964-65*), although at both these sites the excavations lasted for several field-seasons. The Harappan excavations continued in Gujarat at Lothal but soon new sites were added to the list: Rojdi (cf. *IAR* 1962-63), Malvan (cf. *IAR* 1967-68), Surkotada (cf. *IAR* 1964-65) and Desalpur (cf. *IAR* 1963-

64). This was also the time when there were systematic explorations for Harappan sites in Kutch (cf.*IAR* 1964-65). Kalibangan continued to be excavated throughout the 1960s but more Harappan explorations took place in western Uttar Pradesh (cf. *IAR* 1965-66) and Panjab and Haryana (cf. *IAR* 1963-64). An important development in western Uttar Pradesh was the evidence of Ochre-Coloured Pottery and Harappa interrelationship at the sites of Ambkheri-2 and Bargaon (cf. *IAR* 1963-64). In Uttar Pradesh, the excavations of Atranjikhera (cf. *IAR* 1965-66) and Lal Qila (cf. *IAR* 1968-69) were equally important, throwing new light on the Ochre-Coloured Pottery occupation at Lal Qila, which ought to have been named Narayanpur because the site lies in the fields of this village. Of outstanding significance was the proof of the direct association of upper Gangetic valley copper hoards and Ochre-Coloured Pottery at Saifai Lichhwai (cf. *IAR* 1969-70). Noh near Bharatpur in Rajasthan yielded a sequence which was more or less like the one obtained at Atranjikhera (cf. *IAR* 1965-66). In 1963-64, the Noh excavations were undertaken apparently jointly with J. LeRoy Davidson of the history of art department of California university. The name is missing in the subsequent volumes. Inamgaon excavations began in Maharashtra in 1968-69 and 1969-70 (*IAR* 1969-70) and Theur was excavated in 1969-70. Singanapalli, basically a chalcolithic site of the Kurnool area of Andhra, was excavated in 1967-68 (cf. *IAR* 1967-68). Mahishdal and Nanur were among the new chalcolithic sites excavated in West Bengal (*IAR* 1963-64). Kayatha is a major site of this type in Madhya Pradesh (cf. *IAR* 1964-65, 1967-68). Among the early historical sites, Korkai and Uraiyur (cf. *IAR* 1967-68, *IAR* 1968-69) deserve notice in Tamil Nadu where an Indo-Roman trading station was excavated at Karaikadu (*IAR* 1966-67), about 30 km south of Arikamedu. Interestingly, there is a brief reference in the Karaikadu context to 'protonmagnetometric investigation' of the site by a French physicist. One does not know if anything came out of it. Rajghat and Chandraketugarh continued to be excavated in Uttar Pradesh and West Bengal. In Uttar Pradesh, Ahichchhatra was excavated (cf. *IAR* 1963-64). Ter and Paunar (cf. *IAR* 1966-67) were among the excavated early historic sites in Maharashtra (cf. *IAR* 1966-67), with Peddavankur (cf. *IAR* 1967-68) being one such site in Andhra. Among the Andhra early historic sites, Dharanikota (cf. *IAR* 1964-65) is important. The fortifications of the early historic site of Balirajgarh near Madhubani in Bihar were noted in 1962-63, and at Rajgir the excavation focus seems to have shifted to the fortifications of New Rajagriha (cf. *IAR* 1962-63). In Madhya Pradesh, Eran, famous for its chalcolithic and historic levels, (cf. *IAR* 1963-64), was taken up for excavations along with Besnagar where seven pillars were identified from their pits near the Heliodorus pillar which has to be considered a part of the row of these pillars. From centre to centre, the distance between the pillars was 4.25 m. There is no confusion about their existence. In fact, it has been written (*IAR* 1965-66) that "out of the seven pillars in a row, two pillars with Garuda capitals marked the extreme ends; the Heliodorus pillar being in the north and the other in the south". The discovery of an earlier temple at the site of Heliodorus pillar is also important. Tripuri, a chalcolithic to early historical site near Jabbalpur in Madhya Pradesh, came to be excavated in 1967-68 (*IAR* 1967-68). Among the Karnataka historical sites investigated during this period are Udayavara near Udupi, Honavar and Banavasi (cf. *IAR* 1968-69). In Uttar Pradesh, the excavations at Masaon (cf. *IAR* 1967-68) did not identify any fortification. Ayodhya was excavated in 1969-70 (cf. *IAR* 1969-70). Among the Buddhist monastic sites, one has to mention Devnimori (cf. *IAR* 1962-63) in Gujarat, Antichak (cf. *IAR* 1962-63) in Bihar and Rajbadidanga (cf. *IAR* 1962-63) in West Bengal.

Miscellaneous stupa structural sites (cf. Yeleswaram) were reported from Andhra.

If one has to isolate different features among the various explorations and excavations conducted in the 1960s, one may state the following: First, people were coming to grips with prehistory in various parts of the country: southeast Rajasthan, Maharashtra, the Allahabad-Banaras area and the adjacent Vindhyas and the Kaimurs, Andhra, West Bengal, modern Jharkhand and the Garo hills tract of Meghalaya. The work in the Allahabad-Banaras-Vindhya-Kaimur region was followed up with care and took specific shapes in the subsequent periods. Murty's work at Renigunta led to the recognition of a specific upper Palaeolithic phase in Indian prehistory. The work at Chirki was important in its own right because of the profusion of tools in mint condition. The work in southeast Rajasthan led to Misra's systematic study of the prehistory of the region and the same is true of A.K. Ghosh's study of the prehistory of Singhbhum and G.C. Mohapatra's study of the prehistory of Orissa. The academic profile of Indian prehistory was clearly assuming a visible shape in the 1960s, laying the basis of some important publications and formulations in Indian prehistory in the 1970s. In the Neolithic field, the discoveries at Burzahom in Kashmir, the miscellaneous south Indian sites and Daojali Hading in Assam were important, although regrettably, the Daojali Hading work was not followed up. In the area of the chalcolithic, discoveries and excavations went on taking place in many areas including Madhya Pradesh and Maharashtra where Eran, Kayatha and Inamgaon were important additions to the already known long list of sites. The work at the Gangetic sites of Atranjikhera and Noh has a special significance of their own because this had the effect of considerably expanding Lal's work at Hastinapur. The excavations at Saifai proved the association of the Gangetic valley copper hoards with the Ochre-Coloured Pottery and were in that sense of breath-taking importance. Lal Qila or Narayanpur turned out to be an unusual Ochre-Colured Pottery site primarily because of the richness of its painted pottery tradition. The Harappans were studied over the vast region comprising Gujarat, Rajasthan, Haryana, Panjab and western Uttar Pradesh. The sites of Ambkheri and Bargaon amplified the association of Ochre-Colured Pottery with the Harappans and underscored, by implication, the fact of the Harappan merger in the Gangetic mainstream in the east. In Gujarat, the excavations at Surkotada brought out a distinct type of Harappan settlement in Kutch. The nature of Harappan occupation in Kutch was also underlined by the extensive explorations for Harappan sites in Kutch. In Panjab and Haryana, the work on the Harappans was basically exploratory in character but that did enough to highlight the importance of Harappan occupation of the region. Among the historical sites, the work at the southern sites of Karaikadu, Uraiyur and Korkai was important, and in north India, the Ahichchhatra excavations established the cultural sequence of the site. Perhaps the most significant but generally ignored discovery in the field of early history was the discovery of a row of seven pillars, of which the Heliodorus pillar was one. The Antichak excavations were on a grand scale, although only a little of that has been published. The same may be said about the Rajbadidanga or Karnasuvarna/Chhiruti excavations.

The decade of the seventies did not begin with any major change. The Allahabad university work in the Vindhyas and the Allahabad zone went on establishing the stratigraphy of prehistoric occurrences in this belt. In 1971-72, excavations began at Koldihawa and Sarai Nahar Rai. The miliolite formation and its relationship with the local prehistoric sequence came in for attention in this year which also witnessed the beginning of excavations at Bhimbetka. In 1972-73, an unbroken sequence from the late Acheulian to the Mesolithic was worked out in the Bhimbetka rock-shelter III.F.23. More light was thrown on the miliolite formation in Gujarat in 1974-75. In 1975-76, the editor of *IAR* of that year, B.K. Thapar declared that the Survey had adopted the use of terms like Lower, Middle and Upper Palaeolithic, and the Mesolithic and the Neolithic from then on. Hunsgi figured first in *IAR 1974-75* and Patne, the upper Palaeolithic to the Mesolithic site near Chalisgaon, in *IAR 1972-73*. The basic prehistoric modalities of Rewa, Sidhi and Satna were worked out in *IAR 1975*-76 by the Allahabad university. Didwana in western Rajasthan showed its prehistoric column first in 1979-80. Koldihawa (*IAR 1973-74*), Chopani Mando (*IAR 1977-78*), Mahagara (*IAR 1977-78*) and Mahadaha (*IAR 1977-78*) were among the important excavated sites of the decade and at each of them the work was done for multiple seasons. Among the chalcolithic sites, Daimabad (cf. *IAR 1974-75*) and Inamgaon (*IAR 1974-75*) turned out to be highly significant because both of them were horizontal excavations and reported in full. The investigations of the sites of Manda, Kathpalon, Nagar and Dadheri were important steps in the Harappan field which also witnessed a major excavation at Hulas (cf. *IAR 1979-80*). Daulatpur, Balu and Bhagawanpura were three more such sites (cf. *IAR 1975-76* and *IAR 1976-77*). In Gujarat, a number of small Harappan sites such as Zekhada, Pabumath, Kanwal, Valabhi, Nesadi, etc. (cf. *IAR 1977-78*) were excavated. In West Bengal, Bharatpur (cf. *IAR 1970-71*) was a newly excavated chalcolithic site. Jakhera (cf. *IAR 1974-75*) in Uttar Pradesh was also a protohistoric site. Atranjikhera in Uttar Pradesh (cf. *IAR 1979-80*), Dangwada in Madhya Pradesh (cf. *IAR 1979-80*), Chechar Kutubpur in Bihar (*IAR 1977-78*) and Padigutta in Andhra Pradesh (*IAR 1978-79*) were all neolithic-chalcolithic sites. A large number of historical sites were excavated in this decade: Besnagar, Semthan, Bhatgaon-Madhopur, Sringaverapur, Kalingapatnam and Piprahwa and Ganwaria. Malhar (cf. *IAR 1974-75*) and Bhokardan (*IAR 1973-74*) were two more such sites. In Andhra, the major excavated early historic sites were a chain of Buddhist stupa sites, the most important of them being Dhulikottah (cf. *IAR 1975-76*). Both Agroha and Dwaraka were noticed during this period which also witnessed sporadic excavations at Champa and Antichak in Bihar.

In retrospect, there was no major archaeological surprise in the 1970s except the establishment of a proper Mesolithic phase in the central Ganga valley and the adjoining Vindhyas. The excavations at Koldihawa were important, despite controversies. On the whole, the Allahabad university under G.R. Sharma showed an independence of thought and approach which was not repeated in any other Indian university. The northeastern region, regrettably, continued to remain a largely unknown area from where there was hardly any dependable work or date. The southern belt went on having one megalithic site investigated after another, with no addition to the total sum of knowledge except at Hallur where they found an overlap phase between the Neolithic and the megalithic. In all other areas, there was some kind of progress in the archaeological knowledge of the local area, Piprahwa-Ganwaria being a major historical discovery.

SOME PUBLICATIONS OF THE PERIOD

The foregoing discoveries led to an increasing number of publications throughput this period. In the late 1960s, two publications—*The Birth of Indian Civilization* (1968) by B. and F.R. Allchin and *Indian Civilization, the Formative Period. A Study of Archaeology as Anthropology* (1968) by S.C. Malik—deserve mention. The first one was a synthesis of the archaeological data in the framework of the traditional framework of ancient Indian studies and aimed to identify the different linguistic correlates of Aryans, Dravidians, etc. The first one-third of the book was on the Stone Age, outlining its distribution, sequences and typologies. In the case of protohistory, the newly emergent crop of radiocarbon dates was a great help, although in the case of the Indus civilization they uncritically preferred a short chronology between c.2350 and c.1770 BC, putting faith in D.P. Agrawal's assertion in 1964 that this shortened Indus chronology tallied with the Mesopotamian historical evidence limited to the Sargonid period and later. The basic approach of this book to cultural developments in India was no less West-centred than Sankalia's. The four chapters at the end—patterns of settlement, economy and agriculture, craft and technology, and art and religion—put the archaeological data in the confines of Indian ancient history and argue clearly both the nature of the evidence and its bearings on the later history of India (for my earlier comments on the Allchins' book, Chakrabarti 2003, pp. 52-54).

In view of the importance of the Aryan premise in this and other volumes and writings of the period, it may be worthwhile to point out that the mutual inconsistencies in the various hypotheses proposed for the identifications of the Aryans in the archaeological record were clearly reviewed in 1968 itself (Chakrabarti 1968).

S.C. Malik's aim was "to stimulate interest in the development of different approaches to the study of archaeology rather than to present any definitive results" (Malik *ibid.*, p. 14). Quite significantly, he cites the case of an Australian tribe of hunters and foragers "who grow nothing, build nothing, and stay nowhere long", thus leaving little or no trace of their presence in the landscape. The similarity with the Indian Stone Age landscape which shows virtually nothing except artefact clusters is striking. In the Harappan and post-Harappan contexts, he draws attention to the archaeological evidence of three culture-contact situations: the one within the Harappan peasant-urban sphere, the one between the Harappans and other non-Harappan spheres, and the one among the other non-Harappan spheres. He also points out the "increased frequency of these culture-contact situations between the various interacting spheres" and believes that this led to the formation of the indigenous primary Indian civilization. However, Malik did not work out his ideas in detail (for my earlier comments on Malik's book, Chakrabarti 2003, pp. 54-57).

A significant cluster of writings on Harappan radiocarbon chronology and other protohistoric issues came from D.P. Agrawal (1964, 1966, 1971, Agrawal and Kusumgar 1974). Agrawal basically advocated a short Indus chronology (Agrawal 1964, 1966)—c.2300-c.1750 BC—arguing that this bracket tallied with the historical evidence of Mesopotamian contact with the Indus valley, which, according to him, did not antedate the Sargonic period. *Prehistoric Chronology and Radiocarbon Dating* by D.P. Agrawal and Sheela Kusumgar (1974) was basically an inventory of the radiocarbon dates which were available till the early 1970s, with its interpretative framework rooted in Agrawal's earlier publication *The Copper Bronze Age in India* (Agrawal 1971). Agrawal's archaeological ideas are clear from the following:

> The antecedence of the west in most of the cultural traits ... may indicate a west to east diffusion. Thus for the same traits little earlier dates in Iran than Afghanistan and relatively earlier dates in Iran than Afghanistan, and relatively earlier dates in Mundigak than Baluchistan sites should be expected. A trait appearing much earlier in Mesopotamia may thus be of relatively late date in Baluchistan (Agrawal 1971, p. 71).

On the whole, Agrawal's originality lies in his wide use of radiocarbon dates and technical studies of copper-bronze artefacts, only a limited portion of which was attempted by himself. His invocation of the 'ecological factors' did not extend beyond the usual geographical characterisations of different areas.

In their 1974 book, Agrawal and Kusumgar cannot deny that the date of the Neolithic-megalithic phase at Hallur was around 1000 BC but adds that "one can explain such high antiquity only by invoking a sea-route. The Sialk B analogues from Perumal hills, the megalithic similarities with Yemen, etc. do point to such mariner transmission of cultural traits" (Agrawal and Kusumgar 1974, p. 147). They further added that in the diffusion of iron from Iran to India, the Indo-Aryans possibly played a role, echoing what N.R. Banerjee wrote earlier. Regarding the radiocarbon dates, they noted that no calibration was necessary at that stage.

Agrawal published his ideas regarding the archaeological implications of "the metal technology of the Indian protohistoric cultures" in the 3rd issue of the newly instituted journal of *Puratattva, Bulletin of the Indian Archaeological Society* (Agrawal 1969-70). Three groups of cultures—Harappan, Chalcolithic and Copper Hoards—were considered and it was stated that these were essentially independent cultural phenomena.

The Indian Archaeological Society came up as a suitable forum for academic discussions and also for inculcating a sense of organization and proper direction among Indian archaeologists under the leadership of A.K. Narain of Banaras Hindu University in 1967-68, and it specifically mentioned 'natural sciences' as an area of interaction for archaeology in the country. The first issue, in fact, carried an article by Vishnu-Mittre on the interaction between archaeology and plant sciences. The first issue also carried an analysis of the typology of prehistoric tools by P.C. Pant, which was important in bringing about a standardisation of the descriptions of prehistoric tools in Indian archaeology. In the third issue, H. Sarkar and B.M. Pande published an analysis of the 'knot-design from Mohenjodaro and its occurrence in later times', including the Rashtrakuta period land-grants. The fifth issue published the proceedings of a Delhi seminar on the OCP and the NBP.

On the whole, by the beginning of the 1970s, the natural scientific studies found an importance of their own in Indian archaeology, although archaeo-botanical, archaeo-zoological and metallurgical studies had long been known in the subject. All that one has to do is to note that both floral and faunal studies were undertaken on the Indus civilization specimens and M. Sanaullah undertook extensive chemical analyses of the composition of the Indus civilization metal artefacts. However, the significance of D.P. Agrawal's studies lay in the fact that by this time radiocarbon dating had significantly added a dependable chronological dimension to Indian prehistoric, protohistoric and historic cultures, and although his interpretation and approach were out and out diffusionist, uncritical and somewhat cut-and-dried in conclusions on the model of Sankalia and others, the very fact that the significance of natural scientific studies was academically well-accepted by this period lends significance to the relevant studies. The physical anthropological studies of archaeological skeletons were well-rooted in the Indian archaeological tradition, but the examples that one finds both in this and the earlier periods were dominated by racial classifications. In all cases from Langhnaj to Nevasa and more prominently in the case of the south Indian megalithic skeletal studies, the anthropologists concerned thought of the early populations in terms of different racial groups. The racial approach to the Indian skeletal finds began to change partly after the publication of D.K. Sen's critique of this approach in 1964-65 and K.A.R. Kennedy's study of the south Indian megalithic skeletons in 1975 (Kennedy 1975).

In the sixth issue of *Puratattva*, I (Chakrabarti 1972-73) made an attempt to relate the growth of cities in Indian archaeological record to the theoretical literature on the growth of cities in the contemporary archaeological literature, and in the next issue I showed (Chakrabarti 1974) how the different phases of early Indian urban growth could be related to the different political power-structures and how this supported the idea that the kings were the principal founders of cities in the ancient contexts.

A major natural-scientific publication of the period was Gurdeep Singh's article on the Indus valley culture seen in the context of postglacial climate and ecological studies (Singh 1971). This was based on his study of the dated pollen profiles from the lakes of western Rajasthan, and an outstanding finding was the presence of cerealia pollen in the level dated around 7000 BC, which, along with the associated charcoal fragments, was indicative both of human presence and cultivation of cereals in the area as early as this period. Another major point was the evidence of aridity in the region around 1800 BC, suggesting that the decline of the Indus civilization could be related to this phase of aridity.

In 1970, Purushottam Singh published a book on the burial practices of ancient India from the late Stone Age to the beginning of the Christian era, with emphasis on their types, associated materials and eschatological beliefs. A major feature of the book was also a discussion on what was described as "tribal burials". This denoted a clear concern with synthesis of archaeological data in different areas of Indian history. A similar attempt to synthesize was also noticed in a number of books in the early 1970s, beginning with W.A. Fairservice's *The Roots of Ancient* India in 1971. This was primarily devoted to the Baluchistan assemblages and the Indus civilization but also contained a discussion on what was happening outside the Harappan area. The book also contained some detailed sections on the Stone Age materials. B.K. Gururaja Rao offered a summary of the archaeological data available on the south Indian megaliths in his *Megalithic Culture in South India* in1972. The data belonged to Kerala, Tamil Nadu, Karnataka, Andhra Pradesh and central and northern India and dealt with megalithic types, grave goods, skeletal remains, everyday life and the issues of south Indian megalithic chronology and origin. The following sentence sums up his idea: "The black-and-red ware people, after adopting iron and the megalithic cult from the cairn burial folk in the 9th century BC, must have arrived in south India sometime in the 8th century BC" (Gururaja Rao 1972, p. 326). The lower limit of the megalithic culture of south India was, according to him, 8th-7th century BC, with a possibility of going back to c.1000 BC.

On the south Indian megaliths again, L.S. Leshnik published a detailed study entitled *South Indian 'Megalithic' Burials, the Pandukal Complex* in 1974, covering virtually the whole of the territory surveyed by Gururaja Rao earlier: Tamil Nadu, Malabar coast and Coorg, Mysore and Kongunad or Coimbatore area and Telengana or northern Andhra Pradesh. Comparative chronology and typology figured prominently in his approach, with emphasis put on the Taxila material for comparative purposes. A lot of attention was also paid to the Caucasus area and Iran for locating megaliths. The following statements throw light on Leshnik's basic approach: "Westward of India, in the region of Iran, many, if not all of the traits comprising the Pandukal complex occur" (Leshnik *ibid.*: 241); "In the Caucasus region, there are numerous slab cists whose description could without difficulty fit that of the Pandukal specimens"(*ibid.*, p. 243). These opinions finally lead to the conclusion that "the western affinity of the Pandukal complex is established" (*ibid.*, p. 244):

> The opinion that they are the funerary monuments of pastoral peoples in the Persian tradition, who occupied large areas of South India in the centuries between III BCE and II CE has been developed in the previous chapters.

Regarding the Nilgiri burials, Leshnik puts them in the 3rd-5th centuries AD.

A. Ghosh's *The City in Early Historical India* was published in 1973 and tried to evaluate the relevant Indian data in the light of the relevant theoretical literature on the preindustrial urban growth. A major section of the book deals with the different units of settlements, especially *grama* and its variants—*grama*, *nigama* (also called *samvaha*) and *nagara*. There is also a detailed discussion on the depiction of the ancient Indian city in literature. On the impact of iron in Indian agriculture and society his comment is that "in a slow-moving society the impact of iron was slow". This is something which was also concluded by the present author in 1974 (Chakrabarti 1974a). However, according to Ghosh, the exploitation of iron "must have started with the increase of demand from the more advanced regions that lay to the west, from which technology itself may have been borrowed." He asserted that there was nothing to relate the early historic cities to any impact of the Indus civilization. In fact, he seems to be highly reluctant to find any major continuity between the Indus civilization and the later periods. As he puts it, "In building their cities in the early historic period the people were working on a clean slate, with no Harappan nor any other mark on it" (Ghosh *ibid.*,

p. 89). Regarding iron, he accepts without demur the diffusionary hypothesis of the day, and similarly, his belief in the possibility of archaeologically identifying the Aryans was absolute. According to him the Painted Grey Ware people represented the later Aryans whereas the early Aryans could have been represented by the Ochre Coloured Pottery and the Black-and-Red Ware people.

It is thus obvious that till the mid-1970s, the grip of the old conceptual framework of Indian archaeological studies was more or less unchallenged, although Malik tried to deviate from it and offer an anthropological interpretative approach. Although the significance of natural scientific studies was, so to speak, re-discovered by Agrawal during this period, Agrawal did not go beyond the old ideas as far as the diffusionary postulates are concerned, nor did he show any sign of disbelief in the Aryan idea which was neither scientific nor archaeological. However, the impact of the radiocarbon dates was far-reaching, and through such articles as Gurdeep Singh's pollen studies in western Rajasthan, the importance of multi-disciplinary investigations in understanding archaeological problems made considerable headway. The futility of sticking to the Aryan idea was underlined by the present author in 1968, and in his dissertation on "the early urban centres in India, an archaeological perspective, c.2500 BC-c.300 AD", submitted to the Calcutta University in 1972, he viewed the protohistoric archaeological development in India in purely archaeological terms without referring to the Aryans. Further, the concerned data were arranged not in terms of the successions of "Neolithic", "Chalcolithic", "Bronze age" and "Iron age" but basically in terms of geography. The urban frames of both the Indus civilization and the early historic period were tied to the preceding stages of cultural developments with emphasis on the economic and technological developments region by region. From this point of view, it strongly deviated from what had hitherto characterized Indian archaeological thought. The present author also demonstrated as early as 1974 (Chakrabarti 1974b) that the dating of what Banerjee called the pre-NBP iron-bearing levels of central Indian sites like Nagda is likely to date from before 1000 BC, and that along with the date of c.1000 BC from the Neolithic-megalithic overlap phase at Hallur (M.S.N. Rao 1965) and the date of c.1100 BC for the iron-bearing PGW level at Hastinapur, this went against the idea of west to east migration of iron technology. As I wrote, "There is no logical basis to connect the beginning of iron in India with any diffusion from the west, from Iran and beyond" (Chakrabarti 1974b). In the review of radiocarbon dates by Agrwal and Kusumgar (1974), we have noticed how there was a marked reluctance to accept the early radiocarbon date for the PGW from Hastinapur. It was also in 1974 that M.D.N. Sahi pointed out the occurrence of iron fragments in the second and third phases of the chalcolithic level at Ahar, although without claiming any independent beginning of iron in India. Sahi underlined the Ahar occurrence of iron in the Indian History Congress, held in Jadavpur University, Kolkata, in 1974, although his publication on this topic had to wait till 1979 (Sahi 1979). Further, although Gurdeep Singh's premise (1971) of the occurrence of cerealia pollen as early as c.7000 BC in the lakes of western Rajasthan still remains to be archaeologically verified, the very fact that pollen analytical data suggested this possibility was in a sense enough to make us a little aware of other non-diffusionary dimensions of various archaeological issues. The present author's emphasis on a closer examination of the contexts of archaeological data also suggested that the situation could have been different from what was thought earlier regarding the same data. In retrospect, the mid-1970s seem to mark a new way of thinking about Indian archaeology—a way in which the archaeological data alone demand primary consideration.

I believe that one of the reasons why some of us could think of taking a purely archaeological approach to the Indian past was that a new generation of archaeology students came up after 1960 when the teaching of archaeology was taken up in some seriousness in a few universities. Unlike our teachers who looked at ancient India primarily through the prism of Indian literary tradition, we of the post-1960 period could at least focus our gaze on the changing patterns of Indian archaeological data. There is little doubt that the data were changing their patterns quite rapidly. This becomes remarkably clear if one compares Sankalia's *Prehistory and Protohistory in India and Pakistan* of 1962 with his *Prehistory and Protohistory of India and Pakistan* in 1974. A significant aspect of both these books is that they are by and large full of either the author's own work and the work of his Ph.D. students. Sankalia's own work meant the excavations conducted by him and his Deccan College associates in a vast area from Karnataka to Gujarat and from Rajasthan to Orissa. His Ph.D. students also worked essentially in this geographical range. Most of this Ph.D. level research was in the area of prehistory and protohistory, which meant that the concerned researchers could not embroil themselves with the literary tradition beyond a certain point. Whatever was written about the supposed west Asiatic contacts of the pottery and other material traits of the excavated and explored protohistoric sites was mostly bizarre, without even a shadow of logic or commonsense behind it. The west Asiatic pottery shapes cited were not identical with the Indian examples cited by the protagonists of this approach, nor did these supposed parallels represent any specific time-bracket or area which could be related to any specific geographical belt in India. I believe that this gibberish was produced mainly under a blind belief in the axiom of the Aryan invasion and all the correlates this invasion hypothesis is supposed to have in the Indian scenario. By firmly entrenching a tradition in the Deccan College that an Indian site had to be judged mainly by the contacts it had with the outside world, especially in the West, Sankalia caused, in fact, substantial damage to the idea of judging the archaeological history of the land primarily in its own terms. When Ambari was excavated in the early 1970s, I was shown some excavated pottery from the site and I found it comparable with the pottery we found at Chhiruti, the site of Karnasuvarna visited by Hsuang-Tsang in the 7th century AD. I judged the chronology of the site accordingly, and my idea, which was reported in the Bengali daily *Anandabazar*, was later supported by the radiocarbon dates from the site. However, a Deccan College team soon visited the place, and we were treated to the newspaper headlines of Roman contacts of Ambari. Such tendencies to look at Indian sites mainly in terms of their real or imaginary foreign contacts have had somewhat tragic consequences since then. When the site of Bagor was excavated in 1968-70, parallels for the arrowheads found in its Phase II were sought among a wide variety of sites in west Asia, which were not mutually related or represented any definite chronological bracket (Misra 1970). The way V.N. Misra, Bagor's excavator, seeks typological parallels of three hollow-based copper-bronze arrowheads from Bagor among a remarkably wide and largely unrelated sites from the Swiss lakes and Africa to southeast Asia is no doubt a remarkably thorough academic exercise, representing perhaps the Deccan College academic tradition at its best.

> The detailed though by no means exhaustive examination of the distribution in space and time of concave-based

> (including barbed) arrowheads of bronze as well as stone brings out the following facts quite clearly:
>
> (1) Bagor in south Rajasthan marks the eastern limit of the distribution of this class of tools (not including the far-eastern examples which clearly belong to a different cultural province).
>
> (2) Stone prototypes of metal arrowheads are completely absent from the Indo-Pakistan sub-continent.
>
> (3) The main concentration of stone prototypes is in the Caucasus, Europe and Africa.
>
> (4) *Finally, the Indian examples, both Bagorean and Harappan, must originally have been inspired by the western world. It is difficult to pinpoint the exact source but in all likelihood it was the Caucasian or the Aegean region.* (Misra 1970, p. 231, italics added).

The typology of the three arrowhead specimens from Bagor, whose origins Misra sought in the Caucasus or the Aegean, was identified later among the arrowheads at the site of Ganeshwar elsewhere in the Aravallis. In fact, the three arrowheads which figured in Bagor Phase II indicate nothing more than a relationship between the northeastern and the southeastern Aravallis in the second half of the 4th millennium BC, which is roughly the date of the beginning of the Ganeshwar copper metallurgy. To be fair to Misra, in his 1973 publication in *World Archaeology* (Misra 1973), he was much less enthusiastic to seek wide-ranging parallels for the Bagor arrowheads.

Sankalia and Misra are certainly not exceptional in their approach to Indian history and archaeology. The cultural comparisons which Lal and the Allchins offered in their publications, moving between Thrace and north Iran (Shah Tepe) and thinking of the migrations of people to the upper Ganga plain (cf. Lal) and the south (the Allchins) have about the same logic and common sense displayed in different contexts by Sankalia and Misra. A. Ghosh's book on the early historic Indian cities was not free from the Aryan premise and he postulated a sharp break between the Harappans and their successors. In fact, he downplayed the idea of continuity between the Harappans and the later Indian civilization.

The tradition persists even now. One of the major examples of this trend is the invocation of the Bactria-Margiana Archaeological Complex (BMAC) as the source of the miscellaneous designs on some clay objects from Gilund in Rajasthan. That the BMAC 'seals' were by and large metallic and had varying chronological contexts was not of any concern to the proponents of this theory. The BMAC complex was also supposed by an Indian ancient historian, R.S. Sharma, in his book *Advent of the Aryans in India* (2003, new edition) to denote the area from where the Aryans came to India.

The point is that in ancient Indian ancient historical and archaeological studies, the arguments or the logic of the chain of reasoning never played a role—not a major role anyway. The way the Indian and other scholars grabbed chronologically and geographically unrelated assortments of archaeological data in west and central Asia and related them to widely differing cultural situations in India did not have even an iota of archaeological logic behind them, but that was not something which bothered their fellow-scholars. I noticed the absence of such logic in the Aryan hypothesis in 1967-68 and while working on the archaeological data related to the early urban centres in India, I kept clear of this hypothesis and examined if one could offer a logical portrayal of these urban centres primarily in terms of archaeology. In fact, the dissertation rigorously stuck to the implications of its title 'the early urban centres in India, an archaeological perspective c.2500 BC-c.300 AD'. This work is likely to be the only archaeological essay of the period which had the temerity of not mentioning the Aryans at all or remaining silent about the issue of relating archaeology to Indian tradition. This exercise also brought out the details of protohistoric and early historic archaeological developments in India region by region and highlighted their overall patterns, with reference to the distribution, location and morphological features of the relevant city-sites. In a number of ways, this Ph.D. thesis was different from Ghosh's publication on the early historic cities, which was published in 1973. First, it clearly brought out the theoretical understanding of the early urban centres in the contemporary archaeology, with the avowed aim of judging the Indian data in the light of this understanding. The debate which occurred between Gordon Childe's technological and economic approach to the Urban Revolution and Robert Braidwood's and others' social-institutional approach was not raised in Indian archaeology outside this thesis. Interestingly, in his 1973 publication, Ghosh discusses Childe's concept of the Urban Revolution in detail but is silent about the ideas of the Chicago school. Secondly, this was an attempt to view both the Harappan and early historic urban phenomena in India together in a continuous narrative of sequence and archaeological features and thus, turned out to be the most detailed exercise on the understanding of ancient Indian urban centres.

Thirdly, the basic features of the relevant literary data were not ignored and the outline and the idea of an ancient Indian city in literature were broadly compared with the emerging archaeological picture of the town-planning and other morphological features of an early historic Indian city. Fourthly, as far as the theoretical approach to ancient cities was concerned, the work first pointed out the limitations of the attempted sociological definitions of an ancient city and then dwelt on the significance of G. Sjoberg's functional approach, i.e., a city as a settlement serves several functions in a landscape. Finally, the work also fulfilled the function of offering accessible summaries of a vast amount of archaeological data related to the major protohistoric and early historic settlements.

A number of publications increased the international academic profile of Indian archaeology during this period. In 1965, M.S. Nagaraja Rao (1965) published an ethnoarchaeological study of the Boyas of Tekkalakota in the light of his excavations at the site. In 1973, Misra (1973) provided a summary of his Mesolithic excavations in *World Archaeology*. In 1970, A.K. Ghosh (1970) summarized the results of his Ph.D. thesis on "the Palaeolithic cultures of Singhbhum' in *Transactions of the American Philosophical Society*. On the basis of his Ph.D. thesis on the Neolithic sites of the Deccan, K. Paddayya (1973) published *Investigations into the Neolithic Culture of the Shorapur Doab, South India* in 1973 through the publisher E.J. Brill, Leiden. In 1974, M.L.K. Murty (1974) published the results of his excavations at the Billa Surgam cave of Kurnool in Andhra in *Proceedings of the American Philosophical Society*. This was preceded by his analysis of 'blade and burin industries of Renigunta' in *Proceedings of the Prehistoric Society* in 1968 (Murty 1968). In 1973, G.R. Sharma (1968) published the results of his excavations at Sarai Nahar Rai and other Mesolithic sites near Allahabad under the title 'Mesolithic lake cultures in the Ganga valley, India' in *Proceedings of the Prehistoric Society* in 1973. In a sense, these publications are a kind of message to the international archaeology circuit that Indian archaeology had gained from its incorporation in the Indian university framework.

I must point out, however, that the presence of Indian archaeology in the Euro-American university framework was fairly marginal during this period. In the United States G.F. Dales and W.A. Fairservis maintained an interest in Indus archaeology alive, Dales through his excavations at Sutkagendor and Balakot on the Makran coast and Fairservis through his investigations in the Quetta valley and Zhob-Loralai region. There was an American interest in south Indian megaliths, and the representative writings were those of Paul Hockings (1975) who dated the Paikara megalithic burial in the Nilgiris in c.8th century AD and K.A.R. Kennedy's study of *Physical Anthropology of the Megalith Builders of South India and Sri Lanka* (Kennedy 1975), the latter trying to go beyond the traditional racial framework of the excavated megalithic skeletal remains. An offshoot of Dales' interest in Pakistan was a Ph.D. thesis by R. Mughal on the results of his explorations in Cholistan, and although the work was not published till 1997, the manuscript version of the thesis (Mughal 1970) enjoyed some circulation. The French interest of this period in the archaeology of the subcontinent was represented by J.M. Casal at Amri and Pirak. There was no British field-interest in Indian archaeology till the late 1970s when excavations were undertaken at Malvan in Gujarat 1970 (Allchin and Joshi 1995) and Lewan in Bannu in 1977-78 (Allchin 1986). There was an interest in the prehistory and the advent of aridity in the Thar desert and its adjacent regions including Sind on the part of B. Allchin and her associates in the early 1970s (Allchin, Goudie and Hegde 1978). In 1971, the European Association of South Asian Archaeologists marked its formation and first of its biennial conferences in Cambridge in 1971 (Hammond 1973). Since then the conferences have been held regularly at different European venues and although the title mentions only archaeology, there is a large presence of art historians in it. Further, although the name of the association is supposed to mean interested people from Europe, there is a large

American presence in it. It is no more than an exclusive Euro-American club of South Asian archaeologists, and admission of the native South Asians to it is in the form of invitations to a select few who are given free airfare and hospitality. It makes it a point to publish the proceedings of its conferences only in the First World, which has occasionally resulted in these publications being irregular and invariably being very expensive. Besides, these proceedings have very limited circulation in the subcontinent not merely because they are very expensive by the standard of the Indian libraries but also because they are difficult to get hold of. However, for a record of the First World interest in South Asian archaeology, these proceedings are the best source.

From time to time, I have heard it being said by Western South Asian archaeologists that the Government of India did not encourage foreign participation in Indian archaeology. The accusation does not hold ground today. These days, virtually anybody who can raise an Indian collaborator can get a license to excavate in India. However, even before the current period, there are some cases of international participation in Indian archaeology. If one goes through the successive volumes of *Indian Archaeology - A Review*, one does come across Western names as participants in various excavations. Even otherwise, we know that L.S. Leshnik, for instance, worked with V.N. Misra at Bagor, although the collaboration turned out to be sour later. However, the First World applications to excavate in India were somewhat difficult to get cleared by the Government of India in the 1970s and 1980s. As far as I am aware, the policy was initiated by S. Nurul Hasan as the Minister of Education, and one of the reasons for initiating this policy was the fact that Professor Hasan felt humiliated by the British India specialists while he was on a fellowship in Britain. His experience was by no means unusual and the tradition continues unabated. The problem was that Professor Hasan soon came to occupy a position of power in India. Secondly, it may be noted that in the British or other Euro-American universities, the Indian studies are still dominated by concerns with Indian languages, religion, philosophy, and modern Indian history, sociology, economics, etc. Indian archaeology hardly figured in this scheme in the 1970s and 1980s. Thirdly, on the university level, there was hardly any integrated focus on ancient India including its art, archaeology and ancient history. Only Cambridge ran in its 'Oriental Faculty' and Department of Archaeology a full-length course of ancient India up to the Gupta period. The components of this course were Indian prehistory, protohistory, early history, art, architecture, coins and inscriptions. In the Department of Archaeology, this course was followed till at least my retirement from active teaching in 2008. Now that there is no longer an Indian Studies tripos at the University, there is no question of running a course in any aspect of ancient India in what used to be called formerly Faculty of Oriental Studies. The Faculty has now been re-named the Faculty of Asian and Middle Eastern Studies. But even when there was a 'Faculty of Oriental Studies', there was not much emphasis on any aspect of the history and archaeology of ancient India in the 'Indian Studies' tripos. In 1990, I found that the undergraduates opting for this tripos could keep themselves away from anything related to Indian archaeology and ancient history. In the Department of Archaeology (Faculty of Archaeology and Anthropology), however, the students had no problem about expressing a clear interest in the archaeology of ancient India.

I cannot say anything about the place, structure and organization of Indian archaeology in any other Euro-American university. My general impression is that elsewhere the course has always been fragmented. One can study, if one likes, the bits and pieces of ancient Indian history and archaeology. The basic framework is dominated by the language studies. The total framework of Indian archaeology did not generally matter outside Cambridge. It is, however, worth noting that there is a core of ancient South Asia professionals in various Euro-American museums and possibly other organizations. Their main focus of interest is, of course, their museum collections and their expertise is essentially linked to the major items of the collection.

THE CHANGE IN THE WORLD OF INDIAN HISTORICAL RESEARCH (1972)

The financing of research-projects in the Humanities including history, had been till this date the responsibility of the Indian UGC. With the establishment of a new organization, exclusively for the support of historical research, under the auspicies of the then government of India Ministry of Education, Social Welfare and Culture, the primary research funding of history ceased to be the exclusive responsibility of the UGC. The objectives of the new organization were, according to their web statement, the following:

- to bring historians together and provide a forum for exchange of views between them;
- to give a national direction to an objective and scientific writing of history and to have rational presentation and interpretation of history;
- to promote, accelerate and coordinate research in history with special emphasis on areas which have not received adequate attention so far;
- to promote and coordinated a balanced distribution of research effort over different areas;
- to elicit support and recognition for historical research from all concerned and ensure the necessary dissemination and use of results.

The second objective of giving a 'national direction' to the study and writing of history and to have a 'rational presentation and interpretation of history' clearly suggests that the contemporary history establishment of India was not happy with the way things were moving in their field and the necessity of a government control by means of a new organization was felt. The 'national direction', if there can be a uniform national direction in the study of historical writing and research along with its interpretation and 'rational presentation', is primarily dependent on the general consensus of the national body, if any, of historians. In India, the 'Indian History Congress' had so long served the purpose of such a body. One does not understand why in 1972 the necessity of a new government-sponsored body to guide historical research in the country was felt. The attempt to 'guide' historical research in the country was once a familiar feature of the Soviet Block of countries. Apparently, the ideology behind the setting up of a government-controlled organization to finance historical research came from that quarter, and considering the general political situation of the country where the ruling party, Congress, was dependent on the support of the communists, this development was not surprising.

After the war with China in 1962, the Communist Party of India (Marxist) seceded from the Communist Party of India and began to pursue a specific 'Chinese line' instead of the 'Soviet line' of what remained of the former Communist Party'. The people behind the newly instituted Indian Council of Historical Research (ICHR) were all affiliated to, or sympathisers of, the pro-Soviet Party. The important people were three in number: S. Nurul Hasan, the Minister; Satish Chandra, the Chairman of the UGC; and R.S. Sharma, the Chairman of the ICHR. They were all professors of history. They showed signs of a strong partisan approach right from the beginning. Tapan Raychaudhuri, an economic historian of the Mughal period, has written in his autobiographical book *Bangalnama* in Bengali that V.K.R.V. Rao, an earlier education minister of the government of India, had allocated a grant of Rupees three crores for the translation of the volumes of the Bharatiya Vidya Bhavan series into different regional languages and that the new minister had used this money for the formation of the ICHR. One of the first acts of the ICHR was to initiate a programme of translating some books of Indian history into regional languages. The volumes of the Vidya Bhavan series, which were edited by R.C. Majumdar, were ignored and the books which now found place in the politically approved list of 'important books' were all written by the people associated with the ICHR or their favourites. What I also learnt by word of mouth was that long before any of these books was translated, the estimated royalty from the sale of each translation was paid to the concerned authors. Another related development was the publication of school textbooks in history by the National Council of Educational Research and Training (NCERT). These volumes were all written by people eminent in the eyes of the ICHR—R.S. Sharma, the Chairman of the ICHR, and Romila Thapar, among them. Considering that these textbooks were recommended and published by the overarching body of school education in India, i.e., the NCERT, and that there are hundreds of thousands of schools in the country, the number of copies sold of these books must be beyond the dreams of ordinary history-writers.

The issue, of course, went far beyond making a group of history-teachers rich. If one goes back to the sections on 'objective and scientific writing of history' and 'rational representation and interpretation', one realizes that the whole thing had a sinister sub-text. To suggest in 1972 that the writing of history in India before this date had not been 'objective and scientific' and 'rationally represented and interpreted' and that these lacunae called for the establishment of a government-sponsored organization to control the financing of historical research in the country had certainly a dictatorial or fascist tone about it. The leader of the new group, S. Nurul Hasan who later became the Indian Ambassador to Moscow, Vice-Chairman of the Council of Scientific and Industrial Research (CSIR) and 'governor' of a CPI (M)-controlled 'State', could be called a professional historian only because he had a D.Phil in history from Oxford and was a professor of history in Aligarh Muslim University before he was inducted to Mrs. Indira Gandhi's cabinet. His historical papers in mediaeval India were posthumously collected and edited in 2005. Satish Chandra, the UGC chairman of the day, was also a professor of mediaeval India and by 1972 he seems to have had only one major publication, the editing and translation of an eighteenth century text called *Balmakandnamah*. Both Hasan and Chandra belonged to the upper class landed gentry of Uttar Pradesh. Hasan married into the famous Nawab family of Rampur and Satish Chandra was the son of Sir Sita Ram, who was the first president of the Uttar Pradesh Legislative Council (1937-49). R.S. Sharma came from a humble background and worked his way up teaching in various undergraduate colleges and eventually becoming professor of history at Patna University and Delhi University (1973-85). Before being recruited as the chairman of the ICHR, he, unlike his patrons (the minister Hasan and the UGC chairman Chandra, both far above him in government hierarchy), had a string of publications to his credit, two of his major books being *Shudras in Ancient India, a Social History of the Lower Order Down to c.600* AD, his London University Ph.D. thesis of 1956, and *Indian Feudalism* which was published in 1965. Sharma's thesis of Indian feudalism, which he traces roughly from AD 400, evoked a lot of discussion in the 1970s, especially after he became the chairman of the ICHR and thus occupied an important position of power. His emphasis on a series of land-grants from different parts of India during this period as a marker of the royals giving up some of their juridical rights over the donated land to the donees need not mean any feudal tendency because such land-grants seem to denote a remarkable phase of agricultural growth all over the country and also because they date in their earliest from the Satavahana period in the early centuries AD, i.e., before Sharma's postulated period. Besides, it has been pointed out that the total number of such grants considered by Sharma constitute only a small percentage of the total grants available. Sharma's case also gets weakened when one considers his subsidiary hypotheses of 'urban decay' and the absence of trade and commerce during his postulated 'feudal' period. The material data from different parts of the country argue against such decays of cities, trade and coinage. In retrospect, Sharma's principal approach to the study of ancient India distinctly echoed the Communist Party of India luminary S.A. Dange's attempt to view Indian history on the model of F. Engels' *The Origin of the Family, Private Property and State* in his *India from Primitive Communism to Slavery* (Dange 1949). It must be admitted that Sharma was the only working historian of the group, the dispute regarding his ideas notwithstanding. Sharma was soon appointed the Head of the Department of History of Delhi University and thus acquired the power, apart from that of the chairman of the ICHR, to recruit teachers of history to all the undergraduate colleges affiliated to the university. Meanwhile, the Jawaharlal Nehru University had come up in the capital with large-scale government/UGC patronage and the history department, if not the university itself, was completely taken over, right from the beginning, by the believers in the 'progressive' philosophy of the new group of historians just as the undergraduate departments of history in Delhi University soon became full of the history–teachers with the same political orientation. In a nutshell, the framework of history teaching and research in the Indian capital was mostly taken over by the members of the new group. From their positions of power, this group was soon able to form a ruling coterie of historians all over the country.

In retrospect, this period marks the beginning of many features of the current historical research in India. First, everything related to history is now oriented to particular groups of historians and their politics. The enormity of the situation has not yet sunk in. By raising the bogey of communalist approach to historical studies, the new 'progressives' succeeded in consolidating an anti-lobby, i.e., the lobby opposed to the Congress/Communist lobby—in other words, the lobby affiliated to the Bharatiya Janata Party (BJP) and its associates. The only forum which the BJP lobby has and which can remotely be called a forum of professional historians is the Indian History and Culture Society. This Society came into existence well after the Emergency imposed by Mrs. Gandhi in 1975 ended in 1977. Compared to the Indian History Congress, it has few members and the major sign of its activity is its annual conference, which it has never been able to organize independently, not even when the NDA government with the BJP as the major partner was in power in Delhi. The point is that in 1972, historical research in India hardly faced any attack from the BJP or what the 'progressive' lobby called 'communal forces'. Secondly, as a corollary of the first premise, it has become necessary on the part of the new group to keep on talking about Hindu fundamentalism and its various offshoots. The point is that such fundamentalists had been so long very much outside the margins of professional historical research, and by them, I mean the characters who believe in a kind of utopia in the context of ancient India and feel outraged by references to such things as beef-eating in that utopia. Their position was at the lunatic fringe of historical ideas. The references to beef-eating in ancient India were compiled by no less a scholar than Rajendra Lal Mitra in the mid-nineteenth century, but now we find fairly dubious characters among the so-called progressives trying to get some publicity by compiling precisely those references and thus drawing attention to themselves. It appears that by making too much of them, the 'progressives' have made the 'fundamentalists' almost respectable. Thirdly, by extending the progressive/reactionary bipolarism to areas of sensible historical debates, such as the dried-up Sarasvati system and other issues (cf. the idea of Aryan invasions), the 'progressive' group is trying to choke the field of genuine historical dissent. This whole development has been unfortunate and led nowhere except different kinds of skulduggery and divisions among Indian historians. What began as a Communist coup in 1972 has led in various ways to the degradation of historical research in the country, irrespective of the political affiliations of its proponents.

The important question from our point of view is the extent of its impact on archaeological research in the country. I am not sure if many archaeologists benefited from the ICHR research grants. However, the number of retired history/archaeology teachers who got three-year fellowships/grants under the scheme for retired people must have been quite a few. The first major archaeology project financed by the ICHR was the 'dictionary of Indian archaeology' project under A. Ghosh, a retired Director General of the Archaeological Survey of India, in the late 1970s. The work could regrettably be published only in 1989. However, despite its tentative links with archaeology in its early days, the impact of the ICHR on the financing of archaeological research in the universities is undeniable.

At the same time, I must underscore the fact that the attitude of the new 'progressive' group of historians to archaeology was remarkably ambiguous. Neither in Delhi University nor in Jawaharlal Nehru University was there any initiative to set up strong archaeology groups. None of these two major universities in the capital of India even boasted a university museum. As the Vice-Chairman of the CSIR, S. Nurul Hasan could set up, without much of a bother, a national level laboratory for archaeological science, but, as I am aware, he declined to do that. I refuse to believe that these Communists did not realize the potential of archaeology in bringing about a revolution in expanding the horizon of the peoples' history of India. Despite their lip-service to 'progress' and other laudable things, they and their associates were nothing but a group of people who were interested only in self-aggrandisement. The organization they built, the ICHR, may be the first example of an 'academic scam' in modern India, as Arun Shourie has argued with specific evidence of major research funds going waste in his book *Eminent Historians*.

THE WIDENING OF THE ACADEMIC FOCUS: INDIA AND WEST ASIA BEFORE THE ACHAEMENIDS, THE BEGINNING OF IRON IN INDIA, AND THE HISTORY OF INDIAN ARCHAEOLOGY

I have previously pointed out that in the 1960s and 1970s, Indian archaeologists had been concerned with the problem of the archaeological evidence of contacts between India and the area which lies to the west, especially central Asia and west Asia and also with the problem of the beginning of iron in the subcontinent. My review of the entire span of Indian prehistoric and early historic archaeological research, which I had to do connection with my Ph.D. thesis, made me keenly aware of these two problems. Once the Ph.D. work was over, I thought I would focus on them. There was also a third problem, primarily the offshoot of the presence of 'history of archaeology' in our Kolkata MA course. This meant a comprehensive idea of how archaeology had developed stage by stage in the country and what were the basic ideas the subject had lived with. The two articles by S. Roy and A. Ghosh in *Ancient India 9* had dealt with the situation exclusively from the point of view of the Archaeological Survey of India. They were not interested in the development of the subject as an academic discipline. By 'history of archaeology', Sankalia meant the different approaches taken by different archaeologists and he thought that these approaches meant different schools of thought. Allchin's paper in the volume on the historians of India, Pakistan and Ceylon (Philips 1963) outlined the scope of the problem but was far from being a detailed or definitive discussion, which, of course, was also not possible within the scope of a short paper.

Thus, these three problems had occupied my mind after the Ph.D. work was over. Of these, 'India and West Asia before the Achaemenids' was the first choice. It was obvious that the problem was far more than building up an inventory of Indian protohistoric pottery designs and shapes and comparing them with the material from various central Asian and west Asian sites. Under the Achaemenids, the north-western part of the sub-continent up to the Indus plain was a part of the west and central Asian orbit, and right up to the Kushan kings and later this orbit had played a role in ancient Indian history. It was important that one focussed on understanding the geographical, political and economic configurations of this orbit as far as they related to the subcontinent. It would also have to be accompanied by a close analysis of the archaeological data of the different periods.

CHURCHILL COLLEGE, CAMBRIDGE (OCTOBER 1973-SEPTEMBER 1974)

I was awarded Ph.D. degree in 1973 on the basis of the thesis I submitted about a year earlier. In the first half of 1973, I was awarded a Commonwealth Scholarship for post-doctoral studies at Churchill College, Cambridge, for one year beginning in the last week of September and with F.R. Allchin as my academic supervisor. On the Indian side, Professor Barun Dey, a friend of S. Nurul Hasan and certainly an important member of the new progressive group of historians, put in a kind word, on his own, for me to one of the Indian selectors. Professor Dey, a bright history student of Presidency College and later a Nuffield Scholar at Oxford, did not turn out to be an archive-frequenting historian, but he was a well-read person, an excellent academic administrator and a benefactor of many aspiring academics like me. Sometime in early 1973, John Robert Knox, then a Ph.D. student in Cambridge in Indian archaeology, turned up in Kolkata, and his visit to the Department of Archaeology at the university resulted in a life-long friendship. Now that Dr. Allchin is no more, I remember him sitting with his feet dangling from the window ledge of the Indian archaeology section of the Oriental Faculty library and talking about all kinds of things related to archaeology in the subcontinent till he suddenly remembered that his wife would be waiting and he rushed away. The Cambridge libraries then evoked a world in which scholarship and scholarship alone mattered. On my first visit to the UL (University Library), I was simply asked to mention my college and get in, and when I expressed surprise at the lack of any identification, Mr. Clayton of the Library entrance desk simply said, "Let that day be far off when a member of the university has to identify himself." Now that you cannot take a step inside without producing your identification card—and in the Rare Books room, they can ask for identification, if they do not like your face, any number of times—I think of Mr. Clayton from time to time. In the field of ancient Indian history and archaeology, I was preceded in Cambridge by three fellow Bengalis and two Kannadigas or persons from Karnataka. The Bengalis were Harunur Rashid from the Pakistan government's Department of Archaeology, Pratapaditya Pal who briefly taught us in our MA course in Calcutta, and Brajadulal Chattopadhyay who was also from Calcutta and later became an important member of the History department of Jawaharlal Nehru University. Harunur Rashid was at Churchill whereas Pal and Chattopadhyay were at Corpus Christie. The two Kannadigas who were there at the same time were S. Settar and M.S.N. Rao, the excavator of Tekkalakota. They were both at Churchill. Rashid's Ph.D. thesis was on the archaeology of the Mainamati area and many years later, I had the privilege of knowing him and working with him at Jahangirnagar University near Dhaka in Bangladesh. Pal did his second Ph.D. from Cambridge on the architecture of Nepal and eventually found himself in Boston Museum holding the post which the great art historian Ananda Kentish Coomaraswamy once held. Chattopadhyay's thesis was on the ancient currency system of south India but later he specialised in the early mediaeval history of north India. For some reason, M.S.N. Rao did not complete his Cambridge Ph.D.; he had an earlier Ph.D. from the Deccan College. Once the Director of Archaeology of Karnataka, Rao became the Director General of the Archaeological Survey of India for three years in the 1980s. S. Settar wrote his dissertation on the Hoyasala architecture. He taught mostly at Dharwar University and later turned his attention to Jaina texts. I believe that Harunur Rashid came to Cambridge with Mortimer Wheeler's recommendation and was on a Pakistan government grant. The rest were all Commonwealth scholars.

During those days, this scholarship was run by the British Council. I had a very happy experience with the British Council and I came away with the belief that it was one of the best British organizations of its kind. There were not many Indian graduate students in Cambridge at that time. The number of Indian undergraduates must then have been miniscule. An aeronautical engineering Ph.D. student from Bangalore, K. Yegnanarayan, and a political science Ph.D. student from Israel, Warren Young, became good friends of mine at Churchill. Dr. Allchin soon put me to doing some undergraduate 'supervision'.

'New Archaeology' was not something which could be ignored even in Kolkata in the late 1960s. However, in Cambridge it was very much a direct experience, especially in the seminars of D. Clarke. The difficulty of breaking the barrier of the English prose, which was being used, was certainly difficult but even I could make out that the basic reasoning of David Clarke and many others, both in Cambridge and elsewhere, was based on mathematical reasoning and modelling and that those unfamiliar with mathematics, which I was, would have to put enough effort even in going through the first barrier, i.e., the barrier of language. It was, of course, very clear that archaeology had begun to draw people from different intellectual backgrounds and that the way in which they would look at the archaeological universe would not be the way in which traditional Humanities people like me would look at it. Sometimes I have wondered if New Archaeology would not have been more easy to follow if it had begun with the analysis of reasonings hitherto followed in archaeology, pointed out their limitations and move from there. In any case, I decided not to try to tread the path of New Archaeology because in no way would I have been able to pursue it logically and convincingly. It is interesting that in the Indian context, nobody has far showed this grip, and the reason, I believe, is the fact that all of us had come to the subject principally from historical studies. Only K. Paddayya among us wrote a book on this, but the problem with that book is that although he has competently summarized the principles of New Archaeology in its first two chapters, the third chapter, which is about Indian archaeology, stands unrelated to the principles enunciated earlier. In fact, none of the things he mentions in the third chapter is either difficult to understand or unacceptable to orthodox Indian archaeologists like me but I would very much hesitate to accept any of his Indian examples as related in any way to New Archaeology. In the 1970s and 1980s, people like me had to bear always a sense of guilt because they could not participate in all the exciting things which were then done in their subject or even understand the literature in which these exciting things were being written. As the 'post-processualists' walked in, I suppose that people like me felt a little less ashamed, and now that World Archaeological Congress uses the term 'archaeologies' as the title of its formal mouthpiece, we are relieved because that takes in all the diversities with which the study of archaeology has evolved in the world. A problem with New Archaeology was its open aggressive attitude, relegating all those who did not speak their language to academic dust-heaps. For the Third World as a whole, New Archaeology was not something it could cope with and New Archaeology also did not mind its opinion of the Third World archaeology being known. If I remember correctly, the Third World archaeologists were advised by an important New Archaeologist (opinion cited in one of the issues of *Antiquity* of that period) to go to 'mealie fields' if they could not put up with 'science'. However, these days it is nice to read Joan Gero in the website of World Archaeology Congress:

> The discipline of archaeology is no longer the exclusive province of white European upper-class men, and there

> is no going back to a pre-WAC era of exclusionary, hierarchical and scientized knowledge that marginalizes the multivocal archaeology from the peripheries. The question of "who controls the past?" is no longer a conundrum because it must be generally conceded that there are many pasts and they will be known differently from many views.

To be honest, it would be wrong to perceive that the difference between the archaeology of the two worlds has died away. This is far from being the case. The difference between the Third World archaeology as practised by the Third World scholars and the Third World archaeology as practised by the First World scholars is still very much there and not covered by the pious thoughts of World Archaeology Congress.

Coming into contact with Glyn Daniel at Cambridge in 1973 renewed my interest in the history of archaeology, especially Indian archaeology, and one of the first papers I then wrote was on Robert Bruce Foote. Since my student days, it had been almost axiomatic to consider that the establishment of the Asiatic Society in Kolkata in 1784 marked the beginning of archaeological research in India. Even some preliminary study of the relevant material showed that this was far from being the case and that there was a clear concern with Indian antiquities by the middle of the eighteenth century. It also came to light that towards the end of the eighteenth century there was a solidly entrenched opinion that the Brahmins/monks once settled in central Asia and migrated from there to as far west as Scotland. Such ideas of migrations from the east were replaced by the ideas of migrations from the west after 1857.

In any case, there was no way I could go through and check the contexts of all archaeological data suggestive of India-west Asia-central Asia contacts till the Achaemenids in the year I had in Cambridge. I decided to focus only on the section related to the Indus civilization. Eventually, this led to the publication of my book *The External Trade of the Indus Civilization* (Chakrabarti 1990) but this was preceded by a series of papers on the topic in the 1970s (cf. Chakrabarti 1977, 1978a, 1978b, 1978c). It may be remembered that the very identification of the Indus civilization as a Bronze Age civilization was possible only because the Indus seals had previously been reported from the Bronze Age contexts of Mesopotamia. Its dating also significantly depended on a close examination of the range of dating suggested by these contacts. The evidence did not come only from Mesopotamia. The Indus-type seal was reported from Susa in southwest Iran as early as the late nineteenth century. In the 1950s and 1960s, discoveries in Bahrain in the Gulf threw absolutely new light on the Indus relationship with the region. In 1964, Dales highlighted the possible role of Sutkagendor on the Makran coast as an intermediary port between the Indus and the Gulf. The excavations at Tepe Yahya and Shahr-i-Sokhta in Iran in the late 1960s and later strongly underlined the role of southern Iran in the Indus-Mesopotamia contact and the possible independent role southern Iran might have played in this east-west Bronze Age trade. The existence of the Harappan site of Shortughai in the Kokcha valley of north Afghanistan was known only in the late 1970s but the existence of Namazga Tepe with its evidence of Indus contacts was known earlier. The point is that in 1973, one could justifiably think of focussing on the evidence of Indus contact with Afghanistan and central Asia, Iran, the Gulf and Mesopotamia to understand the early phase of India-west Asia relationship. In fact, unknown to me, two Ph.D. programmes were already underway, one in the Institute of Archaeology, London (During-Caspers) and another in the Department of History, Jawaharlal Nehru University, Delhi (Ratnagar). Shireen Ratnagar's book on the topic was not published till 1981 whereas E. During-Caspers had published a number of papers on her work in the 1970s, the most important of these papers being the one on etched carnelian beads (During-Caspers 1972). I began my work by preparing a detailed inventory of the relevant artefacts, including the seals and their contexts both in India and outside. It was a time full of different theories regarding trade. In fact, everybody working between the Gulf and the Indus had their quota of speculations how the trade across the region was conducted (cf. Lamberg-Karlovsky, Kohl, comments on Lamberg-Karlovsky by Chakrabarti 1974c). Without first going through the theoretical literature on trade, I focussed on getting closely familiar with the concerned archaeological situation. This work could not be complete in my first year at Cambridge (1974-75) but spilled over in April-June 1975, and the academic year 1975-76.

One of the first points that emerged was that the Indus-Mesopotamia contact dated back to the period of the Royal Graves at Ur, i.e., around 2600 BC. Etched carnelian beads and long barrel-cylinder carnelian beads, two indisputably Indus products, occurred in the Royal Graves. As far as the etched carnelian beads are concerned, their significance in this context was understood by me before I read During-Caspers' paper on the subject. It appears that in the case of the long barrel-cylinder carnelian beads, I can claim the exclusive credit myself because I was the first one to point out its significance in this context. The evidence of pre-Sargonic Indus-Mesopotamia contact, which could also be buttressed by what Kohl called 'intercultural style vessels' of chlorite/steatite, had tremendous significance on the starting point of the Harappan chronology, showing conclusively that the shorter chronological bracket suggested on the basis of radiocarbon dates by scholars like D.P. Agrawal and F.R. Allchin was not supported by the historical evidence of dating. Later, I also drew attention to the occurrence of Indus seals at Nippur in the Kassite context and thus satisfactorily bracketed the civilization at its later end as well.

A clear understanding of the basic geography of the concerned areas, including the trade routes, was important, and in my case, a three-month stay in Iran with a fellowship of the British Institute of Persian Studies in Tehran was a great help. The material from Sialk and Hissar, which I could study in the Tehran museum, was important in assessing the significance of various theories about the relationship between these sites and India. Fresh Indus material was located at Marlik at the southwestern edge of the Caspian and at Jalalabad near Shiraz in the Fars plain. In both cases, the material was represented primarily by etched carnelian beads but at Jalalabad the long barrel-cylinder carnelian bead-type also occurred. No Indus material was previously reported from the Fars plain, and as the Fars plain lies squarely on the southern Iranian route from India to Mesopotamia, the identification of a site with Indus material in the Fars plain was important.

Theoretically, I tried to visualize the Indus trade in the context of the traditional trade of the entire region, which in some form continues even today. An inkling of this still-continuing traditional trade could be had from my coming across a trader from Irani Baluchistan who obtained some woollen jackets from Karachi in Sind and travelled along the southern Iranian route up to the Fars plain, selling the jackets to individual customers along the way. This experience also strengthened my assumption that the traditional trade between Mesopotamia and the Indus had been primarily overland, and I also argued at some length how there was a perfectly feasible coastal route between southwest Iran facing the Gulf and Baluchistan on the basis of a nineteenth-century army officer's report. The nineteenth/early twentieth century British Indian gazetteer literature helped me in coming to grips with the possible character and scope of the Indus external trade. An important geographical by-product was an understanding of the possible routes the Indus traders could have used across the Hindukush and across the northwestern Indian ranges.

INSTITUTE OF ADVANCED STUDY IN THE HUMANITIES, EDINBURGH UNIVERSITY (OCTOBER 1974-MARCH 1975)

The focus of my studies in Edinburgh was the problem of the beginning of iron in India. I was not satisfied with Banerjee's obsession with the Aryan premise and its supposed links with the beginning of iron among the Hittites of Anatolia and its subsequent migration to India. I found it curious that such an important technological problem in the Indian context should be bogged down in something linguistic. I was also unhappy with the way Banerjee dated the post-Chalcolithic and pre-NBP iron-bearing level of the central Indian sites like Nagda. I could find no reason why this date could not be pushed up from Banerjee's c.800 BC to at least c.1100 BC. However, to give a specific academic frame to my ideas regarding the beginning of Indian iron, I had to do far more reading than I had hitherto been able to do. The fellowship which I received at the Institute of Advanced Study in the Humanities at Edinburgh University for six months allowed me some time to pursue this problem. Professor A.M. Snodgrass, a member of the Board of this institute, was at that point of time interested in the Iron Age of Greece and the Mediterranean, and I suppose that it was due to his intervention that I received the fellowship.

I have always found it useful to define a research problem by examining how the problem began and how it had evolved through different phases of knowledge. The history of research on Indian iron was fascinating from this point of view. I had been intrigued to know that towards the end of the eighteenth century the Royal Society was interested in getting samples of pre-industrial Indian iron analysed and that in the early part of this century, the best iron in the Cairo market was obtained from India. The eighteenth century and earlier reputation of the excellence of Indian iron was as good a point as any to begin my research survey from, and I was soon overwhelmed by the geological and metallurgical interest in preindustrial iron till the 1930s. In fact, some of this early literature categorically expressed the opinion that India must have witnessed the beginning of iron quite early. It was interesting to discover that Panchanan Neogi, who published his book *Iron in Ancient India* in 1913, was aware of this early Western scientific interest in pre-Industrial Indian iron and that he based his book on a synthesis of the relevant historical (both archaeological and literary), ethnographic, geological and metallurgical data. In a sense, I was trying to update Neogi's much earlier work on the subject.

I was also helped in acquiring an ethnographic perspective of the early iron-smelting in India by Valentine Ball's book on the economic geology of India in 1881 and by many other writings, which were published on the subject in the twentieth century including Andrew McWilliams' analysis of the iron smelted at Mirjati village near Jamshedpur in 1922 and Henry Cleere's study of the Singhbhum iron-smelting furnaces in the 1960s. It was also interesting to have an idea of the ubiquity of iron ores suitable for preindustrial smelting all over the peninsular India sand to learn that the Delhi iron pillar was likely to have been formed of iron, which resembled the composition of iron produced in the ordinary preindustrial iron-smelting furnaces. An exhaustive review of the relevant literary sources was no less interesting, and in this I was helped by Edinburgh University's excellent collections of Sanskrit and other literary texts. The synthesis of the major archaeological data posed no problem and a coordinated picture of an independent beginning of iron in India fell into shape. The concerned paper was read out in an institute seminar at the end of my stay, and at the suggestion of Professor Stuart Piggott, who chaired the seminar, the paper was sent to *Antiquity* for publication. A few other publications also resulted from this work, although my book *The Early Use of Iron in India* was not published till 1992. The point is that without a single new discovery, one could look closely at a significant range of Indian archaeological data and offer a clear and convincing alternative. This alternative has been given a substantive archaeological basis by the radiocarbon dates which have since then been accumulated on Indian iron.

THE BRITISH INSTITUTE OF PERSIAN STUDIES, TEHRAN, APRIL-JUNE 1975

What I aimed at, apart from looking for Indus material and studying the pottery collection from some famous sites, was to acquire a first-hand idea of the various geographical regions of Iran and how that helped in the understanding of the distribution of the Indus material. Tepe Yahya and Shahr-i-Sokhta were among the sites visited. Interestingly, from the top of the mounds north of Meshed, one could have a distant glimpse of the famous steppe region of central Asia. The Caspian shore was almost tropical in its lush vegetation and contrasted sharply with the plateau lying to the south of the Elburz. The dividing line between the plateau aridity and the Caspian vegetation is sharp and clearly comes into view as one crosses the Elburz from the Tehran side, passing in the shadow of its highest peak Mt. Davamand (5670 m), which retains some snow even at the height of summer. The section between

Meshed in the northeast and Zahidan in the southeast provides a cross-section of the plateau rim which divides Iran from Afghanistan and Pakistan. Shahr-i-Sokhta lies between Zabul and Zahidan in the southeast, with a railway connection between Zahidan and Quetta, which broadly passes just south of the Chagai hills at the northern border of Baluchistan with Afghanistan. Zahidan was an important point of what used to be known once as Hippie trail, and it was not uncommon there to come across Western travellers who had been as far east as Kathmandu and Vaisali. Along the eastern rim of the Iranian plateau, Urdu is still understood and the general imprint of the subcontinent is, so to speak, in the air. From Zahidan there is a route to Kirman which passes through Bam, and from Kirman one can approach Tepe Yahya which lies in a valley through which the lorry-drivers bound for the Pakistan border used to take a short-cut till 1975. The egress from the Tepe Yahya valley took me to Sirjan from where I passed through Neyriz to reach Shiraz. My first glance at the famous Persepolitan pillars made me wonder who on earth could conceivably see similarity between the freestanding and almost sculpted Mauryan monoliths and the Persepolitan pillars which are integral parts of an architectural composition. From Shiraz, there was a route straight to Ahvaz, passing through the southwestern corner of the Zagros and the famous oil-fields of the Susa region. The French archaeologists' castle at Susa was an ample indication of how the First World archaeology used to be conducted in this part of the world in the late nineteenth century.

While travelling from Tehran to Cambridge, I decided to travel overland, passing through Erzerum, Ankara and Istanbul to reach Bulgaria in Europe. The famous peak, Mt. Ararat, when viewed from the Turkish side, gave the impression of floating lightly in the air. In no way did I become knowledgeable in the archaeology of Iran, but at the end of three months I could at least visualize the locations of the sites where the Indus material was discovered in that country and they were related to the wider network of related routes.

WOLFSON COLLEGE, CAMBRIDGE, JULY 1975-JUNE 1976

Dr. Allchin took a year's leave and I came in as the substitute teacher for Indian archaeology for three 'terms' in 1975-76, having an association with Wolfson College as a 'visiting senior member'. This was the time when I prepared the outline of the three-volumed *A Source-Book of Indian Archaeology*, compiling the material of the first volume (Allchin and Chakrabarti 1979). This was a step forward in the direction of acquiring a more than marginal interest in the history of archaeology in India, although the writing of a full-fledged book on its history till 1947 had to wait till 1987 (Chakrabarti 1988). My interest in the history of Indian archaeology was strictly based on published sources and my main aim was to focus on the basic history of ideas—how different ideas have had their roles in Indian archaeology, and the extent to which we are still carrying on these ideas. I mainly wanted to understand these ideas because these would throw light on the roots and development of many of our current ideas of Indian archaeology. The working out of individual biographies or of the personal background of individual archaeologists was far removed from my concern. I was interested in individual archaeologists only to the extent they influenced the course of development of archaeology in the subcontinent.

There was not much scope of working freshly on the early use of iron in this year but work on 'India and west Asia' went on in bits and pieces. A major paper that I worked out during this period was "India and West Asia—An alternative approach" (Chakrabarti 1977), which made me go into the historical and economic linkages between the different components of what Aurel Stein called 'Indo-Iranian borderlands' and T. Holdich described as the 'gates' of India. The realization that the entire region comprising the southern section of central Asia, the eastern rim of Iran, the whole of Afghanistan and the whole of the Indus valley including Kashmir formed one interacting political and economic interaction zone helped to assess the various categories of artefacts, which are usually put forward as evidence of migrations to the subcontinent in a new light and also offered a geographical model to understand the distribution of such artefacts. In the mid-1970s, the potential of this geographical model was not understood in Indian archaeology.

A STUDY TOUR OF SOME UNIVERSITIES IN THE UNITED STATES, JULY-SEPTEMBER 1976

At the end of the second phase of my Cambridge stay, I received a grant from the JRD IIIrd Fund to visit several universities of my choice in the United States. The support came from Dr. Allchin, who obviously knew the concerned people of this fund well. The institutions I visited were located in New York, Philadelphia, Washington, Cornell, Harvard, Ann Arbor, Chicago, San Francisco, Los Angeles, and Hawai. On the way back to Kolkata, I visited Tokyo and Bangkok, meeting M.A. Konishi in Tokyo. In retrospect, it was a great educative experience, giving me a glimpse of the free spirit of the youth and its warmth in the United States campuses in the mid-1970s. The libraries and the campus bookstores were important places to visit and the campuses themselves carried the impressions of easy organization, academic strength and visionary insights. Mr. Richard Lanier of the JRD IIIrd Fund and Ms. Maureen Liebl, his assistant, looked after the programme with commendable expertise and care. The university museums in their majesty were eye-openers. I saw a fair amount of west Asian and Indian material.

As I look back, the themes I selected for studies between 1963 and 1977 were the protohistoric and early historic urban centres, India and west Asia during the period of the Indus civilization, the beginning of iron in India, and the history of Indian archaeology. None of these themes, as I have shown before, was isolated from the prevailing concerns of Indian archaeology, and from this point of view I was a part of the main flow of my field of study. No book was sent to the press but I did not hesitate to publish articles putting forward my views on each of these four themes. I also helped in some specific ways, as I have pointed out clearly, to give these themes a new shape and direction.

3

Delhi, 1977-1990

PERSONAL NOTES

I was associated with the Department of History of Delhi University for fourteen years but not all of these fourteen years were spent in Delhi. I got a job in the Department of Ancient Indian History, Culture and Archaeology at Visvabharati University, Santiniketan, but could be there only for about 10 to 12 weeks in the winter of 1980-81. The library was inadequate and the atmosphere lotus-eating and insular. In 1980-81 at least, the professors and/or Head of the Departments at the university could not order even a steel cupboard for the Department without first taking approval from the Vice-Chancellor (or, *Mananiya Upacharya* or 'respected Vice-Chancellor', as he is invariably addressed there). One soon realized that this campus, although wholly financed by the central government, was not primarily meant for independent-minded academics. Mercifully, I had kept lien on my job in Delhi and went back. The few weeks which were spent in Santiniketan were devoted to wandering around in the lateritic gravel beds of the campus, which yielded microliths in several localities and also in Birbhum, the district of which Santiniketan is a part. The landscape of Birbhum with its uplands and groves of tall palm-trees is beautiful and holds a special position in the Bengali literature, especially in the novels of Tarashankar Bandopadhyay.

In 1982, I was on a month's fellowship at Allahabad University, thanks to the support of Professor G.C. Pandey who was then the Head of the Department of Ancient Indian History, Culture and Archaeology. He is more of an original philosopher than a historian but his primary textual scholarship is formidable. The foundations of archaeological research in Allahabad were laid during the tenure of his predecessor G.R. Sharma, who could be overpowering to his students and colleagues but whose originality of thought and approach and commitment to research were beyond dispute. The fact that the Indian universities could carve out a niche for research was mostly due to people like him. The highlight of my stay in Allahabad, apart from imbibing the ambience of this old and cultured city, was a visit to the Belan valley and the Sidhi district in the company of the Allahabad University team, which I found to be one of the most formidable field-teams around.

In 1988-90, I was on an archaeology teaching job in the Department of History of Jahangirnagar University in Bangladesh, receiving support from V.C. Joshi who was then a consultant of the Ford Foundation in Delhi, the foundation which sponsored my stay, and Abu Imam who was the coordinator of the archaeology project at Jahangirnagar. The project had also employed Harunur Rashid who had then retired from his service in the Bangladesh government's archaeology directorate. After Bangladesh became independent in 1971, he left his parent department in Pakistan to join the newly formed department in Bangladesh. I returned to Delhi from Jahangirnagar in the middle of 1990 and left for a teaching position in Cambridge soon afterwards. During this period, I focussed on acquiring a field-knowledge of Bangladesh sites and their excavated material. A reassessment of some earlier material and the identification of a prehistoric horizon were made in the process.

It was on March 1, 1977 that I joined the Department of History in the old Faculty of Arts building of Delhi University, which was certainly an improvement on what I was used to in Kolkata. For one thing, it was part of a large complex set in an open space, some of which was given over to gardens and big trees. I remember seeing a hornbill in one of those trees. Secondly, it had students from all over India, lending a vibrant pan-Indian atmosphere to the campus. Thirdly, the Archaeological Survey of India headquarter and the National Museum were not far from the campus and both these places had strong attractions in the form of libraries and professional brethren. The news of whatever was happening in the archaeology of the country soon reached the Survey headquarter. Fourthly, one could easily travel from Delhi to virtually all the parts of the country. That carried a feeling of assurance of its own.

On the negative side, the very fact that it was located in Delhi imparted a bureaucratic atmosphere to it. The ups and downs of Indian politics could distinctly be felt in the campus. Also present was an unmistakable spirit of one-upmanship among the teachers and students. Most of them were determined to be on the make. Both the teachers' and students' unions fought for their rights in various ways, and among the teachers at least it was considered advisable to try to inculcate the favour of one political group or another. The small section of teachers who kept away from the flow of the campus politics or all-India politics generally had their sight on the short-term or long-term stays in the First World campuses. Nothing was wrong with it, but soon the worth of teachers in the social sciences and humanities began to be measured by the number of their visits to the metropolitan universities of the First World and the degree of the patronage they received from that quarter. On the other hand, Delhi University being a metropolitan campus in India, its leading academics successfully developed a patron-client relationship with the academics in the provinces. In various ways, they were actively involved in the running of the major national organizations which were mostly located in Delhi. Their proximity to these sources of academic power made them important in the eyes of their colleagues around the country. Before coming to Delhi, I was unaware of so many shades of power in the Indian academia.

There were also too many 'sahibs'/ 'memsahibs' (Europeanised gentlemen and ladies) in the Delhi academic community. The native *Master-ji* type was not merely rare but also looked down upon. Romila Thapar, a famous 'progressive' lady historian of Delhi, had, according to Tapan Raychaudhuri's *Bangalnama*, acquired a fame for ballroom-dancing in the ship by which she travelled to London for her studies. Raychaudhuri also had travelled to Oxford by the same ship. Historically, it would be interesting to know when the ballroom-dancing types from among the Indian upper middle class had decided to opt for historical studies as a career option. As far as I can make out, this began to happen in the 1950s and 1960s. In the 1950s, the tendency on the part of the upper middle class households was to send their children—the bright ones, among them—to Cambridge or Oxford for their undergraduate degrees and a number of them had stayed on to do a Ph.D. in history.

It was in Delhi that I first became aware of the glaring difference which exists between students who have been to vernacular medium schools and those who have been taught in the English medium institutions. Most of the teachers of History catered primarily to the needs of the students of 'English medium' and occasionally I have wondered if in the Indian universities good marks/grades in the humanities are not almost wholly dependent on how well the students wrote English. There was hardly any decent book for the Hindi medium students, who had to depend mostly on the scrappy 'notebooks' of various kinds. One may also doubt that just because somebody went to Hindi medium schools, his/her Hindi would be good. Because Sanskrit is no longer a compulsory school subject, the students' knowledge of the roots of their regional languages is invariably poor. One is told that there is serious opposition to making Sanskrit a compulsory school subject because Sanskrit is perceived in some quarters as a symbol of Hindu communalism. By not making Sanskrit a compulsory school subject for all Indians, steps have been taken to erase the memory of our Classical tradition from the minds of our future generations. The price will be serious to pay; already one meets students who cannot even read anything in their vernacular literatures. I wonder which kinds of histories of India will they compose.

One may digress a bit at this point to say that one of the nice things about the Archaeological Survey of India is the comparative rarity of people cut off from the country's Classical tradition. Its officers, we were privileged to know, till the mid-1980s were all ladies and gentlemen of formidable scholarship in the ancient traditions. I hardly knew A. Ghosh but I had met him when he was editing two volumes of *Encyclopaedia of Indian Archaeology*. He was basically a student of Sanskrit literature and still enjoys a very high reputation as the Director General. M.N. Deshpande and Mrs. D. Mitra were among the scholarly Director Generals, and even B.K. Thapar may be placed in that company. Regrettably, B.B. Lal decided to have a very short tenure. The persistence of the tradition could be perceived among the senior officers of the time, most of them honest, hard-working and scholarly. K.V. Soundararajan was not a good communicator but H.B. Sarkar was a person from whom we learnt a lot. Something of Sarkar's style of scholarship has passed on to Arundhati Banerjee whose room in the Survey has been my favourite place for many years. Among the current senior officers I personally know, I would rate highly the scholarship of Buddha Rashmi Mani, Simadri Bihari Ota, Pramod Trivedi, C. Dorjee, Dharam Veer Sharma and Shubhra Pramanik. As far as scholarship is concerned, the years under the Indian Administrative Service rule have damaged the Survey beyond belief but mercifully, an average professional officer of the Survey still remains a person rooted in the land. This is something which I would not say about a large section of the Indian university teachers of history and archaeology and their 'English-medium' students.

One of the reasons why the Delhi academia had a distinct smell of bureaucracy was the fact that the profession was full of people who did not succeed in being recruited to the Indian Administrative Service and other Class I Central Services. There were two main reasons why students—mostly boys—from other parts of India, especially from the eastern 'states', had flocked to Delhi for studies. One was the chaos in the academic institutions of their own 'home states' and the second was the notion that it was easier to get better coaching for the various administrative service examinations in Delhi. Although the whole project could mean a lot of expenses for the family, the boy, if successful, would fetch a high price in the marriage market and that would handsomely compensate for the incurred educational expenditure. If unsuccessful, they would try for teaching positions in the university or its colleges, lobbying for patronage from important people of their castes, regional networks or politics. These 'important' people in their turn would use such 'mass-support' to indulge in skulduggery of various kinds in the campus. Some teachers did not like the idea of holding regular classes, and apart from receiving salaries as teachers, they earned money through different business activities such as share-market dealing, running shops and buying and selling land. The human scenario in the Delhi university campus was, on the whole, decidedly intriguing, and it was in Delhi that I first became aware of a vast spider-web of patronage and criminality in the Indian academia. In Kolkata, the scale of things was much smaller and did not have much of a country-wise effect.

Delhi University did not have a tradition of ancient historical research. One of the reasons was that the university was set up as late as 1922 and that in its early phase teaching was confined to a handful of colleges. When I joined the history department in 1977, I could gather the names of only a few ancient India specialists who were members of Delhi university or one of its colleges: Dasarath Sharma who wrote on the Chauhan dynasty and later left for Rajasthan; G. Upadhyay who researched the caste history of the Brahmins; Om Prakash who was a specialist in ancient Indian food and drinks; Devaraj Chanana who investigated the system of slavery in ancient India; and Romila Thapar who published her London Ph.D. thesis on Asoka. Among my colleagues were three ancient India specialists: Devahuti or Devahuti Singhal who authored a book on the king Harshavardhana, Pratipal Bhatia who researched the dynastic history of the Paramaras and later specialized in coins, and D.N. Jha who researched the Mauryan revenue history and was brought to Delhi by R.S. Sharma, the Head of the Department and another historian of ancient India, from his former university in Patna. I was the only archaeologist among these ancient historians.

A number of interrelated developments determined my fate in Delhi University almost from the day I joined it. In March 1977, the very month of my joining Delhi University, Mrs. Indira Gandhi decided to hold elections and was defeated. Among the historians who were ruling over the fellow-historians in her name and the name of her education minister S. Nurul Hasan, the effect of this dislodgment of Congress-Communist Party of India power was catastrophic. The opposing group, which had so long felt suppressed, had found its mouth-piece in S.P. Gupta, an archaeologist of the National museum and reputedly a senior functionary of the RSS. He organized a meeting in the National museum and issued some pamphlets criticizing the school history textbooks sponsored by the previous government. His special target was the book written by R.S. Sharma, the chairman of the ICHR and the Head of the Department of History at Delhi University. Neither the book by Sharma nor its critique by Gupta was academically significant, and when I asked Gupta about it, he gave a candid reply in his characteristic fashion: 'These people, as long as they were in power, did not allow even a single paisa to go to the historians and archaeologists who did not agree with them. How do they expect us to be tolerant now?' The 'reactionary lobby' or 'Hinduttva lobby' or whatever lobby the 'anti-progressive lobby' is currently called came into existence and took the shape of a group, as I have argued before, primarily due to the setting up of a specifically 'left-oriented' and intolerant lobby by S. Nurul Hasan and his protégés. It was the 'other' whose existence was necessary to justify the excesses of the so-called 'progressives' who were in control of the purse-strings of historical research in India. As an apolitical person, I kept out of this fray but the fact that I did not declare my allegiance openly to Sharma and his cohort made them feel somewhat suspicious of me right from the beginning of my presence in Delhi University. Considering that this group facilitated my entry to the university—otherwise there could be no question of my getting a job in the history department of Delhi University in 1977—they were perhaps justified in finding my attitude intransigent.

The second development was more academic. The Backliwal family, a distinguished family of jewellers and art-dealers of Delhi, decided, soon after Sharma had joined History department in 1972, to donate a large collection of 16th-18th century miniature paintings, illustrated and unillustrated manuscripts, bronze figurines, etc. to Delhi University. The Vice-Chancellor accepted the gift, passed it on to the history department and both he and the history department soon forgot all about it. For several years the collection was left locked in tin trunks in a damp ground-floor room of the Arts faculty building. Even the mediaevalists of the Department, who were supposed to do teaching of mediaeval art history, showed no interest in the collection. Unfortunately, for the Department, after a new government was sworn in Delhi in 1977, the Backliwal family found a powerful patron in the changed grouping of power and began to send a series of letters to the Vice-Chancellor asking him what had happened to the art collection donated by them.

The Vice-Chancellor, a chemistry professor, re-directed the question to the history department which suddenly found this collection too much of a bother. Assuming that miniature paintings and orthodox archaeological antiquities are not vastly different, the department passed on the responsibility of looking after the Backliwal collection and setting up a departmental museum for it to their newly appointed archaeology teacher, i.e., me. I took this opportunity to do some reading of mediaeval art history and prepare a proposal for setting up a small 'archaeology and museum unit' in the department with the Backliwal collection as its core. Eventually, a curator and an assistant were employed for the museum and I was designated its 'teacher-in-charge'. I ensured that the essential qualifications of the proposed curator were entirely archaeological and the first curator was S. Jamal Hasan, who had his major excavation experience with the Archaeological Survey of India at Sringaverapur near Allahabad. The money sanctioned for the annual maintenance of the museum and archaeological exploration in 1979 was no more than 15000 rupees, but somehow I went to the field in the company of Hasan in 1980 and surveyed the valley of Kangra in Himachal Pradesh. In 1981, I began the programme of surveying the Chhotanagpur plateau in east India. After a brief spell with me in the east, Hasan joined the Archaeological Survey of India and was replaced by R.K. Chattopadhyay from Kolkata. Assisted by Chattopadhyay, I continued my Chhotanagpur survey till 1987. The Backliwal collection and the archaeological material collected in the course of explorations in Kangra (1980), Chhotanagpur (1981-87) and the Union Territory of Delhi and Haryana (1987), were eventually housed in a museum which came up as a part of the history department. The work in Ranchi in Chhotanagpur and Delhi was privately financed by Nayanjot Lahiri, who was then a Ph.D. student, and her advocate husband Kishore Kumar Lahiri. The catalogue of the Backliwal collection, which was divided into two parts, one carrying the name of Mr. S.S. Backliwal and the other carrying the name of Mrs. S.R. Backliwal, was prepared in active collaboration with Mr. Backliwal who proved himself to be a very civilized and knowledgeable gentleman completely at home in the world of miniature paintings. It was while working with Mr. Backliwal that I realized that the solid understanding of the art objects of various kinds, which basically business persons like

Mr. Backliwal possess, is mostly rare in the academia and that this expertise cannot be neglected by the academics in any way.

My association with Delhi University virtually came to an end in 1988 when I was divested of the responsibility of looking after the 'archaeology and museum unit' of the history department. On the day I received the university Registrar's letter divesting me of this responsibility, I submitted my application for 'long leave' to the university and went to Bangladesh.

The circumstances that led to my divestment of responsibility for the departmental archaeology and museum unit constitute the third line of my professional history in Delhi University and carries the imprint of a singularly murky affair. While organizing the archaeology and museum unit in the department I did not stand for any interference, and this upset people like R.S. Sharma, D.N. Jha and their friends. The colleagues who had confidence in what they studied themselves, were simply not bothered. In 1984, Jamal Hasan and I jointly published *Antiquities of Kangra*, basically a field-report on the results of exploration in Kangra in 1980. This field-report was written by me with material input from Hasan and was submitted as an M.Phil dissertation by Hasan who was registered as an M.Phil student in the Department under my supervision. The examples of joint publication by the supervisor and the student being common in the field-subjects, I did not think twice about getting it published and did not even bother about getting a written consent from Hasan, although otherwise he was very much in the picture. After the book was published, some colleagues—notably D.N. Jha, R.L. Shukla, T.K.V. Subrahmanyam, H.C. Verma, Suhas Chakravarty and P.S. Gupta, all members of the 'progressive' group led by Sharma—raised against me the charge of plagiarizing a student's work and publishing it in my name.

Before raising the matter in the departmental committee and taking it up officially from there, they conspired to get the matter published first as a news item in a Delhi newspaper. A section of colleagues remained neutral because they were told of precisely this conspiracy a few months before I was actually charged. Somebody with close links to the conspiring group informed me of this conspiracy, and when I asked for a written statement from that person, he also gave me that. I was further told that Jamal Hasan was persuaded by the conspiring group to join them by offering the prospect of a college teaching job to him. I showed that statement to several colleagues opposed to the machinations of this variety of 'progressives'. The Vice-Chancellor of that period was a geographer called M. Raza, who was a protégé of S. Nurul Hasan and a member of the 'progressive lobby'. The pressure on him was to get me unceremoniously 'suspended'. The Vice-Chancellor apparently resisted the move because he himself had some publications with his students. The people most vociferous in demanding an enquiry against me were D.N. Jha, P.S. Gupta and Suhas Chakravarty. It must be recorded that a member of the Delhi University Academic Council named Mr. Sankhadhar, an RSS member/sympathiser, first demanded an enquiry against me in the Academic Council after reading about it in a newspaper. Eventually, an enquiry committee was set up and luckily for me that contained one scientist to whom joint publications with students were not unknown. I was exonerated of the charge of plagiarism by this committee in 1988, although it wrote that I should not have allowed the field-report to be submitted as an M.Phil thesis and should have mentioned that it was in fact submitted as an M.Phil thesis.

There is another footnote to add. Sometime in 1987/88 D.N. Jha, the leading person in this matter, became the Head of the Department and wrote to me in that capacity a letter asking me to step down as the teacher-in-charge of the department's 'archaeology and museum unit'. I contested the matter before the Registrar of the university on the ground that I was the only archaeologist in the department and thus had the academic right to be involved in the affairs of its archaeology and museums. Sometime in 1988, before I went on leave to go to Bangladesh, the Registrar informed me that the Head of the Department could give this particular responsibility to any departmental member he liked, archaeologist or no archaeologist. As I had already received the job-offer from Jahangirnagar University, I had no inclination to enter into another phase of correspondence with the university authorities.

The nucleus of an art and archaeology museum was in any case established in the History department by this time, and in the next stage the department or the university should have thought of setting up a much larger 'university museum'. In fact, the universities like Banaras and Panjab have big university museums. The fact that neither Delhi nor Jawaharlal Nehru University possesses such a museum throws a light on the respect which the historians of these universities have for the historical heritage of the country. The way in which the Backliwal collection was allowed to rot in dampness in a room of the Delhi Arts faculty under the care of R.S. Sharma and his cohort at the full height of their power when money for taking care of this collection was available easily is another indication of how little these people, all historians and Communist Party of India affiliates, were concerned with Indian heritage. What upsets me is that even after this phase of the history of the Delhi University's Department of History was over, there was no attempt to nurture the growth of the departmental museum. Two members of the Department, both professors and both among my former Ph.D. students, became members of the University's top management team during this phase and could have played a major role in trying to convert History department's art and archaeology museum into a major university museum of the country. No initiative was taken in this regard, and when Delhi University teachers, including these two former students of mine, talk of heritage, I view that with a lot of cynicism.

The running battle of the 'progressive' historians with me took more time to die out. Nayanjot Lahiri, one of my Ph.D. students, completed the writing of her dissertation when I was away in Bangladesh. According to the Delhi University norm, the supervisor sends a panel of names out of which three names are formally selected. D.N. Jha was then the Head of the Department and took the initiative of replacing my panel of examiners with a fresh panel of his own where some of his close friends were listed. These 'friends', following a long-established Indian university tradition of having Ph.D. theses submitted under the supervision of 'enemies' rejected, would have cheerfully ensured that Nayanjot Lahiri, for no fault of hers, would have had adverse reports on her dissertation. She decided not to submit her thesis as long as D.N. Jha was the Head. However, a section of the Delhi University teachers took up her cause, with the matter discussed in detail in a magazine called *Onlooker* and some Delhi newspapers. The criminalisation of Indian historical education, which began with the induction of communist-sympathisers to Mrs. Indira Gandhi's government in 1972, was rapidly showing signs of bearing fruit in many directions.

The ramifications of this episode kept me busy till 1988, and as I have just noted, even later. The truth also demands that I record that in the Gangetic belt the senior ancient Indian history and archaeology teachers who belonged to R.S. Sharma's caste group of the Bhumihars and included reputedly such persons as G.R. Sharma of Allahabad wanted to have me thrown in the garbage heap.

Truth also demands that I record that in Delhi University or elsewhere I was not entirely without support. The newspaper report (*The Hindustan Times*, 25 January, 1985) was published when I was away in the field in the Santal Parganas, and even before I came back to Delhi, 38 teachers signed a letter protesting against the report. I am not sure if I have ever acknowledged my deep personal debt in print to these colleagues, and to atone for this lapse I do so now, listing their names and subject/institute affiliations as they appear in the document I possess: (1) R. Ramana (Economics, St. Stephen's College), (2) V. Tankha (Philosophy, St. Stephen's College), (3) Ashok Vohra (Philosophy, St. Stephen's College), (4) Upinder Singh (History, St. Stephen's College), (5) Sumit Guha (History, St. Stephen's College), (6) Tapan Basu (Hindu College), (7) Nayanjot Lahiri (Hindu College), (8) S.K. Jain (Hindu College), (9) Tripta Wahi (Hindu College), (10) A. Mittal (Hindu College), (11) S.M. Rai (Hindu College), (12) Amitav Ghosh (Sociology, Delhi University), (13) Tanika Sarkar (St. Stephen's College), (14) Pratipal Bhatia (History, Delhi University), (15) Aparna Basu (History, Delhi University), (16) Sumit Sarkar (History, Delhi University), (17) Manoranjan Mohanty (Political Science, Delhi University), (18) N.N. Agrawal (Hindu College), (19) Hari Sen (Hindu College), (20) O.P. Kaushik (Hindu College), (21) Parasara Mishra (Hindu College), (22), A. Chakravarti (Sociology, Delhi University), (23) Dilip Simeon (Ramjash College), (24) A. Majid (Agro-Economic Centre, Delhi University), (25) Rana P. Behal (Deshabandhu College), (26) Indu Agnihotri (Vivekanand Mahila College), (27) Chitra Joshi (Nehru Memorial Museum), (28) Rashmi Pant (Indraprastha College), (29) Bishwamoy Pati (S.V. College), (30) Kapil Kumar (Nehru Memorial Museum), (31) R. Naqvi (Hindu College),

(32) Uma Chakravarti (Miranda House), (33) Saroj Malik (Hindu College), (34) Gaurav Dutt (Hindu College), (35) Vijay Singh (Satyavati College), (36) S.C. Bhargava (St. Stephen's College), (37) Madhu Dubey (St. Stephen's College), (38) Aditya Bhattacharya (St. Stephen's College).

In an open letter against the newspaper report, which I circulated in the campus, I wrote the following about the above-mentioned letter signed by 38 academics:

> Many of the above-mentioned colleagues do not know me personally. The fact that all of them stood in my defence (at a very short notice and that too in my absence) has been an extremely moving experience for me on personal level.

Among them, I knew Tripta Wahi and Vijay Singh well. Ms. Wahi did her Ph.D. in London and Mr. Singh his degree from Christ's College, Cambridge. They were anti-establishment to their bones and associated with most of the 'agitations' against the university authorities and the little 'progressive' despots of History department. Many of these colleagues have earned well-deserved reputation in their own disciplines, and I take some pride in the fact that they were all in my favour. I possibly take a lot of pride in the fact that Amitav Ghosh, the celebrated novelist, signed the letter in my favour.

Another moving experience was the fact that some of my MA students entered my room and gave me quietly a 'good wish' card, declaring their confidence in me. The card bore the signatures of Kalpana Krishan, Ramesh Kumar Singh, Sonia Singh, Pradeep K. Tiwari, Ruchit Vohra, Atul Rawat, Singdha Singh, Kiran Singh and Iqbal Singh. As college teaching jobs of History in Delhi University depended in those days on the sweet will of the R.S. Sharma group, it needed extraordinary courage for these young people to declare their faith in me.

Karam Tej Singh Sarao, a former student of mine and a teacher of history in Kirorimal College, went completely out of his way to support me thick and thin through this period. He is proud to be a Jat Sikh, and having known him I respect the sense of pride the Jat Sikhs possess. Unstinted support also came from Shabanam Suri and Rajni Nanda, both now Delhi University senior teachers. Among the departmental colleagues before the formal enquiry committee set up by the university to investigate the charge of plagiarism against me, which was published in *The Hindustan Times* of 25 January, 1985, Sumit Sarkar, Pratipal Bhatia and Devahuti Singhal clearly supported me. According to Professor Sarkar's statement, "The matter was first raised by Professor D.N. Jha at an M.Phil committee meeting on 15.1.1985 when Dr. Chakrabarti was absent on field-work. In view of Dr. Chakrabarti's absence, discussion was not allowed. The *Hindustan Times* report alleging "academic piracy" appeared on 25.1.1985. "

Further, he acknowledged that "he had been informed by Dr. Chakravarti in September 1984 that a number of colleagues including the then Head were planning a smear campaign against Dr. Chakravarti. One of the first steps would be a newspaper report". Sumit Sarkar was a well-known member of the historians' group, which came into prominence after S. Nurul Hasan *et al.* had emerged into prominence. At that point it needed great moral courage for him to support me. I also gratefully acknowledge the support lent by Pratipal Bhatia ("justified Dr. Chakravarti's conduct") and Devahuti Singhal ("she had the greatest respect for Dr. Chakrabarti's scholarship and his tremendous courage of conviction"). Both of them were apolitical, although Devahuti was the principal founder of the Indian History and Culture Society, which was later taken over by S.P. Gupta. The seed money of all real estate developments of the Indian Archaeological Society in the 'institutional area' of south Delhi was donated by Professor Devahuti Singhal and her husband Professor Damodar Singhal. That seed-money was a huge amount in the context of the 1980s and Indian archaeology should not forget them.

Support also came in good measure from outside the university history and social science circle. In a letter addressed to me on August 30, 1985, Amar Nath Maitra, a Chemistry 'reader' at the university, wrote:

> I fail to understand how such a controversy can occur in the first place. This is the most normal procedure (i.e., joint publications with students) in the world of scientific-technical research and publications. I have published myself all my joint works either with my supervisors or my M.Phil and Ph.D. students. I have also presented the research results of my students as their co-authors in two international symposia.

S.K. Ghosh of the Saha Institute of Nuclear Physics, Kolkata, and S. Ray of the Department of Physics, Kalyani University, wrote to me in the same vein. In an extraordinary show of courage, J.R. Knox of the British Museum wrote a letter to the Vice-Chancellor of Delhi University on the letter-head of his Museum (22 March 1985):

> I am sure you will agree that this matter is as regrettable as it is unfair. I hope that by now scholarly and colleaguely reason will have prevailed and that Dr. Chakrabarti's reputation will have emerged unblemished by this slur.

The archaeological community was not silent, although it was not possible for the government officers of the Archaeological Survey of India to lend their names to such controversies. However, it was unlikely to have been possible for S. Jamal Hasan, an Archaeological Survey employee by that time, to embrace limelight in this controversy without the tacit support of some of his superior officers or without their consent. S.P. Gupta, Secretary of the Indian Archaeological Society, wrote a detailed letter to the editor of the *Hindustan Times* (28.2.1985) arguing that "as far as the archaeological community is concerned, Dr. Chakrabarti's role in the whole affair has been absolutely normal—he was fully within his rights to publish this report as its first author even though a part of it was used by his assistant to earn M.Phil. Our information reveals that Shri Jamal Hasan has been made a scapegoat by Dr. Chakrabarti's detractors in his department". On 20.2.1985, V.N. Misra and M.L.K. Murty wrote to the editor, the *Hindustan Times*, on the letter-head of the Deccan College arguing that "Dr. Chakrabarti has done absolutely nothing wrong, ethically or legally, in publishing the results of joint field-work under joint names". In a letter to the editor, *Times of India*, dated March 8, 1985, D.P. Agrawal of the radiocarbon laboratory of the Physical Research Institute, Ahmedabad, decided to point out a malaise of the Indian university system:

> Any active research worker in the present University system incurs the wrath of other mediocre and inactive teachers. And I think the Hindustan Times journalist has played into the hands of such politician teachers without talking to the accused teacher... Such irresponsible behaviour of journalists and teacher politicians will only demoralise honest teachers who attach more importance to research than their own petty benefits. Please note that Dr. Chakrabarti resigned the permanent professorship at Vishwa Bharati to be able to do research even as a Reader at the Delhi University.

In 1988 the Registrar, Delhi University, laid down the university's policy regarding the archaeology and museum unit of the history department: "The overall control of the Museum and Archaeology of the Department of History is that of the Head of the Department and ... he can assign this function to any teacher or member of staff at his discretion" (Ref.No.SPA/

R-40, March 24, 1988). On 7.4.1988, Dr. Dilip Simeon, a member of the Academic Council, pointed out in a letter to M. Raza, the Vice-Chancellor, that

> the decision to give the Head of Department (History) power to put a specialized unit under the charge of any member of the staff (teaching or non-teaching) is a matter with serious academic implications for all specialized research units, including science laboratories, in the University. The matter, therefore, ought to be discussed by the Academic Council before the decision is actually implemented.

The matter was not pursued as I soon left for Jahangirnagar University. I am not particularly aware of what happened to the Delhi University Department of History's 'archaeology and museum unit' after I left it. However, I am glad to note that in the past three or four years, an individual teacher of the Department of History, R.C. Thakran, undertook excavations at one or two Harappan sites in Haryana and Rajasthan. This is a happy development and one hopes that archaeology will somehow develop in the university. Historically, it is worth recording that Thakran is a member/ former member of the Department of History's 'progressive group' represented by R.S. Sharma, D.N. Jha and others. The fact that Thakran has taken the initiative of doing excavations shows that my experience cannot be attributed specifically to any political grouping belonging to the right or left. As I have noted, the first move against me in the Academic Council was initiated by a member of the 'right' group. Moreover, what had come to pass as the progressive group of Indian historical studies unfortunately soon turned out to be a crowd of unscrupulous self-seekers in the history departments of various north Indian universities, including Kolkata, Aligarh, Allahabad, Delhi, Jamia Milia and Jawaharlal Nehru. The group seems to be thriving even now, and when I find the so-called 'eminent historians' and others declaring their support for fellow 'eminent historians' in various Indian newspapers, I cannot help but ponder over the sheer audacity of a group of people who in all these years have not risen above their original position as 'campus goons' protected by politicians.

During my Delhi days, the National Museum could boast of a number of scholarly persons: S.P. Gupta whose books on central Asia and Mauryan art are valuable contributions, Shashi Astana who started as a protohistorian but shifted later to art history, and Chhaya Bhattacharya who studied the Stein collection of central Asian materials in the National Museum.

THE GENERAL TRENDS OF DISCOVERIES AND WRITINGS IN THE LATE 1970S AND 1980S

The publication of *Puratattva*, the annual bulletin of the Indian Archaeological Society, became regular by the 1970s. The relationship between this Society and the Archaeological Survey of India was initially lukewarm but with the induction of B.K. Thapar of the Survey as the editor of *Puratattva* things changed for the better. The number 8 issue of the journal, which was due to appear in 1975-76 but appeared in 1978 contained a section on 'archaeology and tradition' in which there were many arguments in favour of literature-archaeology correlation in India and some against. In early 1977, a new Society, the Society of Indian Prehistoric and Quaternary Studies with its headquarter in Pune was established. The inaugural issue of its journal or annual bulletin, *Man and Environment* was released in the Indian Archaeological Society's annual conference in Jaipur in December 1976. Since then the two Societies have held their annual conferences together.

Because of the poor finances, the new journal was unstable for the first few years but once money began to flow from the Ford Foundation, it was taken to Pune where it has long been operating as a house journal of the Deccan College. The Ford Foundation money was available mainly due to the initiative of V.C. Joshi, who was a 'consultant' in the Foundation's Delhi office.

For its unstable early years, I played a role in maintaining the regularity of its publication. It was a world of cheap hand-composed presses in Karolbagh or Kingsway Camp in Delhi but the copies were delivered with clock-like regularity every year to S.P. Gupta's office in the National Museum. Gupta then carried the copies to wherever the Society's annual conference was held.

There were a few clear developments in the prehistoric studies of this period. First, in *Puratattva* 7 (1978), V.N. Misra offered a layer-wise techno-typological analysis of the Acheulian artifacts from Bhimbetka, possibly the first Indian site where such a sequence was obtained. Secondly, throughout the 1980s, Misra and his associates undertook a detailed stratigraphic study of the Palaeolithic occurrences in west Rajasthan in the light of soil analyses. This was preceded by the study of soil profiles of various Stone Age sites of west India, including Rajasthan desert by B. Allchin, A. Goudie and K.T.M. Hegde (1978) but under Misra and his associates, the scope of palaeo-environmental studies became much wider. This culminated in the publication of a dated prehistoric profile of the region in 1988 (Misra, Rajaguru and Raghavan 1988).

Thirdly, in the central Ganga plain and the adjacent eastern Vindhyas including the Sidhi area of Madhya Pradesh, G.R. Sharma and his associates' work flowed in three directions. Their earlier study of the prehistoric profile of the Belan valley was extended to the Sidhi district of Madhya Pradesh in collaboration with J.D. Clark and his team from Berkeley, California. The excavation of the upper Palaeolithic site of Baghor I with its piece of stone-bearing lamination marks in the shape of a vulva and the excavation of the Mesolithic camping site of Baghor III are noteworthy in this connection. The second aspect of the work of Sharma's Allahabad team was that the Belan valley work was continued through the excavations at Chopani Mando, Mahagara and Koldihawa and led to the postulate of a mesolithic to early rice cultivation transition in this region. As I pointed out earlier (Chakrabarti 2003, p. 88),

> This was a claim of extraordinary historical significance in the annals of post-Independence Indian archaeology. Whereas the people of the two major power-centres of Indian archaeology, the Archaeological Survey of India and the Deccan College, had kept an extraordinary large chunk of their minds focussed on such issues as the Aryans, the archaeological veracity of Indian tradition and 'prehistoric colonisation of India', an archaeogist from Allahabad University tried to demonstrate the relevance of alternative dimensions.

Moreover, their excavations at the Mesolithic sites of Sarai Nahar Rai, Mahadaha and Damdama revealed not merely the economic and settlement details of these sites but also a large number of human skeletons (cf. Pal 1984, 1986, Kennedy, Lovell and Burrow 1986). Sarai Nahar Rai was excavated in the late 1960s and early 1970s but Mahadaha was excavated in the late 1970s and Damdama still later.

Fourthly, there was the introduction of the settlement-subsistence approach in prehistory pioneered by K. Paddayya (1982) in the Hunsgi valley, Karnataka, M.L.K. Murty (1981, 1985) in Kurnool and D.R. Raju (1988) in Cuddapah. These are important pieces of work based on a close study of the find-spots and assemblages of stone tools, eco-system and the available plant and other resources of the concerned areas. The most detailed work in this regard was undertaken by Raju, who took his clues from the food-habits of the Yanadis of his field-study area and concluded that "the upper Palaeolithic hunter-gatherers relied on aquatic food-resources for their subsistence as much as on game and wild vegetal foods" (Raju 1988, p. 93). Fifthly, there was an expanding research-interest in several fields: animal remains, metrical analysis of stone tools, detailed reporting both in the light of geomorphology and Stone Age technology, study of the micro-wear of stone tools, geochronology and prehistoric art. The significance of the Indian Pleistocene fauna with special reference to the Siwaliks was highlighted by G.L. Badam in 1979 (Badam 1979). In 1986, R.V. Joshi and Anupama Kshirsagar (1986) drew attention to the fluorine of the bones and its dating potential, along with the impact of fluorine on the fossilisation process of bones. Thermoluminiscent dating of Rajasthan sand dunes was done by Singhvi, Sharma and Agrawal (1982) and V.D. Gogte's and M.L.K. Murty's ESR dating of the Kurnool caves was the first example of such dating in India (Gogte and Murty. Metrical analysis of stone tools figured in the writings of Claire Gaillard (1989) and Cheryl Semans (1981), with G. Corvinus (1981, 1983) providing an example of geomorphological reporting of the Stone Age material of the Pravara basin. J. Jacobsen's study of the Late Stone Age cultural adaptation in the central Vindhyas (Jacobsen 1980) is another important study of the period. A.R. Marathe's study of the geochronology of the Hiran valley (Marathe 1981) was followed by M. Baskaran and others' more specific article on the geochronology of Palaeolithic cultures of the area (Baskaran *et al.* 1986). After the discovery of the fossil hominid at Hathnora, there were attempts to understand its stratigraphical context both in the light of its animal bones and associated stone tools (Badam *et al.* 1986). In the same vein, mention may be made of J. Armand's reporting of his excavations at the Durkadi Nala (Armand 1983) and B.C. Verma and J. Srivastava's study of the early Pleistocene and earlier character of the Palaeolithic industries of the outer Siwalik belt in the Sirmur district (Verma and Srivastava 1984).

The study of prehistoric art, mostly in the Late Stone Age context, took off with a study of the painted rock-shelters of India by V.S. Wakankar and R. Brooks(1976) and Sankalia's *Prehistoric Art in India* (1978) was followed by E. Neumayer (1983), V.N. Misra and Y. Mathpal (1979) and Mathpal (1984). The knowledge of Stone Age India was reviewed by Misra (1989) and among the monographs of the period, one may mention the volume on Konkan by S. Guzder (1980) and the one on the chopper-chopping tool tradition of India by V. Jayasawal (1982).

If one takes an overview of Stone Age research in India in the late 1970s and throughout the 1980s, one realizes that this became multi-dimensional during this period. In the field of Late Stone Age studies, radiocarbon dates had already begun to play a major role, but ESR, thermoluminiscent and other geochronological dating methods made their appearance during this period. The number and context of these dates were limited but the fact that they had been applied to Indian Stone Age studies was a major step forward. The multidimensionality of the Stone Age was also reflected in an increasing concern with the environmental background of sites, a rigorous approach to stratigraphy and the belief that a better insight into the use of landscape by the Stone Age communities could be obtained by studying the use of the same landscape by the local hunter-gatherers.

Protohistoric sites were excavated in all the major regions. Ramapuram, a chalcolithic site, was excavated in

Andhra in 1980-84, with Banahalli and Watgal, two Neolithic and later sites of Karnataka, being excavated in 1983-87 and 1988-89 respectively. Taradih (1983-89), Maner (1984-90), Chechar Kutubpur (1988-89) and Senuwar (1986-87) were the Neolithic sites excavated in Bihar during this period. In West Bengal, the major excavated Chalcolithic-Iron Age sites were Bahiri (1981), Mangalkot (1986-90) and Dihar (1983-85). In U.P., the chalcolithic identity of the trans-Sarayu area was firmly established at Narhan (1983-87) and Jakhera in Etah in the Doab proper showed the association of iron with Black-and-Red Ware. The Ochre-Coloured Pottery base of the site of Sringaverapura was revealed in 1983-85. Chalcolithic sites of minor character continued to be identified and excavated in Madhya Pradesh and Maharashtra. In Rajasthan, the discovery of early metallurgical levels at Ganeshwar (1983-84, 1987-89) and related sites was an outstanding event. Among the Harappan sites in Haryana, Balu (1978-80,1983-87), Banawali (1983-84, 1986-88) and Kunal (1985-86) were important and in Gujarat, there were Nageshwar (1983-84), Ratanpura (1984-85), Rojdi (1982-86), Nagwada (1985-90), Shikarpur (1987-90), Kuntasi (1987-90), Oriyo Timbo (1989-90) and Dholavira (1989-90 and later). In Panjab, Rohira was excavated in 1982-83. The late Harappan level was identified at Sanghol in 1977-78 and 1980-81.

A chain of early historic sites, including the remains of Buddhist stupas, was identified in Andhra (cf. Thothlakonda, 1987-90, Ghantasala 1984-85, Vaddamanu 1983-85), with Sannati (1986-89) being a major site in Karnataka. In Uttar Pradesh, Sravasti (1986-89) and Purola (1988-89) were both early historic sites. Like Sravasti in U.P., Arikamedu in Tamil Nadu was taken up for re-excavations in 1989-90.

Several theoretical trends are noticeable along with these and other discoveries. One of these was a shift in the settlement analysis as revealed in M. Lal's *Settlement History and Rise of Civilization in the Ganga Yamuna Doab*, George Erdosy's *Urbanisation in Early Historic India* and Rima Hooja's *The Ahar Culture* (1988). Two archaeological reports, one by R.C. Gaur on Atranjikhera (Gaur 1983) and the other on Inamgaon by M.K. Dhavalikar, H.D. Sankalia and Z. Ansari (1988), were also important in this context, with both of them bringing about a significant change in the understanding of settled communities in the Doab and Maharashtra. Dhavalikar's synoptic volume, which took into consideration the excavated data from other relevant Maharashtra sites (Dhavalikar 1988), was also an important publication in this regard. In the field of Harappan studies, a detailed study of the distribution of Harappan sites in India was published by J.P. Joshi, M. Bala and J. Ram (1984) and although the labelling of each site as 'early','mature' and 'late' may be disputed in many cases, this was a pioneering and painstakingly researched paper. There was a significant paper on the course of the Ghaggar-Hakra by Yash Pal *et al.* (1977) and in the case of Gujarat, there were two decent settlement studies of the Indus sites by K.N. Momin (1984) and R.N. Mehta (1984).

Another important trend was a major shift away from the conventional pattern of human skeletal studies, with the study of Inamgaon skeletons by J.R. Lukacs and S.R. Walimbe (1986) setting a new direction. The new questions addressed were those of population continuity, palaeopathology, palaeodemography, etc. Additional scientific dimensions to protohistoric studies were added by B.C. Deotare(1983) and A. Kshirsagar (1983) by their search for phosphate and nitrogen contents of the soils of the relevant sites.

Throughout this period, one notices a distinct and recurring concern with the history of technology and mining, beginning with the publication of H.C. Bharadwaj's *Aspects of*

Indian Technology (Bharadwaj 1979), which was a collection of the results of a limited number of miscellaneous materials. In 1989, R.N. Singh's emphasis was exclusively on the technical analysis of ancient glass (Singh 1989). K.T.M. Hegde's review of 'scientific studies in Indian archaeology' in 1985 (Hegde 1985) was a marginal attempt in this regard. In the 1980s, P.T. Craddock (1987, Craddock *et al.* 1989) published extensively on the history of Indian zinc and brass. The importance of the history of preindustrial Indian mining was also outlined by the present author in 1986 and 1988 (Chakrabarti 1986, 1988). This was the offshoot of his earlier interest in the history of ancient Indian iron and the later interest in the history of ancient Indian lead and silver (Nanda and Chakrabarti 1985, 1989).

Some major studies of the Indus civilization appeared during this period, including a collection of papers edited by G.L. Possehl (1982). Many of these papers were important in the context of the time. Another relevant publication of the period was *Frontiers of the Indus Civilization* (Lal and Gupta 1984). S. Ratnagar's *Encounters*, which basically discussed the archaeological evidence of the trade contact of the Indus civilization with the Gulf, west and central Asia, appeared in 1981 (Ratnagar 1981) and linked the growth of this civilization to Mesopotamia's needs for raw materials. In my review of the book in *Puratattva*, I pointed out that according to Ratnagar's argument, the position of the Indus civilization in relation to Mesopotamia was about the same position held by India in relation to the British empire as a supplier of raw materials. That a so-called sophisticated anthropological jargon or a desperate eagerness on the part of most of the Indian archaeologists and historians to be one of 'them', i.e., the western archaeological and historical community, can lead to a fairly disastrous theoretical position in relation to the nation was amply driven home by Ratnagar's book.

My own detailed discussion on the Indus external trade took a data-oriented view and argued that the nature of this trade had to be understood in the context of the traditional trade, which persisted in the relevant areas till the nineteenth century and later. Among the new Harappan explorations, mention should be made of the study by S. Bhan and J. Shaffer (Bhan and Shaffer 1978) in northern Haryana.

Miscellaneous publications covering different areas, such as the Brahmaputra valley (R.D. Chowdhury 1985), central Assam (N.D. Chowdhury 1985), Kangra (Chakrabarti and Hassan 1984), *Panchala* region (S.B. Singh 1979), etc. were also a feature of the period. Such area studies were accompanied by a number of general reviews (cf. Misra and Bellwood 1985, Dikshit 1985, Deo and Paddayya 1985) and two major works of synthesis, one by D.P. Agrawal (1982) and the other by B. and F.R. Allchin (1982).

Agrawal, "more at home in the technicalities of dating, metallurgical analysis and palaeoclimate and less in historical and archaeological data" (Chakrabarti 2003, p. 99) prefers to restrict himself to generalizations reminiscent of ecological determinism. His summary of the archaeological data remains competent but is marred by gross diffusionary assumptions that the technologies from the early Palaeolithic to the Iron Age have a late start in India and 'cultural influences during various periods can be traced to West Asia, China, Central Asia and Southeast Asia'. In the Indus context, Agrawal inexplicably forgets to discuss the significance of Shortughai. B. and F.R. Allchin's *The Rise of Civilization in India and Pakistan* offers a more pleasantly integrated synthesis of the archaeological data, but remains mired, like their earlier *The Birth of Civilization in India and Pakistan* (1968) in Aryanism of one kind or another. They also expect "at least two main periods of Indo-Aryan migration into north-western India and Pakistan, the first or early period dating from around 2000 BC and the second some six centuries later" (Allchin and Allchin 1982, p. 301).

On the whole, the late 1970s and the whole of the 1980s witnessed multifaceted developments in Indian archaeological studies. The basic details of the preceding outline of the history of relevant archaeology were earlier summarized by me (Chakrabarti 2003, pp. 73-120). On one level, some early assumptions regarding India's archaeological developments were questioned in and about this period (cf. the independence of the beginning of iron technology in India, a better precision in Harappan chronology, etc.) but on a different level, such questionings had hardly affected Indian archaeological thought, as the monographs by Agrawal, and B. and F.R. Allchin amply demonstrate.

MY RESEARCH THEMES, PUBLICATIONS AND FIELD RESEARCH, 1977-90

Some of the publications of this phase are based on research undertaken in the immediately earlier phase.

A Geographical Approach to the Study of India: West Asia Contact

For instance, the paper "India and West Asia—An Alternative Approach" (Chakrabarti 1977) derives from my study of the pre-Achaemenid perspective of India-West Asia contact, which I pursued in 1973-74. In retrospect, this paper, although it clearly defines the traditional archaeological and historical interaction between the southern part of central Asia, the Indus valley, the eastern rim of Iran including its northeastern and southeastern sections, and the whole of Afghanistan, and sets out the possible lines of contact with the areas east of the Indus valley, suffers from a rather limited use of the data based on political and economic history covering this broad region period by period. As far as I am aware, this fuller discussion still remains to be done and the geopolitical identity of the Oxus to the Indus stretch still remains to be fully worked out area by area and period by period. The major implication of this geopolitical zone or interaction sphere in Indian archaeology and history is two-fold. First, miscellaneous artefacts of central and west Asiatic affinity in various segments of the subcontinent's northwestern region including the Indus valley may not be anything except indicators of trade contacts over this interaction area. Secondly, to be of significance in the context of India to the east of the Indus, any cultural or political movement or influence has to be firmly established first to the east of the Hindukush. It is this region which witnessed the forays of different political powers to India from the Indo-Greeks to the Muslims. On the whole, while trying to pinpoint lines of diffusionary movements of any kind to India from beyond the Hindukush, one should do far more than focussing on general similarities and tracing straight lines on that basis. One must try to fit one's premise in the context of the subcontinent's known geographical alignments.

I developed this idea primarily on the basis of T.F. Holdich's *The Gates of India, Being a Historical Narrative* (1910) and *The Indian Borderland 1880-1900, Being a Personal Narrative of Twenty Years* (1901). It would be exciting to work out fully the political and economic geography of this vast terrain but even in an outline form, this introduces some geographical order to the vast mass of historical data which have frequently been offered as examples of 'foreign invasions' of India. Our premise, on the other hand, suggests that most of these so-called 'foreign invasions' emanated from south of the Hindukush, an area which must be considered a part of the Indian world in itself.

The External Trade during the Harappan Period: Evidence and Hypotheses

This paper is rooted in my concern with the various nuances of the historical geography of India. It is not directly related to my attempt to understand the external trade of the Indus civilization. My book on this topic was published only in 1990 but in the form of an extended summary, this was circulated in the seminar on the Indus civilization at the Indian Institute of Advanced Study, Simla, in the autumn of 1977, and along with this there were papers on the Indus seals at Nippur (Chakrabarti 1978a), the occurrence of reserved-slip ware in the Harappan context (Chakrabarti 1978b) and the occurrence of Indus beads in Iran (Chakrabarti and Moghadam 1977). The paper on the Indus seals in Nippur highlighted their implications for the terminal point of the Indus chronology, highlighting the continuity of this civilization to the Kassite context of c.13th century BC. An in-depth analysis of the reserved slip ware, which had so long been considered Mesopotamian imports or items of Mesopotamian derivation, showed that their Indian occurrence could not be linked to Mesopotamia. In the case of the Indus beads in Iran, the most notable point was their occurrence along the northern and southern west to east routes in Iran. Further, their occurrence in the Fars plain was an important geographical addition to the list of the various Iranian areas where such beads were found. The overall summary circulated in the Indus seminar in Simla in 1977, which was expanded into a book in 1990, had the following salient points about it. First, the data were clearly tabulated and analysed in depth with the geography of the entire region providing the context of these data. For instance, it was clearly argued that the Hindukush passes were in use during this period and the entire chain of passes in the sub-continent's western hills was clearly enumerated. As far as the much-used term 'Meluhha' to denote the area of the Indus civilization is concerned, I pointed out the difficulties in making such straight correlations as argued by I.J. Gelb and did not advance beyond claiming that this term might have included some parts of the Indus distribution area but never denoted exclusively this distribution zone. This was in strong contrast to some attempts to put 'Meluhha' in Gujarat based on disputable archaeological arguments (Chakrabarti 1975) and irrelevant linguistic reasoning (During-Caspers and Govindankutty 1978). In view of the assumption which had gained ground after the discovery of the Indus material in the Gulf region and the excavations at Suktagendor on the Makran coast by G.F. Dales that the maritime links of the Indus civilization were possibly more important than its overland links, I pointed out the traditionally overwhelming importance of overland trade throughout the concerned region, including a possible link-up with the Gulf area itself through southern Iran. I further argued that the general pattern of the Indus external trade could not have been much different from the pattern of traditional trade between the Indus region and central and west Asia. Equally importantly, in view of my analysis of the total range of data, I pointed out that the basic quantum of this trade could not be as large as it is generally supposed, which strongly contrasted with S. Ratnagar's supposition (Ratnagar 1981) that the Indus civilization was a very important supplier of raw materials to Mesopotamia.

History of the Use of Metals

As a continuation of the article on the beginning of iron in India in 1976 (Chakrabarti 1976), there were a number of articles on various related aspects of the topic, such as iron ores (Chakrabarti 1977a), early Indian literary references to iron (Chakrabarti 1979), review of research on early Indian iron (Chakrabarti 1977b), pre-industrial iron-smelting (Chakrabarti 1984a) and a detailed study of the archaeological evidence of iron in the northwestern subcontinent including an exhaustive examination of the date of the Baluchistan cairn burials (Chakrabarti 1979). Meanwhile, articles on Indian Iron Age were contributed to at least three seminars (Chakrabarti 1984, 1985a, 1985b). These culminated in the publication of a book in 1992 (Chakrabarti 1992). Somewhat related to this interest was a publication on the problem of tin in early India (Chakrabarti 1979), which reviewed not merely the basic protohistoric and early historic archaeological evidence but also the related geological, literary and ethnographic evidence. The section on the literary sources was marginal but in the case of ethnography, interesting evidence emerged from Bastar and Giridih where the cases of preindustrial tin-smelting were noticed. Interesting evidence regarding the distribution of tin ores emerged from Bastar and Chhotanagpur, especially Giridh. In the context of the general interest in tin in archaeological literature, this was a detailed assessment of the relevant Indian context. Similar examination of the situations regarding lead and silver were published jointly with Rajni Nanda (Nanda and Chakrabarti 1985, 1989).

History of Indian Archaeology

A general survey of the development of Indian archaeology was published as an article in 1982 (Chakrabarti 1982) but the three other papers of the period dealt with the nineteenth-century background in much greater detail (Chakrabarti 1981, 1979a, 1979b, 1981). Although not specifically concerned with the history of Indian archaeology, the first volume of *A Sourcebook of Indian Archaeology* (Allchin and Chakrabarti 1979) arranges data in sections like 'background' and 'early methods' to highlight the historical development of the subject. These articles provide a substantive prelude to the author's *A History of Indian Archaeology from the Beginning to the Present* in 1988 (Chakrabarti 1988).

Trade Routes of the Historic Periods

Although not based on field-work, the author's study of the early historic routes of Kashmir (Chakrabarti 1984) integrates the basic evidence of geographical writings on the subject and was followed by a close examination of the hypothesis of a southern route to China through Manipur and Bhamo jointly with Nayanjot Lahiri (Chakrabarti and Lahiri 1986). The geographical aspects of the problems are in both cases clear and specific, based on different explorers' reports.

Survey of the Kangra Valley

After a formal recurring grant was sanctioned for the Archaeology and Museum Unit of the Department of History, I focussed on the Kangra valley as a survey area. There had been miscellaneous informations about this valley: the occurrence of terrace-related Palaeolithic tools in places like Dehra Gopipur, Haripur and Guler, which was explored by B.B. Lal several years back; the report of 'upper palaeolithic' type of tools made of limestone at Ror by G.C. Mohapatra; the sculptures of the Kangra fort and the Vajreswari temple of Kangra; the early 13th century temple of Baijnath; the rock-cut temple-complex of Masrur of c. 8th century AD; the Buddhist complex of Cheturu, which may date from the early centuries AD; the early Brahmi and Kharosthi inscriptions of Kanhiara and Pathiar; and finally the miscellaneous reports of tribal coins in the ancient *Trigarta* territory of which the ancient Kangra was supposed to be a part. Thus, there was little doubt that archaeologically Kangra was an interesting region with a long sequence of occupation. In fact, while discussing Alexander's invasion, Vincent Smith in his *Early History of India* mentions one *Sikandar-ka-Kila* in the context of the Kangra area. In the 10th century, Sultan Mahmud of Ghazni attacked the Kangra fort and successfully removed, according to his chroniclers, an immense amount of loot. In the more recent context, Kangra was home to a major tradition of Indian miniature painting and home to a number of shrine spots (cf. the *Jwalamukhi* temple), including the Vajreswari temple.

Geographically, the Kangra valley is the western segment of the long sinuous valley which begins near Pathankot on the west and continues up to Kulu via Mandi on the east. Basically, this comprises the lower and upper parts of the Beas. In the north it is bordered by the high ranges, including the Dhauladhar, and in the south it is mostly broken country following the edge of the Siwaliks right up to Anantapur Sahib and the adjacent areas in Panjab. Beyond Mandi, one can approach not merely Kulu but also the area towards Simla through Bilaspur. On the west, Jalandhar lies beyond Pathankot and is considered the capital of the ancient *Trigarta* country. As Kangra is considered part of ancient *Trigarta*, it apparently has a geographical tie-up with the Jalandhar region, which implies that it had a close interaction with a large part of the Panjab plains. The major areas in the hills which are easily accessible from Kangra are the areas around modern Dalhousie and Chamba, and through them a significant section of the western Himalayas comes within the orbit of Kangra. The Nurpur fort stands as a kind of western bastion of the valley and gives access to Pathankot, Dalhousie, Chamba and the area to the east including Kangra, Dharamsala and Palampur. The last place is a centre of the tea industry of Kangra and the fact that there was a conscious attempt on the part of the Government of India to establish a trade in tea between Kangra and Tibet suggests that Tibet was not inconceivably far from the orbit of Kangra.

All these discoveries and geographical perspectives no doubt exercised an influence on my mind for selecting this valley as an archaeological survey area. However, the most important thought in this regard was the location of the Harappan site of Manda in Jammu, from which side the Kangra valley is accessible via Pathankot. That the Harappans had contacts with the Panjab Himalayas was proved by the identification of Deodar trees (*Cedrus deodara*) at Harappa.

The result of my survey in the company of S. Jamal Hasan proved negative in this regard, but what it was eventually able to offer was a total archaeological perspective of the valley and a better understanding of its position in the historical cross-currents of the country. It is not that we could achieve a lot—not more than a month could be spent in the field with our resources—but confronted with the millions of small to large boulders in the Beas cliffs at Dehra-Gopipur and Haripur-Guler, we wondered if any other stone tool type except the chopper-chopping variety could be fashioned out of the raw material available in this region. Equally problematic was the supposed association of the stone tools with the postulated Beas terrace system, which was no doubt imitated from the Soan valley terrace systems postulated by H. de Terra and T.T. Patterson. Not being geologists/geomorphologists/geographers, we could not reach any opinion of our own in this matter but wondered if all level stretches along the banks of Himalayan rivers have to be called terraces because the formation of such level stretches can take place also due to the clearance of jungles in the hills by their side. Our study of the Palaeolithic occurrences in this area yielded nothing significant. The only prehistoric industry which merited attention in this context was the flake industry from Ror. Such an industry was reported from Jammu and the industry as a whole was compared with the Neolithic Hissar culture of the 6th-5th millennium BC central Asia by V.I. Ranov. Considering that Ranov is a distinguished archaeological authority on Tadjikistan, his opinion in this regard is very important and has to be followed up on the Indian side by excavations at Ror industry sites. The Brahmi and Kharosthi inscriptions of Kanhiara and Pathiar below Dharamsala, which mention the digging of a tank and the establishment of an *Arama* or monastery and may date from the second century BC, are in a sense problematic because we have no satisfactory answer for its location. As far as we could ascertain, this is not directly on any route and the only major route that we can think of in this connection is the route from Pathankot to Kulu and the Simla area via Mandi or Bilaspur. It appears that this route had an early historic identity. There are apparently Buddhist ruins at Cheturu near Gaggal and on the basis of the size of the bricks, which can still be located on the top of its small hill, it can be dated to the early centuries AD. This is the only sign of Buddhist occupation that we noticed in the valley. A Jaina *Adinatha* image has been reported from within the Kangra fort.

The fact that by the early 13th century AD the Pathankot-Kulu corridor retained, if not increased, its importance is shown by the Baijnath temple inscription of AD 1204, which records the dedication of this temple by two brothers who were sons of a merchant. The place was called *Kiragrama* but the area which had a king named Jayachandra was the part of ancient Trigarta. In fact, looking at the whole Pathankot-Kulu alignment, one would claim that this was a kind of corridor with ancient spots in or around it. The Masrur rock-cut temple complex, which is possibly not earlier than the 8th century AD, lies far to the west of Baijnath along this corridor. Nothing is known of the immediate background of this complex but a number of rock-cut *Sikhara*-type temples are connected with a central shrine dedicated possibly to Siva. The only trace of early historic settlement that we could locate in Kangra was in a road-side cliff at Ror. The early historic pottery assemblage which is associated with an iron knife is clear and dates from c.200 BC. The knife was subsequently found to bear traces of quenching. The traces of early mediaeval occupation are abundant in the valley, notably in and around modern Kangra where from inside the fort sculptures dating from c.7th-8th century AD have been found in some quantity. The Vajreswari temple in the Kangra town contains a number of sculptures dating from c.10th century AD and later. Kangra retained its identity in various forms till the reign of Sansar Chand in the late 18th to the early 19th centuries when it was handed over to Ranjit Singh of Panjab. The 16th-century Krishna temple of Nurpur fort still impresses one both with its grandeur and ornate decoration. Every winter, the nomadic Gaddis who lived at the heights above Dharmasala in the summer used to come down to camp inside the Kangra fort.

From my point of view, the Kangra exploration cannot be called successful because it failed in its main task of identifying a Harappan occupation of the valley. It, however, made me exposed to a well-defined valley with a variety of geographical and archaeological possibilities, and I learnt not merely how to conduct explorations in this Himalayan terrain in the shadow of the Dhauladhar but also how to weave a basic history of the region on the basis of geography and archaeological monuments. I was also impressed by the way this valley in the Panjab Himalayas was tied to the main flow of archaeological developments elsewhere in the country. The typical 'Sunga bowl' with incurved rim of c.200 BC occurred in the roadside cliff at Ror, and the sculptural style of Masrur of c.8th century AD repeated the sculptural style of the contemporary central India. For me that was also a lesson to learn.

Chhotanagpur Survey, 1981-87

Its core area is modern Jharkhand, comprising the old British Indian districts of Singhbhum, Ranchi, Hazaribagh, Palamau and Santal Parganas. From its highest level in the Netarhat plateau of Ranchi, the land descends in slopes till the lower surfaces of Orissa and West Bengal are reached. In Orissa, Mayurbhanj, Keonjhar and Sundargarh districts mainly bear the imprint of this plateau and in West Bengal the concerned districts are Birbhum, Burdwan, Bankura, Purulia and Midnapur. Some scholars consider Purulia to be within the core area of the Chhotanagpur plateau. In West Bengal, the impact of the plateau on the alluvial landscape to the west of the Bhagirathi can be seen in places right up to the bank of the river in the form of ripples of uplands in the landscape. This can be observed as far east as Kherur in Murshidabad. In human terms, the interest of this plateau lies in its mineral resources—copper, tin, iron ores, lead and gold in varying proportions and with extensive traces of preindustrial mining in all cases—and stones, including semiprecious stones of various kinds. Timber was also plentiful. This block of land to the southwest corner of the Ganga plain was naturally a major source of raw materials for the valley.

Miscellaneous pieces of information about the archaeological possibilities of the whole region have been available since the nineteenth century. That was also the period when there was considerable anthropological focus on the various tribal groups of the area, including its hunting-gathering communities. There were reports of the occurrence of the Palaeolithic and other stone tool types in the region, along with the reports of megalithic burials, preindustrial mining and smelting of copper, tin and iron, and some early mediaeval temples and sculptures. In recent years, there was systematic focus on the area's prehistory in the writings of scholars like A.K. Ghosh, G.C. Mohapatra and others. However, the area retained many uncertainties regarding its archaeology. In the plains adjacent to it, especially in West Bengal and Bihar, there was a rich evidence of black-and-red ware village settlements but it was not known if the settlements marked by the use of this pottery reached the plateau area at the doorstep of its distribution area in the plains. The archaeological potential of the region as a source of different minerals was not also properly appreciated. There were reports of the so-called 'Asur burials' from the Ranchi and adjacent areas, which yielded copper implements in plenty. There was no clear idea of their chronology.

My interest in the region was kindled by my brief work in Birbhum during my short stay in Santiniketan in the winter of 1980-81. The lateritic belt of this and other western West Bengal districts is clearly related to the Chhotanagpur uplands, with plenty of black-and-ware settlements in the region. My reconnaissance in Birbhum made me keen to understand the stratigraphic profile of a black-and-red ware settlement site, and for this purpose I selected the site of Bahiri near Santiniketan. Because of the severe limitation of my Delhi University resources, it had to be a small-scale excavation. I went back to Birbhum after my return to Delhi in 1981 to work out the stratigraphic sequence of Bahiri. There was a variety of pottery types apart from the plain and painted black-and-red ware in its Period I. Some of the slipped red wares had painted designs on the model of the chalcolithic pottery of many other sites both of West Bengal and elsewhere. There were bits of copper, bone-tools, a smelting furnace or oven, traces of mud walls and mud-plastered courtyards. Most interestingly, in three of my seven trenches there were pieces of iron slag right on the top of the natural soil. In view of the association of the 'chalcolithic pottery', this occurrence of iron slag was decidedly interesting and previously unreported. In the upper part of the section, there was a wide occurrence of iron ores—in fact, chunks of locally available lateritic ores in profusion. Period II of the site was early historic, as shown by the clear evidence of a piece of Sunga terracotta. This was followed in Period III by a massive foundation wall of presumably a Buddhist establishment which seems to have extended well beyond the periphery of the area of occupation we had been exploring. The C-14 dates of Period I were around 1000 BC and from that point of view the occurrence of iron in the lowest section of the site was not at all surprising. The interesting part is the way iron makes its appearance without bringing about any change at all in the chalcolithic make-up. Also interesting is the presence of tin in the copper bit from Period I, which was analysed by P.K. Chattopadhyay, a Durgapur metallurgist with keen interest in the study of ancient metallurgy. He also analysed the iron knife that we found at Ror in Kangra and showed the signs of quenching. I am very thankful to Dr. P.K. Chattopadhyay for kindly analysing the specimens he got from me. The nearest source of tin at Bahiri was the tin deposit of Giridih in Chhotanagpur, and in one sweep this ties up the plateau area as a source of metal ores with the Bhagirathi plain of West Bengal. The basic archaeological documentation of Bahiri was published in the 6th volume of *Man and Environment* in 1982, with adequate drawings of pottery shapes and designs and other illustrative material. In 1982, this was unusual in West Bengal archaeology. Although many black-and-red ware sites had been excavated by then, there were not many clear pottery and other illustrations.

The initial reaction of the West Bengal archaeologists to the find of iron slag in the lowest level of occupation at Bahiri was one of disbelief and cited as an example of my incompetence to dig. However, there was slow acceptance of the idea that iron could occur in what may otherwise be called a chalcolithic assemblage. It is not that there is no iron-free chalcolithic context in West Bengal; in my single trench at the site of Arara (Santaldanga) in Burdwan, there was a clear iron-free level, but the point to note is that in West Bengal iron made its appearance by 1000/1200 BC. Later, I asked Dr. Shyam Chand Mukherjee of the West Bengal State Directorate of Archaeology, who was closely associated with Pandu Rajar Dhibi excavations in the 1960s, if they found iron in the early level of that site as well. He answered in the affirmative adding that they used to throw away pieces of iron assuming that somehow they fell by way of tree-roots from the top. He held a Ph.D., if I remember correctly, in Vaishnava literature and worked in West Bengal archaeology for many years. I remember him as a fine scholar and kind gentleman.

I remember my Bahiri days with pleasure. The gentleman who owned the land containing the site where we excavated was very kind and helpful, allowing us to stay in one of his mud houses in the village and ensuring that Jamal Hasan and I were comfortable. My wife also joined me there for some time. Jamal Hasan worked hard, adapting himself well to the Bengal village life. The villagers were friendly and invariably helpful, including the chief of the local village council or *Panchayat*. Bahiri was not the only early historic site that we encountered in Birbhum. Kotasur on the bank of the Mayurakshi river near Saithia was a fortified settlement and apparently the early historic capital of the region. Later, I identified it with the capital of the ancient kingdom of Gauda.

In 1982, we were in Purulia, a district full of eroded lateritic uplands and detached chains of hills. Jamal Hasan had left Delhi University by now and I was accompanied in the field this year by Rupendra Kumar Chattopadhyay, the new curator of the archaeology and museum unit of Delh University. He remained my field-associate till 1987 and joined me again in 1991-94. Not for a day did he cause any problem in the field. His enthusiasm to locate stone tools and other sites was immense. We located a fairly rich area of Stone Age artefacts in and around the Ayodhya hills in the western section of the district. This complex of hills formed a kind of inverted bowl, on the top of which we found rich scatters of microliths including fine small cores of crystal quartz. At Sirkabad, on an outer slope of the range, there were rich flake-blade assemblages. This is an area which merits further investigations. At Dabha near Baghmundi, we located a distinct upper Palaeolithic complex and in the area around Balarampur there were stone tools of all sorts including the Acheulian handaxes and fine upper Palaeolithic blades and cores made of blackish chert. Purulia has a singularly wide distribution of early mediaeval ruins, notably temples of both stone and brick, and many sculptures, a dominant portion of which is Jaina. We did some documentation work at these places, although at sites like Pakbira and Budhpur, regular excavations should be conducted. At Boram near Jhaldah, there is a knot of Pal period brick temples which need proper conservation and documentation. Near Jhaldah again, the high grounds at the base of the local hills invariably contained microlithic clusters.

In 1983, we were in Bankura, R.K. Chattopadhya's home district. He already did some work here and took me to the sites he was familiar with. We also studied stone tool occurrences on our own and documented the major early mediaeval sculpture and architecture of the district. The work was followed up subsequently by Chattopadhya's Ph.D. work, which has been recently published as a monograph. The Susunia hill area of Bankura was thoroughly explored by the West Bengal State Directorate of Archaeology before we went to the area, and a catalogue of stone tools from the area was also published by this directorate. Unfortunately, they employed villagers on daily wage for exploration—at the start of the day they were given a few stone tools and asked to look for similar specimens throughout the day. At the end of the day, there were good collections of stone tools, and after some weeks of collection of this type the countryside ran dry of stone tools, although no attempt was made to understand their mode of occurrence or stratigraphy. Susunia is a beautiful hilly area and the hills of Biharinath in the same general area have also yielded Palaeolithic tools, the first discoveries at Biharinath being made in the nineteenth century by the geologist Valentine Ball. There is an inscription of c.4th century AD in the Susunia hills, mentioning Pokharna as a royal capital. Pokharna, or the modern village of Pokharna on the south bank of the Damodar, is also Chattopadhya's village and we explored the site staying at his house. The section of the Damodar cliff clearly showed the historical sequence beginning with the pre-Christian era, and in the village itself there were abundant traces of black-and-red ware occupation. I interpreted Pokharna to be the capital of an early historic kingdom based on the resources of the forested belt of southwest West Bengal. The evidence of early historic and earlier black-and-red ware occupation was also found at Dihar on the bank of the Dwarakeswar river. The chalcolithic level of West Bengal has recently been found to date from 2000 + BC at Dihar.

In 1983, we worked in Burdwan and Midnapur, taking in the distribution of all varieties of sites in these two districts. One of the most rewarding experiences was the identification of the prehistoric sequence of the Bankathi area on the bank of the Ajay river in Burdwan. An Acheulian handaxe was found embedded in a particular level of the lateritic conglomerate deposit of the area. A middle palaeolithic implement was found in a higher level and upper palaeolithic implements occurred still higher. Microliths occurred in a sandy deposit at the top. There was a bed of sterile mottled clay below the lateritic conglomerate deposit. The sequence was not obtained from a single spot but the collective evidence from the area was certainly what we have described. The problem is that lateritic conglomerate does not appear even to a non-geologist like me, to be a primary deposit. If stone tools occur in a sequence in this deposit, we have to understand the original beds in which this sequence was apparently formed. This sequence, as we later found out, occurs over a wide area not merely in the western section of West Bengal but also further west in the Chhotanagpur plateau, such as Singhbhum and Mayurbhanj. So, if we have to understand much of eastern Indian Palaeolithic sequence, we have to understand the original story of deposition The story of this deposition has not yet been worked out. In Midnapur, the artefactual concentrations were mostly in southwest Midnapur in the area of the Suvarnarekha valley and also in the forests near Belpahari. The Belpahari forests also showed signs of copper mining at Chhedapathar. The most famous early historic site of Midnapur is Tamralipta or modern Tamluk, which was an unfortified city. There is no evidence that the ancient city has been substantially destroyed by the Rupnarayan river, on whose bank it stands. This famous ancient port town has never been subjected to horizontal excavations. It was the capital of ancient *Suhma* and I have inferred that in the Mauryan period it was under the administrative control of Tosali, identified with Radhanagar near Jajpur in Orissa.

It was also in western Midnapur that we found the orthodox gravel>silt cycle of Palaeolithic sequence of the Peninsular rivers. We observed the cemented gravel deposit below the bridge over the Tarafeni which we approached from Sildah. There were strings of microlithic occurrences along the Bhairavbanki river in the same area.

After surveying the basic archaeological features of the *Rarh* districts of West Bengal, i.e., the districts at its western margin, we focussed in 1984 on Singhbhum, now in Jharkhand. One of the most important aspects of Singhbhum is its copper belt, which contains many clear signs of preindustrial mining in the shape of massive shafts. We studied this belt but could not find any way of dating them unless we could get some of the old shafts cleared and collect the old mining materials such as water pots, ropes, timber, etc. Although Singhbhum was surveyed for its Palaeolithic occurrences by A.K. Ghosh, we considerably extended the distribution of Palaeolithic sites in the district. We also took due notes of the old temples including the one at Ichhagarh which we visited in 1961. In the hilly upland belt south of Jhikpani and north of Hatgamaria, we located some massive core tools—handaxes—which were difficult to lift even by two hands. We did not have any doubt about their being artefacts. The problem is that we never had the chance to investigate the area again. The issue needs further research. In Singhbhum, Palaeolithic tools were also located in the Sarenda forest which is renowned for its quality of *Sal* (*Shorea robusta*) trees. One day we journeyed from Noamundi to Manoharpur through the forests and although archaeologically it was a barren stretch, the beauty of the forests was unforgettable. In the area of the Rakha mines, one could see the outline of forest fires on the hill tops from a distance. A major site of Singhbhum was Barudih which was earlier interpreted as a Neolithic site because there was a profusion of Neolithic celts at the site. What the earlier workers ignored was that these celts occurred in association with wheelmade plain black-and-red ware and iron. The subsequently done radiocarbon dates put the site in the second half of the second millennium BC. The location of a black-and-red ware settlement in Singhbhum clearly suggests that there were direct settlements of the people from the plains during this period in the Chhotanagpur plateau possibly for its raw materials.

If one journeys by bus from Siuri in Birbhum to Dumka in the Santal Parganas district, one sees at one point the whole rampart of the Rajmahal hills cutting off this portion of the Santal Parganas from the plains. This is a spectacular natural landscape in the border between West Bengal and Jharkhand. In 1985, we were in the Santal Parganas, but before entering the Rajmahal hill belt or the Damin area, we hardly found any evidence of prehistoric occupation. Barren days can be very demoralising in the field and we were having too many of them. We were camping at Shikaripara south of Dumka, and at Kendpahari south of Shikaripara we located our first prehistoric site in the Santal Parganas. Soon we found a whole network of what we deduced to be upper Palaeolithic sites throughout the length and breadth of the Rajmahal hills. The point is that the tools of the Damin hills are made of a reddish type of material and easily distinguishable. At some places we came across acres of spreads of this material, proving that all these sites located at the foot of the hills or even in the open lands of this area are upper Palaeolithic occupation sites, the like of which can certainly not be seen in eastern India. Only in a certain section of Palamau have I come across upper Palaeolithic spreads of this proportion, but there the dominant material was a fine-grained quartz, including crystal quartz. These upper Palaeolithic spreads of the Rajmahal hills deserve excavations rather urgently, but in all these years I could not go back to them. I have given a photograph of the Kendpahari site in my *Oxford Companion to Indian Archaeology* and I do hope that someday this site will be excavated. The Rajmahal hills rise straight from the side of the Ganga before it goes in the direction of Bengal and constitute one of the lovely hilly terrains of eastern India. The spread of the upper Palaeolithic industry that we have called the Damin industry may have its spread also outside the Damin area, but it remains to be worked out in the field.

The other Chhotanagpur districts were Ranchi, Palamau and Hazaribagh-Giridih. In Ranchi in 1986, the focus was on the so-called Asur burials. The Ranchi work was financially supported by Nayanjot Lahiri, who was the co-author of the Ranchi report. Our assessment regarding the Asur burials was that they dated from the early centuries AD and showed evidence of interaction with the cultural elements of the plains. They could even mark the presence of a secondary state in the Ranchi plateau and the adjacent region during that period. On the top of the Netarhat plateau we eventually traced a preindustrial iron-smelter to his village, but that being the season of rains, he was not working. However, we can state that preindustrial iron-smelting lasted in the Netarhat plateau at least till 1986. There were also lithic occurrences at some places in the district. Apart from the lithic occurrences, the main interest of Hazaribagh-Giridih lies in their mineral resources. Most significantly, there was preindustrial mining of tin in Giridih. Upper Palaeolithic tools occurred profusely in Palamau. I still remember some of the large spreads of upper Palaeolithic tools in Palamau. At Ranka Kalan near Garhwa, the Chhotanagpur plateau slopes away towards the Sarguja plain. There were lithic occurrences in the hill-slopes near Garhwa. It is also from the direction of Palamau that the plateau slopes away in the direction of Aurangabad in Gaya. My Chhotanagpur work was rounded up by undertaking a brief survey of the districts of Mayurbhanj and Keonjhar in Orissa. We took a traverse following the Mayurbhanj-Keonjhar alignment and linked it up with the Chaibasa area of Singhbhum.

The Chhotanagpur survey's main purpose was to assess the archaeological potential and significance of this plateau region as a whole. From this point of view, I consider the work to be a success. A basic archaeological frame of the region has been put forward in my *Archaeology of Eastern India: Chhotanagpur Plateau and West Bengal* (1993).

The Survey of the Prehistory of the Union Territory of Delhi and Haryana

People have reported stone tools in the Delhi ridge from time to time, but there was no coordinated attempt to assess their general distribution and stratigraphy. In 1986, with the financial support of Nayanjot Lahiri, an attempt was made to make this assessment. It resulted in the understanding of lithic occurrences in the Aravalli hill system of Delhi and its adjacent parts in Haryana and we could also focus on their stratigraphy. The work resulted in a publication in 1987 (Chakrabarti and Lahiri 1987). In retrospect, what was surprising was the sheer scale of occurrence of stone tools in and around Delhi. I also realized that the entire inner zone of the Aravallis in this sector remains unsurveyed. Subsequently, the Archaeological Survey excavated the Stone Age locality of Anangpur, an area also studied by us. Due to the stone quarrying activities, the existence of prehistoric sites in the Aravallis near Delhi is in severe jeopardy.

A Survey of the Preindustrial Mines of Rajasthan

This survey was jointly conducted with J.G. Shaffer of the Case Western Reserve University in 1982. Professor Shaffer spent an academic year in the Department of Anthropology of Delhi University in 1977-78 as a Government of India fellow. The entire cost of the 1982 survey came from his budget. We got on well together during his prolonged stay in Delhi, and when our joint proposal to the Government of India for research in the Chhotanagpur plateau was not successful, he decided to familiarise himself with the old mining areas of Rajasthan. Our plan was to visit the major known mining areas along the Aravallis from Khoh Dariba near Sariska to the Zawar mines near Udaipur. The places we visited were Kho Dariba, Ganeshwar and Baleshwar localities, Khetri copper mine area, Ajmer, Aguncha lead mine near Bhilwara, Rajpur Dariba between Bhilwara and Udaipur, the archaeological site of Bagor, and finally, the Zawar mines. Each of the mining places contained abundant remains of preindustrial mining in the form of old shafts and slag. We collected slag specimens from each of these places but regrettably this collection, while with P.K. Chattopadhyay for analysis, got lost. This is the reason why there is no publication on this work, although what I remember about the sites we visited got indirectly into some of my publications. A few wood specimens were collected from the old mining shafts and the dates were published in the publications of the radiocarbon wing of the Physical Research Laboratory of Ahmedabad. An indirect consequence of this survey was a detailed publication on the traces of old mining in the Aguncha lead deposit, which was found out to be essentially a polymetallic deposit. We persuaded the geologist of the Aguncha field to undertake a detailed investigation, which was published in *Man & Environment* (subsequently reprinted in the second volume of *A Source Book of Indian Archaeology*). Thus, this survey was not entirely in vain, and I have a deep sense of gratitude to Professor Shaffer for making the survey possible. It was a very educative trip. If I had not seen the hundreds of old shafts of different sizes in the Aravallis and in the Singhbhum hills, I would not have been able to appreciate the sheer scale of mining activities in preindustrial India.

The Writing of 'Theoretical Issues in Indian Archaeology', 1986

The eight lectures (changing concerns of Indian archaeology; diffusion as an explanatory mechanism of India's archaeological development; the problem of literature-archaeology correlation; geographical approaches; prehistory, transition to food-production and urbanisation; agriculture; metallurgy; and finally trade), each of which critically examined some crucial areas of Indian archaeology, were prepared under a weekly seminar series organized kindly by J-C Gardin of the French CNRS at Ecole des Hautes Etudes en Sciences Sociales in Paris in April-May, 1986. The collection of essays was published in 1988 (Chakrabarti 1988). One of the abiding areas of my interest is how the ideas in these crucial segments of Indian archaeology have developed over time. This is far more than historiography. These are problems intimately linked with the future progress of Indian archaeology, and as not many of us are concerned with the broader picture beyond the areas with which we are personally concerned, such critical appraisals are important and provide grounds of discussion. From this point of view, I consider it an important piece of work.

After the Paris stint, I collaborated for about three weeks in Cambridge with a British Council grant to finalise the second volume ('Settlement, Technology, and Trade') of *A Source Book of Indian Archaeology*. Regrettably, that could not be published till 1997. The help rendered in this context by a senior lady of the British Council in Paris is unforgettable.

The Writing of 'A History of Indian Archaeology from the Beginning to 1947', 1987

A three-month stint in the Cambridge libraries in early 1987 with support from Charles Wallace Fund through the Ancient India and Iran Trust helped me to finish writing my book on the history of Indian archaeology till 1947. One of the highlights of the book was to point out that the beginning of archaeological researches in India took a systematic and academic form not with the establishment of the Asiatic Society in 1784 but around the middle of the eighteenth century when scholars like Anquetil du Perron and Carsten Niebuhr openly advocated in their writings the need for a systematic survey of antiquities in India. The book also drew attention to the voluminous descriptions of Indian monuments in the writings of the European travellers to India from the seventeenth century onward. In the case of William Jones, it was argued that his main task was to relate India to the scheme of the Biblical theory of creation and that the ascription of ancient Pataliputra to the site of Patna, which had hitherto been ascribed to him, was in fact achieved by James Rennell. The main inspiration to do archaeology in the field in India came from James Prinsep and the book, apart from highlighting Prinsep's achievements, underscored the manifold achievements of his contemporaries who published and/or collected many field-data. The true academic successor of Prinsep was Alexander Cunningham, whose biography was written earlier by Abu Imam. However, the sole focus of the Cunningham chapter of my book was what he achieved from the field-archaeological point of view and the point of view of the archaeological geography of the country. Going through the work of Cunningham and his contemporaries in the multi-volume 'Cunningham Reports' was a major task and told fully the story of how India was fully mapped for archaeological sites.

The period between the retirement of Cunningham and the coming of John Marshall as the Director General of the Archaeological Survey of India in 1902 is generally passed over in relevant discussions rather quickly but we adequately highlighted the character of a whole range of architectural, inscriptional and more orthodox archaeological publications of the period.

The entire phase of Indian archaeology from 1902 to the coming of Mortimer Wheeler in 1944 was dubbed by me as the John Marshall period of Indian archaeology, arguing in detail how the foundations of modern Indian archaeology, as we currently perceive it to be, were laid down during this period not merely by John Marshall but also by many of his illustrious subordinates and contemporaries—Maulavi Zafar Hasan, Ghulam Yazdani, M.S. Vats, R.D. Banerji, R.P. Chanda, Aurel Stein and many others. The discovery of the Indus civilization was the crowning achievement of this phase and we took care to emphasize how such a discovery was taken in its stride by the Archaeological Survey of India under Marshall's steady guidance. The long series of excavations that he got opened up at Mohenjodaro and Harappa and the three volumes of *Mohenjodaro and the Indus Civilization* that he masterfully edited added a completely new chapter to Indian history. More than that, his perception that this civilization was deeply rooted in the Indian soil, a premise which has been more than adequately substantiated by later research, amply highlights his commanding academic grip of Indian historical and archaeological situations. The different aspects of the historical India were also clearly elaborated under this guidance, which also witnessed the complete ramification of the scope of conservation and preservation work in India.

Although there were some years between the departure of John Marshall as the Director General in 1929 and the coming of R.E.M. Wheeler to the same post in 1944, Wheeler made Marshall the target of his criticism, much of which was unjustified. However, Wheeler had no understanding of Indian history and he came here primarily as an efficient excavator and organizer of archaeological affairs. The Archaeological Survey joke that I heard in this context was that under Wheeler anybody who could draw a good section became an archaeologist and historian. At the same time, in the limited period of four years available to him Wheeler introduced India to the concept of archaeological planning and the techniques of stratigraphic excavations. On the whole, he introduced modernity to Indian archaeology.

One of the important aspects of my book was to examine the ideas behind the archaeological work of different periods. I also examined how the tradition of Indian archaeological research was built up and how we, the modern Indian practitioners of the subject, belong proudly to this tradition. There was also a detailed chapter on the development of prehistoric studies, highlighting how the basis of such studies was laid down securely in the second half of the nineteenth century.

Bangladesh

I consider my stay in Bangladesh in 1988-90 academically productive. The Jahangirnagar University campus was well-wooded and beautiful, and the co-ordinator of the Foundation archaeology programme, Professor Abu Imam, was a fine gentleman. He published a scholarly book on the life and work of Alexander Cunningham. He studied archaeology at the Institute of Archaeology, London University, when Gordon Childe was its director. Professor Harunur Rashid, the third professor of the programme, was a nice and friendly individual, and I learnt a lot about the old set-up of archaeology and

Bangladesh from him. I found the campus very rich in bird life, and it was a pleasure to watch closely some birds closely associated with traditional Bengal. There was also something of traditional Bengal among the teachers and other senior people of the campus whom I came to look upon as friends: friendly, open-hearted and generous without even a shadow of malice.

It took me some time to get familiar with the basic archaeological issues of Bangladesh. There were many excavations but there was not much attempt to offer an integrated account of the material in terms of the general archaeological developments of the subcontinent. Not much attention was even given to assess the true archaeological potential of particular areas and sites. One such area was the Lalmai hills, where attention was solely given to the Buddhist monastic relics of the post-Gupta phase. And yet, the Lalmai hills had Pleistocene deposits and also naturally occurring chunks of fossilwood. The area deserved a look from the point of view of locating prehistoric industries. In early January 1989, I went on a private visit to Mainamati and the Lalmai hills and succeeded in locating a fossilwood industry which I argued to be upper Palaeolithic. Further explorations on behalf of the University in April of the same year led to more finds. Subsequently, the industry was found to compare closely with the late Anyathian fossilwood industry of the area south of Mandalay in Myanmar. The only comparable find in India was in the adjacent Tripura but there the geologist who found the material did not understand the mixed character of the assemblage and devised an imaginary stratigraphic sequence from the Acheulian to the Neolithic at some of his sites. The map-distance between Tripura/Lalmai hills and Mandalay is about 500 km, and on the basis of this simple fact alone I can claim that this must denote a spatially impressive prehistoric spread, regarding which nothing is known except its general stratigraphic position and typology.

That punchmarked coins had been found at a place called Wari Bateshwar near the old course of the Brahmaputra was known for a long time. However, it appears that the site was not explored by archaeologists to assess the context of these finds, and the large amount of information collected by a father-and-son team of the village remained neglected for years. A brief visit to the site in the company of Professor Abu Imam and others made it clear that it was a fortified early historic site and that its location near an old course of the Brahmaputra and the present course of the Meghna suggested a port site. The site was subsequently excavated by Professor S.S.M. Rahman of Jahangirnagar University with excellent results. The site is now dated to c.450 BC.

The only other well-known early historic site of Bangladesh is Mahasthangarh in the Bagura district. This district has been well-surveyed both by the Bangladesh government department and Professor S.S.M. Rahman. Mahasthangarh was supposed to be excavated jointly by the Bangladesh department and the archaeology section of the Department of History of Jahangirnagar University. The formalities were also completed in this regard. By this time the French expressed an interest at the site and the Bangladesh department changed its position in favour of the French. I was told this by Professor Imam. I also gathered that the French got the right to excavate the site as a background part of the French aid package to Bangladesh. That was the general impression of the Bangladeshi archaeologists of the time in the government. I decide to mention the issue here as an example of the often ignored fact that the First World interest in the Third World archaeology is mostly political.

There was no lack of Buddhist monastic sites in Bangladesh and Jahangirnagar University in my time participated in the excavations of the Bangladesh government at the mound of Harish Chandra Rajar Bari at Savar not far from the campus. This turned out to be a monastery of the post-Gupta period.

It was in an empty cotton mill complex at Savar that I witnessed the majesty of a *Palash* (*Butea frondosa*) tree of gigantic proportions. The tree was in full bloom from the bottom to the top, and although Chhotanagpur is supposedly the home ground of *Palash*, I never saw the tree in such majesty there. I made my obeisance to the tree and realized why some trees were imagined to be *Vrikshadevatas*, 'tree deities'. Personally, the only occasion when I saw a tree being directly worshipped was somewhere in Barabanki near Lucknow.

I took the opportunity of my long stay in Jahanhirnagar University to go around Bangladesh, visiting most places associated with my and my wife's early life. This also included visits to archaeological sites and by the time my Jahangirnagar tenure came to an end, I had developed a fairly clear idea of the archaeology of Bangladesh. My *Ancient Bangladesh, a Study of the Archaeological Sources* (1992) was written on that basis.

I came back to Delhi in 1990 and soon left for Cambridge. As I have noted, my stay at Delhi had its tumultuous years, including a close brush with the underworld of Indian historical studies but this is where I came across students and teachers from all parts of India and imperceptibly became a part of the main flow of archaeology in the country. Some of my students have made their own impacts on the Delhi academia. So, although I was not successful in giving a secure base to the archaeology and museum unit of the Department of History, Delhi University, the years were not academically wasted.

4

Cambridge, 1990-2011

PERSONAL NOTES

I joined Cambridge University on December 1, 1990. The post against which I joined was a 'joint post' of the Faculty of Oriental Studies and the Department of Archaeology. The post which my predecessor F.R. Allchin held was not a 'joint post' but belonged exclusively to the Faculty of Oriental Studies. As he was about to retire, the Indian section of the Faculty thought that the cause of the post would be better served by shifting it to some other branch of specialisation. The Department of Archaeology, on the other hand, had a regular teaching course in Indian archaeology, which was taught by Dr. Allchin. So, when the Department of Archaeology came to know of the Faculty of Oriental Studies proposal, it objected to the idea of changing the scope of the post because that would affect its Indian archaeology teaching programme. Eventually, the scope of the post was allowed, initially at least, to remain unchanged and administratively the post came to be considered a 'joint post' of the Oriental faculty and the archaeology department. I was completely unaware of these and related developments when I joined the university. I was told of them later by an archaeology colleague, T. Whitelaw. I opted to be an administrative part of the Oriental Faculty because that is where my predecessor taught and that is the place I had known most during my earlier stays in Cambridge.

When the question of my 'confirmation till retirement age' came up, the Indian section of the Oriental faculty objected to the idea on the ground of my supposed incompetence as a teacher. I contested the claim and the matter got prolonged till 1995 when I was confirmed in my job. As the Indian section of the Oriental Faculty appeared doubtful of the suitability of my presence in that faculty, I was allowed to shift base to the Department of Archaeology. The first few years of my life in Cambridge were thus both uncertain and traumatic, for which I suppose I have to thank exclusively Cambridge's "India experts" of the time. I thank Professor Lord Colin Renfrew of the Department of Archaeology most warmly for being the only person I could turn to for advice in those days within the university.

My years in Cambridge archaeology were uneventful but I doubt if I succeeded in being a part of the Cambridge collegiate set-up. Considering that Cambridge is a collegiate university, this is an important point. In my eighteen years as a regular 'university teaching officer', I never got the chance to be a college fellow or even a college Director of Study, although my archaeology colleagues in the identical positions, some of whom joined the university later than me, did not apparently have any problem in this regard. Both my predecessor (F.R. Allchin) and successor (C. Petrie) have been college fellows. I am aware that in many other subjects 'university teaching officers' who look different and sound different have had no difficulty in being awarded college fellowships. So, this appears to be an archaeology-specific situation. It is certainly possible that the concerned people did not consider me fit to be a college fellow/Director of Study.

I retired on 30 September 2008. I had to pay for the removal of waste paper from my room on that day and having thus made the room fit for the next occupant, I handed over the keys to the departmental office and walked out. More than a month later, I was told that emeritus professors without major research grants could not be issued working computers and that even in the matter of issuing them suitable desk space, the point of their having/not having major research grants was important. I realized that in my post-retirement phase, I had better avoid seeking favours from important Cambridge archaeologists and get on with my business by roaming the university libraries and the general computer work stations.

This is what I do at present.

CAMBRIDGE IN THE ANCIENT INDIAN HISTORICAL AND ARCHAEOLOGICAL STUDIES

Formal interest in the ancient Indian studies in general did not begin in the University till the appointment of E.B. Cowell as Professor of Sanskrit in 1867. He applied for the job on 18 May 1867 and delivered his inaugural lecture on 23 October in the same year. He began his study of Sanskrit at Oxford under the guidance of H.H. Wilson. He went to India in 1856 as a professor in Presidency College, Kolkata and was appointed in 1858 as the principal of the government Sanskrit College there. His task was "to introduce more of Western knowledge through an increased study of English, without impairing the efficiency of the Sanskrit studies". In addition to his official duties, he also tried to make himself familiar with "the traditional learning of the Pandits". If his application were successful, he declared that he would promote the study of Sanskrit "both as a philological pursuit and as the great means of understanding and sympathising with the people of India". His application was positively endorsed by a number of people including Max Muller of Oxford, Monier Williams of Oxford and Bishop Cotton of Kolkata. Max Muller (letter dated 10 May, 1867) pointed out how the professor of Sanskrit at Cambridge was expected to teach Sanskrit, modern Indian languages and comparative philology and how in all these three branches of learning he was the best person available. Monier Williams (letter dated April 29, 1867) also endorsed his "claims to be a teacher of young Englishmen, many of whom are destined hereafter to discharge the duties of rulers towards our Indian subjects". Bishop Cotton (letter dated 11 July, 1867) did not consider it right "to omit the fact, as bearing on a professorship in a Christian University", that he was not a person whose interest in India was confined to philology and ancient learning *but that he was also "actively desirous to see it a Christian country" and that his influence in any position "would be exerted with a distinct reference to that great end"* (italics added).

Cowell's inaugural lecture dwells at length on the basic characteristics of the Sanskrit literature and its importance in the discipline of philology but finally seeks a more mundane and direct justification for it in the portals of the University.

> But I think there is yet a higher interest in Sanskrit than any supplied by the study of the language or the literature for its own sake. It is the key to understand India. The vernaculars of the North can never be properly mastered without some knowledge of Sanskrit, for all are closely connected with it; and in some, as in Bengali, nine-tenths of the vocabulary are directly derived from that language. Bengali bears as close a resemblance to Sanskrit as the Romaic does to ancient Greek—both depend on the old language for all their richness and power. But Sanskrit is still more important as enabling us to understand and feel with the people of India. It will be a growing danger for our empire, if we send out young Englishmen to govern millions of subject Hindus with no sympathy for the

> subject race, with no feeling but contempt for their customs and habits of thought. If they only look on them as barbarous and childish – as the degraded serfs of an inferior race, — they may raise revenue and try to administer justice; but no sympathy will exist between the ruler and the ruled, and our empire will be built on the sand. But it is impossible for one who knows anything of Sanskrit to feel contempt for the Hindu even in his present condition, humiliated though he has been by the long centuries of Muhammedan intolerance and tyranny. The love of Sanskrit must inspire the true student with an interest in the welfare of the Hindus. We see in our day India beginning to free herself from the ignorance and superstition which have so long enthralled her, and I cannot conceive of the Sanskrit scholar as an apathetic looker-on in the struggle. But need I say only the *Sanskrit scholar?* We remember the generous enthusiasm which stirred the heart of civilized Europe, that Greece might be free; and surely something of the same glow may well warm the heart of England, that her great dependency, India, may under her rule share the blessings of Western civilization and Christianity. (Cowell 1867, p. 19).

During his tenure, Cowell did not produce any historical work, although he is known for the translations of many ancient texts including the Buddhist Mahayana texts and the Jatakas. Although he was no ancient historian, his inaugural lecture adequately highlights the cross-currents of ideas behind the establishment of the Sanskrit professorship at Cambridge.

The next Sanskrit person was Cecil Bendall, who succeeded Cowell as professor of Sanskrit in 1903. He is primarily known for his collection of Buddhist manuscripts from Nepal for the University. As a fellow of Gonville and Caius College, Cambridge, he published a paper entitled "On European collections of Sanskrit manuscripts from Nepal:

Their antiquity and bearing on chronology, history and literature" (Bendall 1882), which began with Brian Houghton Hodgeson's donation of more than 300 Buddhist-Sanskrit and Tibetan literature to French and English scholars around the middle of the nineteenth century. The second major gift of such manuscripts—more than 400 of them—came from Dr. Daniel Wright, Residency-Surgeon at Kathmandu, and went primarily to Cambridge University. Besides their literary interest, these manuscripts were "of the highest palaeographical and historical importance". Bendall points out that "the collections, however, have a distinctly historical value. A tolerably complete series of dates of Nepalese sovereigns from the beginning of the XIth century AD onwards, is obtainable from the colophons of these MSS." Their historical interest is not limited only to Nepal: "five of the Cambridge collection, and one at least of the Hodgeson collection of the Royal As. Soc. of London, are dated by years of the reigns of sovereigns of Bengal". Bendall adds an appendix to this publication, giving a general table of the kings of Nepal (AD 1008-1457) with dates from manuscript and other sources. Bendall, although a Sanskritist, thus made an outstanding historical contribution. His *Catalogue of Buddhist Sanskrit MSS in the University Library of Cambridge* was published in 1883, and after that he undertook two tours in Nepal and parts of India chiefly in the interests of the University library. In 1884-85, he collected 500 Sanskrit MSS and 90 MSS in 1898-99. The chronology of the early Nepalese kings and some Gupta kings was helped by the inscriptions discovered by him.

Bendall was succeeded by Edward James Rapson in 1906, and of all the Cambridge Sanskritists, his contribution to ancient Indian historical studies is the most. He is remembered principally for his editorship of *The Cambridge History of India, I, Ancient India* in 1922. He himself wrote four chapters for this volume: 'Peoples and languages', 'Indian native states after the period of the Mauryan empire', 'The successors of Alexander the Great', and 'The Scythian and Parthian invaders'. This is proof enough of his comprehensive grip over ancient Indian history. His attitude to the general character of ancient Indian history is clearly reflected by what he wrote in the chapter on peoples and languages.

> It is true that the civilizations which have been developed in India have reacted, and that Indian religions, Indian literature, and Indian art have spread out of India and produced a deep and far-reaching influence on the countries of Further Asia; *but the migrations and the conquests which provided human energy with which these civilizations were created have invariably come into India from the outside* (italics added).

He also wrote a small volume, *Ancient India from the Earliest Times to the First Century* AD, mainly for the candidates of the Indian Civil Service examination. Among other things, Rapson was an authority in both numismatics and palaeography. His major palaeographical interest ran in the direction of Kharosthi. He published Kharosthi inscriptions discovered by Aurel Stein at Niya and other places in central Asia. In numismatics, he is principally known for his British Museum *Catalogue of the Coins of the Andhra Dynasty, the Western Kshatrapas, the Traikutaka Dynasty and the 'Bodhi' Dynasty*, which was published in 1908. He also wrote a general book on Indian numismatics, *Indian Coins* (1897).

H.W. Bailey became professor of Sanskrit after Rapson's death in 1937, retiring in 1967. As John Sheldon points out in his essay on Bailey in *Encyclopaedia Iranica*, although his teaching duties involved him in Vedic and Sanskrit, he published little that was principally concerned with these languages. His studies were principally in the field of the comparative study of Iranian languages and notable for ground-breaking work on the Middle Iranian Saka language of Khotan. No special interest in the ancient history of India can be attributed to this eminent linguist, unless we take into account the fact that in 1946 Charu Chandra Das Gupta, one of our teachers in Kolkata, was awarded Ph.D. for his thesis *The Development of the Kharosthi Script* under his supervision.

History was also outside the research interest of Bailey's successor, John Brough who remained the University's Sanskrit professor from 1967 to 1984. His major publications are *The Early Brahmanical System of Gotra and Pravara: A translation of the Gotrapravaramanjari of Purusottamapandita with an introduction* (1953) and *The Gandhari Dharmapada* (1962). His *Poems from the Sanskrit* (1968) is a sensitive and warm piece of translation of Sanskrit verses.

It appears that the chain of regular Sanskrit professorships came to an end after Brough's death in a road accident in 1984. The first person to hold a personal chair in the subject was K.R. Norman who retired in 1992. Primarily a Pali scholar, he published an authoritative history of this literature, *Pali Literature*, in 1983. However, he had a deep interest in the language and text of the Asokan inscriptions and extensively published on them. He did not write on ancient Indian history but ancient Indian historians fruitfully use his annotations of the texts of the Asokan inscriptions. In 1985, he and F.R. Allchin jointly published *Guide to the Asokan Inscriptions* in *South Asian Studies, 1*.

The first person to receive a regular teaching and research appointment in the field of ancient Indian history and archaeology at the University seems to be J.E. van Lohuizen-De Leeuw, who wrote a Ph.D. thesis on *The 'Scythian' Period, an Approach to the History, Art, Epigraphy and Palaeography of North India from the 1st century* BC *to the 3rd Century* AD (1949) before she came to Cambridge in 1951. She was in Cambridge till 1959 and it is not easy to locate if she published anything important during this period. Her interests also extended to southeast Asia, on the architectural and sculptural traditions of which she published extensively in later life. Her academic approach was essentially technical and grammatical.

The person who occupies, after Rapson, much of the Cambridge academic scene in ancient Indian history and archaeology is F.R. Allchin (1959-90), although his interest in ancient Indian history proper had been somewhat marginal. His literary training in Sanskrit and Hindi and the architectural training he pursued before opting to study Hindi and Sanskrit made him well suited to author lucidly written and illustrated publications. His reports on his small-scale excavations at Piklihal and Utnur, two small sites of the Raichur Doab in modern Karnataka, are excellent examples of its kind, and in the case of Utnur, it incorporated one of the earliest radiocarbon dates in Indian archaeology, 4120 +/- 150 B.P. uncalibrated. His book written on the basis of these excavations, *Neolithic Cattle Keepers of South India: A Study of the Deccanese Ash Mounds* (1963) offers an explanation of the burning of cow dung of the Deccanese ash mounds by using both ancient literature and recorded ethnographic practices. The way he tries to link the ceremonial burning of cow dung with certain seasonal festivals like *Holi* and *Pongal* was novel in the context of the time. On the whole, Allchin's study of the south Indian Neolithic was a major step forward in the south Indian Neolithic studies after Wheeler's and B. Subbarao's bare excavations at Brahmagiri and Sanganakallu. Much later, he collaborated with the Archaeological Survey of India to excavate Malvan in the coastal mainland Gujarat but after his south Indian work, his major field-interests now shifted to other parts of south Asia: Afghanistan, where this led to the publication of a jointly edited volume on the archaeology of Afghanistan and a research monograph on the pre-Islamic fortress of Shahr-i-Johak with one his students; Sri Lanka, where excavations were initiated at Anuradhapura with another of his students; and Pakistan, where his earlier collaboration with A.H. Dani of Peshawar University was not successful but where under Dani's successors he excavated Tarakai Qila and Lewan in Bannu. A monograph was published on the Bannu work. An important part of his work in Pakistan was the identification of the Gandhara Grave Culture pottery at Taxila, which considerably pushed back the antiquity of this famous site.

Although not a person to question any entrenched hypothesis strongly or pose critical questions regarding the entrenched interest groups of the subject, Allchin wrote clearly and sensibly, often suggesting his familiarity with diverse ethnographic, historical and archaeological aspects of the sub-continent. I have elsewhere commented on *The Birth of Indian Civilization* and *The Rise of Civilization in India and Pakistan*, which he co-authored with his wife. Whereas Sankalia even in his 1974 book *Prehistory and Protohistory of India and Pakistan* adopted a format which was reminiscent of a dictionary, the Allchins adopted a more readable approach. Their *Origins of a Civilization, the Prehistory and Early Archaeology of South Asia* basically summarized their old ideas. Apart from the three volumes of *A Source Book of Indian Archaeology*, which he co-edited with me, he also edited *The Archaeology of Early Historic South Asia*, composing most of the chapters himself.

The reason of Dr. F.R. Allchin's wide acceptance in Indian archaeology circles extends beyond this long series of books and other publications. The Ancient India and Iran Trust, of which he and his wife are co-founders, succeeded in getting the control of a scholarship of Charles Wallace Trust to bring

Indian archaeologists and ancient historians of their choice to Cambridge for 3 to 4 months. This continued for nearly two decades, and there had been long queues of Indians to the Trust for this privilege. When an academic grant is more or less personally controlled by one or two academics—and regretfully this seems to be the dominant custom in some Third World specialities in many Western universities—the importance of those academics in the eyes of the concerned hopefuls goes up manifold, and this is exactly what happened in the case of the Allchins (and a number of other British and European academics that I can think of) in India. The language of the memorial notices published after his death in 2010 in the Indian archaeology journals, *Puratattva* and *Man and Environment*, is a proof of the glowing devotion with which the people he networked with in India are capable of writing about him. For instance, V.N. Misra (2010), a retired Director of the Deccan College, seems to compare him with Mahatma Gandhi:

> When Mahatma Gandhi died in 1948, Albert Einstein said, "generations to come will scarce believe that such a one ever trod the earth in flesh and blood".... Words spoken by Einstein about Mahatma Gandhi can almost equally aptly be applied to Prof. Allchin.

Although in his obituary of Dr. Allchin in *Puratattva*, K. Paddayya, another retired Director of the Deccan College, avoids any comparison with Mahatma Gandhi, the tone of his writing remains equally effusive.

My own assessment is that the academic impact of the Ancient India and Iran Trust, which with its British and American Trustees is something of an Euro-American body, on Indian archaeology has been marginal. The main reasons are highly personalized selections and the fact that most of the selected scholars have had no clear academic focus. In recent years, especially under the guidance of Sir N. Barrington, a former British High Commissioner to Pakistan, the Trust has fruitfully expanded the scope of its activities.

The series of biennial conferences of European archaeologists working in south Asia began in Cambridge at the initiative of the Allchins in 1973. It soon converted itself into another exclusively Euro-American body and has come to include in recent years people who do not have much to do with south Asian archaeology.

I find no reason to include such exclusively Euro-American bodies as parts of the Cambridge academic tradition in ancient Indian history and archaeology, although both of them began in Cambridge and one of them is based there.

Dr. Allchin was succeeded by me (1990-2008), and at this point I have to record my field-research and major publications of this period, as I have done in the context of Kolkata and Delhi and as I have done in the context of the previous ancient Indian history and archaeology UTOs or 'university teaching officers' in Cambridge. Whether I have been allowed to be a part of the Cambridge collegiate set-up or not, and whatever may be my personal opinion of my experience in the Department of Archaeology, my publications as a university lecturer, professor and emeritus professor have to be considered part of the tradition of Cambridge contribution to the study of ancient India by the concerned teachers.

MY PUBLICATIONS, 1990-1995

It is useful to record that my research career before I joined Cambridge embraced the following major topics: (1) *Early Urban Centres in India—An Archaeological Perspective, c.2500 BC-c.300 AD*; (2) *India and West Asia before the Achaemenids*; (3) *The beginning of iron in India*; (4) *History of Indian archaeology from the beginning to 1947*; (5) *Theoretical issues in Indian archaeology*; (6) *Kangra valley survey*; (7) *Survey of the Chhotanagpur plateau and its adjacent areas;* and (8) *Bangladesh survey*. By 1990, books were published only on the topics 2, 4, 5, and 6 but on the rest I could publish till then only individual papers. In its published form, the topic 2 took the form of *The External Trade of the Indus Civilization*. My first academic task in Cambridge was to select a new field-programme and catch up with the publications of what I researched earlier.

I caught up with the publications by 1995. In 1992, I published *The Early Use of Iron in India* and *Ancient Bangladesh, a Study of the Archaeological Sources*. In 1993, my Chhotanagpur volume was published as *Archaeology of Eastern India: Chhotanagpur Plateau and West Bengal*. In 1995 I published the revised version of my Ph.D. thesis under the title *The Archaeology of Ancient Indian Cities*. I have explained the scope of these publications in the previous chapter, i.e., the chapter on Delhi.

SELECTING A FIELD AREA: THE GANGA PLAIN, 1991-2001, 2003-2005

The selection of my field programme from 1991 onwards depended on what I like doing in the field with my time and resources and what I think is significant about it. This is also linked to what I had already done in the field. To reiterate, my independent field-work comprised primarily survey work in three major chunks: the Kangra valley, Chhotanagpur plateau and Bangladesh. I could have extended my Kangra work to other parts of Himachal Pradesh, but somehow that did not appeal to me. The Chhotanagpur work, which led to my appraisal of a large variety of sites and its relationship as a resource area to the eastern section of the Gangetic valley, could certainly be followed up with profit, but that would have needed excavations and multi-disciplinary work. In fact, I would have loved to excavate the upper Palaeolithic clusters of the Damin belt of the Rajmahal hill, but my application for funds for this was rejected.

I found the idea of personally coming to grip with the archaeological geography of the Ganga plain as a whole very exciting. First, despite innumerable piecemeal discoveries both in the recent and earlier periods, there has been no overall personal evaluation of the locations of archaeological sites in this plain since the days of Alexander Cunningham in the late nineteenth century. Secondly, such a personal evaluation would offer insights not merely into the locations and probable functions of the relevant settlements but also provide clues to how these places formed parts of a wide communication network. I thought that if I could have an idea of how the archaeological sites in the whole of the Ganga plain from the Bhagirathi estuary to the Siwaliks lay disposed over this vast landscape and were mutually linked forming parts of an ancient network of communication, I would have a much better perception of the ancient history of this plain and its geographical nuances. I felt that I could pull this off with my scanty resources and whatever little I understood of the history and archaeology of this land. I was fortunate in this case to receive the support of the Society for South Asian Studies. This was before the control of the Society was taken over by all sorts of India experts in Britain. The primary focus of the Society during that period was ancient India and Dr. D.W. MacDowall was one of its major figures. In conjunction with a subsidy given every year by the Cambridge University travelling expense fund, the grant was just about enough to keep myself and one or two persons in the Ganga plain every summer from 1991 to 2001 and from 2003 to 2005. In all, the programme lasted 14 years.

In my first volume on the archaeological geography of the Ganga plain, i.e., *Archaeological Geography of the Ganga Plain:*

The Lower and the Middle Ganga (2001), I dwelt at length on my approach to this survey. On the basis of a long literature survey dealing not merely with the survey work conducted in Indian archaeology since its inception but also with its theoretical milieu of historical geography, archaeology and history, I reached three major points.

> The first point is that the early preoccupation of Indian archaeology with historical-geographical issues is shared by the early stage of archaeological research in such textually rich areas as Greece and Rome and the biblical world of the eastern Mediterranean. From this point of view the publications of Cunningham and Stein conform to an already understood pattern. However, what sets the Indian situation apart is that the beginning made by such early writers was not systematically followed up in the subsequent stages. One can witness the beginning of individual traditions such as systematic settlement surveys, site-catchment analysis and attention to geo-political issues, political geography, routes, etc. but these traditions did not coalesce into an integrated approach to the study of historical geography of the subcontinent. The task of materialisation of the past—the task of relating Indian ancient history to the ground—has thus remained seriously incomplete. ...
>
> The second point is that the aims we have set for ourselves—i.e. the study of the ancient settlements of the Ganga plain with reference to their locations, territoriality or political geography and routes—are in no way outside the scope of academic research in modern archaeology, history and historical geography. ...
>
> On our third focus, i.e. the routes, the literature in the context of Britain, Europe and the Americas is much more voluminous than we think ... As Braudel put it in the context of the Mediterranean ... "The Mediterranean is the sum of its routes, routes along the rivers and routes

along the coasts, an immense network of regular and casual connections, the life-giving bloodstream of the Mediterranean region" (Chakrabarti 2001, pp. 55-56).

In 1991, R.K. Chattopadhyay of Delhi University, who was with me in my Chhotanagpur survey, joined me in my survey of the Maldaha and Dinajpur sections of West Bengal or the Mahananda plains. He helped me also in 1992, 1993 and partly in 1994. The Maldaha-Dinajpur zone, which is a part of the ancient Varendra tract falling in both West Bengal and Bangladesh, had traditional historical linkages with a vast region in many directions: (1) the Tarai area of Jalpaiguri and Cooch Behar; (2) Sikkim and Bhutan which contained mineral sources in their foothills and had some routes to Tibet passing through them; (3) the northern plain of the Brahmaputra and access from it to Myanmar, south China and Tibet; (4) Bangladesh, Arakan and beyond; and (5) the Bhagirathi delta. In a sense, this is Ganga plain's opening towards Tibet, Assam and northern Myanmar and south China and from this point of view, this forms a major geo-political zone. Regarding the administrative capital of the ancient geographical unit of Pundravarddhana, Mahasthangarh, I pointed out that "this was a place that looked towards a vast area of Asia on its north and east: the plateau of Tibet, the fertile plain of the Brahmaputra, the hills and valleys of north Burma extending up to south China, and finally, the Arakan coast and the Irrawaddy valley itself (Chakrabarti 2001, p. 72). It was also well-connected to the Bhagirathi plain to the south by an arterial route network. This route network was clearly described by me in connection with my Chhotanagpur work:

> Apart from the lines of riverine communication furnished mainly by the Bhagirathi system at the southern end of which were Chandraketugarh and other sites further south, there was a major arterial route in West Bengal

> which linked the entire area from the Barind tract in the north in modern Maldaha and West Dinajpur to the Rupnarayan delta and the coastal Midnapur in the south. We feel that the major early historic inland towns and cities of West Bengal were linked in various ways with this aeterial line of communication and its feeders. The Rajmahal zone was very important because it was here that the route from Barind and the route from the middle Ganga valley through ancient 'Anga' or the modern Bhagalpur-Sahebganj area both entered the Bhagirathi plain. The western bank of the Bhagirathi in the district of Murshidabad saw this line moving in two directions. One came up to Katwa, also on the Bhagirathi, turned a little to the interior, crossed the Ajay-Kunur confluence at Mangalkot, and moved towards the modern town of Burdwan. Another line from Murshidabad went towards Birbhum, passing through places like Panchthupi in Murshidabad and eventually came to Mangalkot. From this section onwards there was only one route up to Burdwan. There one crosses the Damodar river and moves on straight to the Garh Mandaran area near Arambagh. The road now goes off to Chandrakona towards the west or southwest. From Chandrakona one travels via Ghatal towards Tamluk whereas another route from the Chandrakona area goes to the Midnapur town area with a view to joining the road to Kalinga via the Midnapur coast ... From the Burdwan area it is also possible to enter Bankura and pass on to the south via such places as Dihar. Pokharna is across the Damodar in the Panagarh section of Burdwan and must have had some links with the route we have mentioned (Chakrabarti 1993, pp. 207-208).

Thus, our selection of the Mahananda plains as a survey area was not a casual decision but based on the understanding of the regional historical and geographical factors. The basic field-notes were taken on the individual sites studied by us, and as small to large collections of early mediaeval sculptures were found associated with them in many cases, we tried to draw up brief catalogues of all the sculptures that we encountered in the field or in miscellaneous collections. A major early mediaeval feature of this area is the presence of very large water tanks such as *Tarpan dighi, Mahipal dighi,* etc. Tarpan Dighi, for instance, is a 30-35 hectare tank associated with a modern village lying on the top of a large mound. The tank once yielded an inscription of the Sena dynasty king Lakshmanasena.

The basic political units, of which Maldaha and Dinajpur were parts, were two *Visayas* or districts of *Kotivarsa* and *Kuddala Khataka,* both parts of a much wider administration division called *Pundravarddhana Bhukti.* Their core areas were identified. There were also problems of historical identifications of some places like Amati, Jagaddala monastery, etc. In the case of Amati, the problem was to determine if this represented the capital city of the Pala king Ramapala in the first half of the twelvth century AD. On the basis of some textual evidence, this identification was satisfactorily acceptable whereas in the case of the Jagaddala monastery mentioned in Sandhyakara Nandi's *Ramacharita,* the place lay near Pakuahat and Bamangola.

In 1992, we shifted our survey area to the western bank of the Bhagirathi or the Mayurakshi-Ajay-Damodar-Rupnarayan plain. In addition to R.K. Chattopadhyay, we had in our team Nayanjot Lahiri of Delhi University, and some members of the West Bengal State government directorate of archaeology (P.K. Mitra, Tapas Bandopadhyay, Dilip Dattagupta and P.N. Malakar) including its chief Gautam Sengupta who offered his unqualified support to us during this work. The major historical linkages of the area are with the Bhagirathi mouth and the eastern bank of this river in West Bengal, part of the course of the Ganga in Bihar, the Mahananda plain, the coastal Orissa and the Gaya-Banaras area, the last linked by a route through Chhotanagpur.

Along with a few early historic urban sites, most of the surveyed sites of this region were found to be black-and-red ware sites. Observations were made on their distribution, size and elements of trade. This was followed by a careful assessment of the location of early historical cities and the issues of political geography. The existence of an early historic political unit was considered probable in the modern Farakka area of Murshidabad. In later time, more important was the political unit of Gauda which in the seventh century had its capital at Karnasuvarna, but in the early historic period, according to our surmise, the capital was Kotasur on the bank of the Mayurakshi near Sainthia in Birbhum. As a political unit, *Radha* had two divisions, *Uttara Radha* and *Dakshina Radha*. According to us, the early historic site of Mangalkot at the confluence of the Ajay and Kunur was the capital of *Uttara Radha* whereas Pokharna on the bank of the Damodar was identified by us as the capital of the southern Radha. Tamluk or Tamralipta was the capital of the political territory of *Suhma*.

In 1993, in the company of R.K. Chattopadhyay, I moved to the Bhagirathi delta and the West Bengal coast line, studying mostly the early historical sites of the region. There were three preliminary issues: the past and the present configurations of the drainage lines, especially of the Ganga/Bhagirathi; the problem of the extent of the estuarine mangrove forests or the Sundarbans south of Kolkata; and finally, the issue of the changing coastline of the Midnapur coast. The changes in the course of the Bhagirathi below Kolkata from the early historic period to the modern times can still be traced more or less clearly. The sites of the early historic and early mediaeval periods are concentrated along the old course. Regarding the extent of the Sundarbans, I cited the opinion of H. Blochmann (cited in Hunter 1875, pp. 380-381) that "the northern boundary of the jungle, has, on the whole, remained stationery since 1582". Regarding the coastline, I argued that it did not undergo any significant change to affect the distribution of archaeological sites. The two major early historic sites of this belt are well known: Chandraketugarh and Tamluk, one in the Bidyadhari river system east and northeast of Kolkata and the other in the Rupnarayan delta southwest of Kolkata. I tried to assess the archaeological evidence on both these sites and took into consideration the chain of related sites The identifications of *Vanga*, *Suhma* and *Dantabhukti*, the three concerned ancient geographic units, were important. The western boundary of *Vanga* was the old course of the *Bhagirathi* whereas its eastern boundary was possibly the Vikrampur area of Bangladesh. *Suhma* lay to the west of *Vanga* and is a large part of the modern Midnapur district lying to the west of the Bhagirathi with Tamluk or Tamralipta as its principal city. On the basis of the information supplied by W.W. Hunter (1876, pp. 20-21), we argued that the administrative division of Hijli in the early British records might denote the ancient Suhma. The Hijli tract, about 2844 sq km in area, was important both for paddy and salt manufacture and was transferred from Orissa to Bengal in the seventeenth century during the reign of Shahjahan. We argued that *Suhma* or the ancient Hijli tract was possibly administered from the city of Tosali which we now identify with the mound of Radhanagar in the Jajpur area of Orissa. The principal city of *Vanga* was Chandraketugarh but its ancient name is not known. The antiquity of the term *Dantabhukti* is possibly not earlier than the 11th/12th century AD but its identification with Danton on the Midnapur-Orissa border is acceptable. In my 2001 publication (Chakrabarti 2001, 154), I mistakenly identified the city of Dantapura of the Buddhist sources with Radhanagar in the Jajpur area.

Dantapura, the capital of Kalinga, has to be placed in the Vamsadhara delta near Srikakulam.

In 1994 I sought the collaboration of the Bihar government's directorate of archaeology, which was represented in the field with me by Ajit Prasad, S.K. Jha, Kumar Anand and A.C. Verma. All of them were very co-operative and nice, and I owe a special thanks to Mr. Prasad for his background support throughout. Dr. P.C. Prasad, Director of Bihar State Archaeology was also a source of great support. We focussed on studying the distribution of sites in south Bihar between Rajmahal and the Karmanasa river. This belt basically conformed to the ancient geographical units of *Anga* and *Magadha*. Champa was the capital of *Anga* or the Bhagalpur-Munger area. Regarding Champa, our observation was the following:

> The image of an artificially raised citadel which was protected both by a revetment wall and a ditch, and overlooked a river-bank area of occupation meant for the ordinary people, lends a forbiddingly stern grandeur to this ancient city which certainly dominated the river-traffic to the east at this point, and it would not have been at all unusual if an octroi on this traffic was levied here (Chakrabarti 2001, p. 167).

Champa is a suburb of modern Bhagalpur, and in the Bhagalpur museum there is a red sandstone female image of the early centuries AD from the Kheri hill, which lies near Shahkund. Not far from this sector is the Mandar hill, which is famous for its tank-dedicatory inscription of the queen of the late Gupta king Adityasena of the 7th century AD. The chronological range of the variety of rock-cut sculptures that one observes on the Jahangira hill at Sultanganj is c.500-1200 AD. Beyond Munger, the main ancient settlement area comprises Uren and Lakhisarai, both of which possess sculptures of the early mediaeval period. The Lakhisarai area has some *Yakshini* figures of the early centuries AD at Nongarh.

Moving to the Patna-Ara belt, one faces the ruins of ancient Pataliputra at the site of modern 'Patna City', but there are remains of the early historic period at Maner, Masarh, Buxar and Chausa. The Ara belt has the temple-sites of Deo Markandeya and Deo Baranarak, both famous for their images of the sun deity. The Mundesvari temple, roughly of the 7th century AD and the city-site of Nindaur are the prominent sites of the Kaimur area. There are many sites with Buddhist and other images in the Gaya, Bodhgaya and the neighbouring areas. In the Nawadah sector, the large and fortified early historic city site of Devangarh lies in an U-shaped valley on the northern side of a range which separates it from Hazaribagh. There is also no lack of sites in the Rajgir-Nalanda-Bihar Sharif–Pavapuri sector but they are mostly monastic and temple-sites including many sculptural relics. I dispute the idea of two Rajagrihas, Old and New. I believe that the capital of Rajagriha was located at the site of the so-called New Rajagriha whereas the so-called Old Rajagriha, which lies in the hill-girt portion, could denote the area with religious structures. There could be a third Rajagriha at the Giriak hill and that could possibly serve the function of a trade centre. In my Chhotanagpur volume, I argued that the raw materials of the Chhotanagpur plateau were mediated through Rajgir which was within easy reach of Devangarh. The ancient Magadha comprised a number of distinct geographical terrains: the Ara or the southern Son plains including the Buxar-Chausa stretch, the Kaimur plateau in the southwest, and towards the east, Gaya-Bodh Gaya, the Rajgir hills, the Nawadah plateau and the rich agricultural plain between the Rajgir hills and the Ganga.

Among the major lines of movement in south Bihar, one is the alignment of the Ganga from Chausa to Rajmahal and the other is the one which enters Bihar crossing the Karmanasa and crosses Gaya-Bodh Gaya to go east and eventually reach Anga. There are many feeder routes such as the route between Rajgir and Patna.

North Bihar, which I surveyed in 1995 in collaboration with the archaeologists of Bihar government, is noted for its ancient geographical units of *Videha*, *Mithila*, *Tirabhukti* and *Vajji*. These are mostly overlapping territories, which is a sensible hypothesis considering the undifferentiated terrain of north Bihar. As I wrote,

> ....the archaeological core of north Bihar seems to lie in its central north-south segment, roughly between the Sitamarhi/Vaisali-Ganga/Gandak line on the west and the Saharsa-Khagaria line on the east.

The major early historic fortified sites such as Vaisali, Katragarh, Balirajgarh, Kopagarh, Mangalagarh (in Samastipur) and Naulagarh and Jai Mangalagarh (in Begusarai) belong to this belt. Manjhi on the northern bank of the Ghaghra belongs to the Champaran-Siwan-Gopalganj-Chhapra zone, which may not be the part of the Videha belt. The Saharsa-Madhepura-Khagaria-Purnea-Katihar belt in the east has early historic material but there is no conclusive proof of an early historic city-site. Sikligarh outside Banmankhi in Purnea may be such a site but its character is still uncertain.

The alignment of some routes is clear-cut in north Bihar. As I pointed out earlier,

> First, having crossed over to the Konhara Ghat–Ram Chowra section on the Gandak, one could move up to Vaisali, Kesariya, Lauriya Areraj and Lauriya Nandangarh, and then travel in two directions: either to Padrauna-Kusinara via the Jatahi crossing over the Gandak or towards Rampurwa on the way to the Nepalese terai. ... In the Sitamarhi-Madhubani sector, of course, the land towards Nepal is open and can easily be crossed at a

> number of points, one of which may be Sursand. To the east, the modern Saharsa-Purnea line of movement ... seems to be rooted in antiquity... The course of the Ganga obviously provided an easy line of lateral movement in this sector ... (Chakrabarti 2001, p. 206).

In 1996, in my survey of the trans-Sarayu plain between the western border of north Bihar and the Ghaghra/Sarayu, which separates this plain from Oudh, I was joined by R.N. Singh of Banaras Hindu University. He was with me every season till the completion of my Ganga plain survey in 2005. My long collaboration with Banaras Hindu University owes its impetus to the academic warmth and interest of Professor Purushottam Singh to whom I have an immense sense of gratitude. Another person who has been kindness incarnate in later years in Banaras is Professor Parasnath Singh.

Our initial problem in 1996 was to determine if modern Padrauna could be identified with Pawa where the Buddha stopped in his last journey to Kusinara. The route from Vaisali in north Bihar would have taken Buddha past Kesariya to the Pipra Ghat crossing of the Gandak and then to the Jharmatiya-Usmanpur sector of the eastern section of the Sarayu plain. Kusinagar would have come next and we felt that there was a greater chance of Pawa falling in the Jharmatiya-Usmanpur sector than at Padrauna, which was considerably out of the way. The ancient territorial units of the Sarayupar or trans-Sarayu plain included primarily Kosala, Malla, Sakya and Koliya. The dominant unit was Kosala, the position of whose capital Sravasti "suggests that it was located to control not merely the territory up to the Gomati beyond the Ghaghra but also the Siwalik terrain and the sweep of the Sarayupar plain through modern Basti and Gorakhpur up to its borders with the ancient kingdom of Kasi" (Chakrabarti 2001, 227). From Sravasti in the west to Naugarh-Piprahwa in the east, there is a clear corridor of movement and "it is possible that the location of Sravasti has also something to do with this Kapilavastu route" (*ibid.*, p. 227). The territorial units of the Mallas, Sakyas and Koliyas lay in the eastern part of this corridor. According to my estimate, the Malla territory may fall close to the Gandak in the Jharmatiya-Usmanpur area before Kusinara whereas the Sakyas and the Koliyas lay in the terai area up to the Nepal Siwaliks and included the sites of Piprahwa-Ganwaria, Tilaura Kot, Banarasi Kalan, Sonpipri, Sirsiadih, etc. In addition to Sravasti, the major urban centre, there were sub-centres like Tilaura Kot, Sohgaura and Chardah.

The Pataliputra-Lumbini route passed through the Sarayupar plain. While travelling from Pataliputra, the route crossed the Ganga for Ballia at Buxar, and passing through a chain of sites like Pukka Kot in Ballia, reached Khairadih where the Sarayu or Ghaghra was crossed for Bhagalpur. I inferred that the so-called *Bhim-ka-Chhari* or 'Bhim's pillar' at Bhagalpur was an Asokan pillar, although uninscribed. From Bhagalpur the route followed the northern bank of the Ghaghra to reach Kopia from where the route to Mahadeva and Bansi and from there to Piprahwa and Lumbini is straight and easy. Among the other distinctive features of the Sarayupar plain, we noticed the frequency of large marshy, lake-like depressions locally known as *Tals* and inferred that they might contain in their general area Mesolithic habitations (Chakrabarti 2001, p. 228). In view of the subsequently discovered evidence of early rice cultivation at Lohuradeva, this observation was important.

The focus of attention in 1997 was the Ballia-Banaras sector. In the Ballia area, Pukka Kot, Tika Deori, Lakhnesar Dih and Khairadi which, as we have noted, fall on the Pataliputra-Lumbini alignment and are major sites. Nahush-ka-tila behind modern Ghosi market is a fortified early historic centre in the Azamgarh sector whereas in Ghazipur, Masaon Dih is the major centre of this period, although we could not ascertain whether it was fortified or not. The Gupta period temple-site of Bhitari is in this area. Apart from Rajghat/ Banaras, Bairant in the Chandauli section seems to be a major early historic site of the Banaras region and the same can be said about Agiabir on the bank of the Ganga between Banaras and Mirzapur. On the other bank of the Ganga, the Ahraura-Robertsganj-Mirzapur sector has an importance of its own mainly because this region straddles the routes which go out of Banaras for central India and the Deccan. Ahraura has a minor rock-edict of Asoka and Belkhara near it has possibly an Asokan pillar (uninscribed). There are ancient remains on the Panchrukhi hill in the outskirts of Robertsganj. The Robertsganj plateau or the Sonbhadra plateau is also full of black-and-red ware sites.

Apart from its archaeological sites, the Banaras sector is important from the point of view of some major routes, notably as the receiving point of the routes from the east which came from places like Azamgarh and Jaunpur and as the starting point of the routes for Sasaram, Ahraura and Mirzapur. The Sasaram-Ahraura-Mirzapur routes are parts of main pan-Indian routes. For Sasaram, the route went past Bhuili, Chakia, Mundesvari, Nindaur, etc., and this eventually led to both Rajagriha and Pataliputra. Through Ahraura, for which the route went past Bhuili, the route climbed the Vindhyan plateau at Sukrit and went to the old Son crossing near modern Chopan with Surguja in mind. From Surguja, the modern Chhattisgarh area was accessible in the direction of both Andhra coast and Maharashtra. The Mirzapur route also took one in the direction of central India and the Deccan via Rewa. At Mirzapur, this route was joined by the route which came from Sravasti via Jaunpur and the combined route climbed the Vindhyan scarp near Lalganj-Halia. From the point of view of pan-Indian routes, Banaras was a major nodal point and played an important role in keeping open the links with the Sasaram sector in the east and central India and the Deccan in the west.

The 1998 season was spent to study the Jaunpur, Sultanpur, Faizabad, Pratapgarh and Allahabad areas. Rakesh Tewari, Director of the Department of Archaeology, Government of Uttar Pradesh, joined me and R.N. Singh this season. The collaboration with the U.P. Government's Department of Archaeology continued from this year to the end of our Ganga plain survey in 2005. A better idea was obtained of the routes towards the Deccan this season, especially from the Allahabad area. In the Jaunpur sector, a notable find was that of Zafarabad or Manhej, a fortified early historic site lying at the junction of Banaras-Jaunpur and Mirzapur-Jaunpur alignments. In the Faizabad sector, we noticed the importance of Surhurpur in the Jaunpur-Ayodhya alignment. From Akbarpur, which is located on this alignment, a route leads to Tanda where the Ghaghra is crossed for Basti from where Lumbini, among other places, is accessible. The Sultanpur sector lies on the traditional route from Ayodhya to Sringaverapura and Prayag/Allahabad, and the sites we considered important in this sector—Garha, Isauli, Narayani and Dakhinwara—seem to be linked to this route. Isauli and Gokula are fortified whereas the others, although unfortified, are major sites. In the Banaras-Allahabad sector, there is a chain of sites along the alignment of the modern Grand Trunk road. Although there are ancient localities within the modern city limits of Allahabad, there was no ancient city here. We felt that Jhusi on the opposite side of the Ganga was the site of the ancient Prayag. We further felt that the Asokan pillar of Allahabad was *in situ* and not shifted to its present place from Kausambi. Among the major early historical sites of the

Pratapgarh area, Chauharjan was possibly the most important because of its citadel-like construction overlooking a bend of the Sai river. A Mathura-type sculpture was noticed at Bihar.

The route which came out of Allahabad for Rewa, central India and the Deccan, went past the fortified early historic city Bhita to reach Shankargarh-Mau where it was joined by a route coming out of Kausambi across the Yamuna. Shankargarh-Mau lie a little downstream of Kausambi and marked probably the site of the major ferry point of the ancient Kausambi. We encountered the site of Balakmau, which is located on a route which comes from Kausambi to reach the Pratapgarh area and crosses the Ganga at Kara which is a major site on the Ganga in this sector. The modern Allahabad-Fatehpur axis was also rooted in antiquity. Mahagaon or Mahagrama, the site of a well-preserved high and nicely rounded mound on this route, is an ancient marker of this route. The route to the Deccan from Allahabad and Kausambi went from Sharnkargarh-Mau to Rewa, climbing the Vindhyan scarp at Sohagi Ghat and/or Baldaha Ghat or Ala Ghat to reach Teonthar on the way to Rewa. Sohagi Ghat marked the site of the ancient stupa of Deor Kothar. Before excavations were undertaken at the site by P.K. Mishra of the Archaeological Survey of India, we inferred that the antiquity of this stupa should be Asokan because there was a complex of Satdhara-type stupas at the site, along with the presence of a small and simple railing enclosure in the form of *Suchis* or coping stones. Mishra's excavations corroborated this inference.

In 1999, we explored the sites between Pratapgarh and Sitapur, dividing them into the Allahabad-Rae Bareli-Pratapgarh-Fatehpur and Lucknow-Bara Banki-Unnao-Kanpur-Sitapur sectors. We classified the mounds of Paithan, Mohan, Galatha and Parsarwa as mounds of local significance. The mounds of Kotra, Manikpur, Dalmau, Jajmau and Dhruva

Tila on the Ganga and Reh and Musanagar on the Yamuna were classified as mounds of more than local significance. Manikpur was possibly the most important of the river ports on the Ganga in this area. Reh and Musanagar on the Yamuna were both important as river ports. Jajmau marks a major crossing point of the Ganga in the Unnao sector, taking one almost straight to the crossing of the Yamuna at Musanagar (beyond Ghatampur) which in turn led to central India. Jajmau stands on an arterial route linking a part of the Oudh plain and lower Doab to central India and the Deccan and is thus a major site of the Ganga plain. Musanagar marks the starting point of a route from the Ganga plain to central India and the Deccan through the Betwa valley. The modern city of Lucknow contains at least two ancient localities (Lakshman Tila and Qila Faridnagar), and among the important sites of the region, mention may be made of Sanchankot, Nimsar, Manoadih and Newal.

In 2000, we focussed on the sites between Kanauj in the central Doab and Kashipur at the foot of the Nainital Siwaliks, studying them in three sectors: Hardoi-Kanauj, Shajahanpur-Bareilly, and Kashipur-Pilbhit-Sitapur. This region witnessed the development of the major early historic cities of Kanauj, Ahichchhatra and Kashipur. Kanauj possibly stood near the confluence of the Kali with the Ganga and we agreed with E.R. Neave's observation in 1911 that the modern town of Kanauj was only a 'mere fraction of the ancient city'. Regarding the significance of Ahichchhatra and the miscellaneous early historic and later sites of the Pilibhit-Kheri area, we pointed out that this area lay on a route coming from the Tanakpur area of Nepal and that trade with the hills and Nepal had played a significant role in the life of the people of this area. I further argued that this argument had a major implication for our understanding of Ahichchhatra as a site.

> This was the most important site in this corner of Uttar Pradesh which has not merely a rich agricultural hinterland but also close links with the U.P. hills and Nepal. Trade coming from these sides had its most important mart at Ahichchhatra. To an extent, modern Bareilly plays this role.... Ahichchhatra may be considered its much larger and more significant ancient counterpart.

Regarding Kashipur we inferred that it was the administrative centre of a kingdom/province, which included a part of the U.P. hills from Kotdwar to Almora and Nainital. It was likely to be the capital of the post-Mauryan *Kuninda janapada* whose coins have been reported from precisely this area of the U.P. hills.

Among the other major sites, one notes Lakhmapur in the Hardoi-Kanauj area, which is possibly a large and undisturbed monastic site at a bend of the Garra river, a tributary of the Ramganga. This was possibly closely related to Kanauj by a river network. Sahabad in the same sector is a large early historic mound containing possibly a 300-m square citadel enclosed by a moat. Ahichchhatra possesses around it a number of stupa sites, some of which are likely to be early. Many sites of this region have been destroyed by agricultural operations. For instance, Hargaon in Sitapur, an apparently early site reported by A. Fuhrer, no longer exists on the ground. The same may be said about many sites in the Pilibhit-Kheri and Ahichchhatra areas.

The sites in the vicinity of Kashipur have also been largely destroyed.

In 2001, our focus was on the Farrukhabad-Etah-Budaun-Mainpuri-Etawah region of Uttar Pradesh. The major sites of the Farrukhabad sector are Kampil and Sankisa. Although Kampil is about a 30-acre-site without any evidence of fortification, there is an apparently extensive and brick-walled site with evidence of occupation between c.200 BC and early centuries AD at the neighbouring site of *Raja Drupad ka Kila*. On the basis of the location of the site of Patiali, we inferred that there was an old route between Kampil and the modern Etah area.

> On the whole our impression is that Kampil marks an important archaeological area in the sense that there is apparently a cluster of ancient sites in and around the place, although we would not press any claim for its significance as 'a Mahabharata city'.

On Sankisa, a fortified site with a somewhat circular periphery of more than 5 km based on the Kali Nadi, our observation is the following. It was the most important administrative centre of the central Doab in the second half of the first millennium BC and later. In terms of routes, it was advantageously located. The villagers point out a ferry crossing of the Kali Nadi, beyond which the road leads to Mainpuri and from there to Agra and Mathura. It is also easy to move in the opposite direction towards Kanauj and beyond. Sankisa also offers an easy access through Etawah, where Chakranagar is located, to the trans-Chambal region of central India. The importance of Sankisa seems to be related to its strategic location at this intersection of routes. In Etah, Atranjikhera is the most well-known site lying on a straight route between Ahichchhatra and Mathura. The excavator's identification of Atranjikhera with the site of *Veranja* of the Buddhist sources did not appear to us to be satisfactory. It was further noted that from Etah there was an approach marked by some high mounds (cf. Awagarh, Jalesar) towards Mathura. The importance of Ahichchhatra-Mathura alignment via Atranjikhera becomes clear when we think that it is marked by such major sites as Awagarh and Jalesar. The Mainpuri sector has a number of very imposing sites (cf. Rizor Khas,

Param, Sakit, all 80-100 acre-mounds with about 20 m height). They stand by the side of the Etah-Sikohabad alignment and thus on the main Etawah-Mathura route.

A number of small settlements located on the banks of the marshy depressions, called *Tals*, and small rivers characterise the Budaun sector. A few larger settlements such as Wazirganj Fair Ground, Bisauli and Ujhani are, however, present in the area. Wazirganj seems to mark the site of a large religious establishment. Bisauli marks the approach to Ahichchhatra from the Budaun side and has possibly a small Kushan period fortified complex to guard the Ahichchhatra segment of the Mathura-Ahichhatra route. Ujhani was the first major settlement on the eastern bank of the Ganga after it was crossed at Soron.

In the Etawah sector, the most important early historic city-site is Chakranagar located in the Yamuna ravines and offering access from the Etawah side both to the Gwalior and Gujarra segments of Madhya Pradesh. The most imposing mound of the Etawah sector is Kudarkot (c.18 m high, 80-85 acres in extent and with extensive structural remains) but many of its villages are located on high mounds, which look like hills from a distance.

In 2002, I could not be in the field in the Ganga plain. I was back in 2003, studying the sites in the Agra-Mathura-Aligarh-Bulandshahr sector. This sector offers easy access to Bhind-Morena and Gwalior of Madhya Pradesh, and through them, to Malwa and Rajasthan. Mathura, the centre of Krishna legend, is not merely connected with Rajasthan but also with the Gangetic areas to the east. Bulandshahr denotes an area with its own network of links with the uppermost part of the Doab.

The Agra sector does not have any ancient city except Bateshwar, which lies at the threshold of Bhind-Morena and Gwalior and has traditional links with Shikohabad, a place on the general west-east alignment of the Gangetic valley. Till the early twentieth century, the Bateshwar area's chief export trade was with Rajasthan and central India. We took due notes of all the alignments of communications in the Mathura sector: (1) Mathura to Vrindavan along the Yamuna and from Vrindavan to Raya across the Yamuna; (2) Mathura to Chatha and Delhi; (3) Mathura to Sonkh and perhaps to Govardhan; (4) Mathura to Govardhan via Aring and Anyor; (5) Mathura to Bharatpur; and finally, (6) from Mathura to Parkham and beyond. The last three alignments are towards Deeg and Bharatpur, and there is no doubt that in the maintenance of links between the Ganga-Yamuna plain and eastern Rajasthan, the Mathura district played an important role. In the Aligarh sector, Sankara on the Ganga was a major early historic site and on one of the routes from Mathura to Ahichchhatra, the Ganga was crossed here from the Mathura side. In Bulandshahr, the major site of Ahar was a major crossing point of the Ganga in the direction of the *terai* region of U.P. and beyond. Another impressive site is Indor, which was no doubt a major regional centre in the fertile landscape of Bulandshahr.

In 2004, the focus was on the Meerut-Moradabad-Bijnor section of western Uttar Pradesh. The highlight of this study was the extensive distribution of sites of the Harappan tradition in this region. The traditions of incised wavy lines and black-painted red ware go back to Early Harappan Kalibangan, i.e. the general Early Harappan tradition of Rajasthan, Panjab and Haryana. This does not mean that the tradition that we have observed at various sites of the Ghaziabad-Meerat-Moradabad-Bijnor area has to be given the same chronological status as the Early Harappan sites of Rajasthan, Panjab and Haryana, but this does represent in a general fashion the manifestation of an Early Harappan tradition in western Uttar Pradesh. This tradition forms the base of the Harappan tradition of this region. In the light of this general premise of ours, there is no reason to suggest neat divisions between, or successions from, Early to Late Harappan here. The Ochre-Coloured Pottery tradition was no doubt linked to the Harappan tradition, but one cannot yet put it in any firm 'early/mature/late' Harappan bracket.

A few massive sites occur in this region along the eastern bank of the Yamuna: Loni, Mandaula I, Katha, Kurdi and Isopur. They possibly mark the traditional crossing points of the Yamuna in this sector. The traditional importance of the Kashipur area in providing access to the hills is also suggested by the existence of sites with Painted Grey Ware here. Another traditional entrance to the hills, the Kotdwar-Pauri area, has the NBP-associated site of Moradhwaj near Najibabad.

In 2005, we concentrated on the study of sites in the Saharanpur-Muzaffarnagar-Haridwar area where we found no reason to change our opinion arrived at in the previous season that Harappan sites of western Uttar Pradesh cannot be pigeonholed into 'early', 'mature' and 'late' as many scholars have previously done. We also reviewed the archaeological evidence from the major points of access to the U.P. Himalayas (now Uttarakhand) from the plains and concluded that this part of the Himalayas was effectively opened up from the plain in the second half of the second millennium BC. We also argued that there was a valid ground to think that the famous pilgrim spots of Yamunotri, Kedarnath and Badrinath had acquired their holy status by c.1000 BC, i.e., by the time of the Painted Grey Ware.

What I have offered above is only a very brief and disjointed summary of what we considered to be some implications of the general distribution of sites throughout the Ganga plain from the Bhagirathi estuary to the hills of Uttarakhand.

MY PUBLICATIONS, 1996-2003

The Ganga plain work was complete in 2005 and the first volume of its report in 2001. However, between 1999 and 2002, I pursued another field-programme along with the Ganga work. It was the work on the archaeology of the routes which linked the Ganga plain with the Deccan. The book on this work was not published till 2005. So, here I have put my publications between 1996 and 2003 together. The Deccan routes book was my next major publication.

Although my publication on the archaeology of Hinduism in 2001 (Chakrabarti 2001) was only in the form of a paper and not that of a book, as all other relevant publications are in the present context, it seems to be the first attempt to analyse a cogent body of archaeological data to lead to an outline of the basic archaeological history of Hinduism. The title of this paper lent its name to the theme of a *World Archaeology* (vol. 36, no.3) issue in 2004.

In 1992-93, Nayanjot Lahiri was in Cambridge as a Commonwealth Fellow, and we decided to publish a study of the early use of copper and its alloys in ancient India. The book was published, under the joint authorship of myself and Professor Lahiri, as *Copper and Its Alloys in Ancient India* in 1996 and basically synthesised the relevant geological, archaeological, ethnographic and literary data. In retrospect, our survey of the geological evidence of the distribution of copper, tin and lead ores was thorough, and the only section which needs major incorporation of data in this context is that on tin which has since then been known to contain a major deposit around Tosham in Haryana, a major Harappan belt in its own right. There was no problem about archaeological, literary and ethnographic documentation. One of the interesting archaeological points to emerge was the link between the upper Gangetic valley 'copper hoards' and the

Harappan tradition. Further, attention was drawn to how antennae-hilted swords, a typical type of such 'hoards', was distributed along certain well-defined routes to as far south as almost the tip of the southern peninsula and as far west as Gujarat. Among other things, it was demonstrated that the general preference for a pure copper tradition was not so much due to the absence of technical know-how to use alloys as to a marked preference for ritualistically pure, unalloyed copper vessels.

Socio-politics of the past has been an integral part of archaeological literature since the first World Archaeological Congress in 1986. Further, a study of Orientalism by Edward Said had been available since 1979. I studied the issue with reference to Indology and showed that the Indian studies in the West were not merely deeply conditioned by Orientalism, one of whose basic principles was racism, but also this is something which has continued almost in an undiluted form in the modern context. The book was published in 1997 under the title of *Colonial Indology: Socio-Poiltics of the Ancient Indian Past*, thus initiating an academic study of socio-politics in ancient Indian studies.

The Centre for Archaeological Studies and Training, Eastern India, which is financed by the Government of West Bengal, asked me to deliver a number of lectures on east Indian archaeology. The lectures were published in 1998 under the title of *Issues in East Indian Archaeology*. In the same year, I published a book in Bengali, *Bharatvarsher Pragitihas* ('Prehistory of Bharatavarsha'), as a volume in a series of historical books from Kolkata.

In 1999, I published a major synthesis of India's archaeological history from the beginning of the Stone Age to the early historic foundations. Its focus was entirely on archaeological data and ignored all references to migrations, etc. unless this was clearly borne out by archaeology.

In 2001, the first volume of the results of my Ganga plain survey was published as *Archaeological Geography of the Ganga Plain: The Lower and the Middle Ganga*, with a long chapter on the theoretical basis of this work in the context of historical geography and archaeology.

One of the two books I published in 2003 was *Archaeology in the Third World: A History of Indian Archaeology since 1947*. Apart from tracing India's post-Independence archaeological development and the problems of heritage management and conservation including those related to political unrest, conflict of identities, communalism, etc., this book further argued that the Third World archaeology has a number of common denominators and that the history of archaeology in post-Independence India may be an example of many of these denominators. In the same year, I published *The Archaeology of European Expansion: Gujarat, c.16th-c.18th Centuries* on the basis of the brief and preliminary fieldwork I undertook jointly with Chris Scarre and Judith Scarre of Cambridge in Surat and elsewhere in Gujarat towards the end of 2000. This book discussed the historical context of Gujarat, especially Surat, during this period and argued how India could provide a fruitful area of investigation in European-contact situation in archaeology. Much of this historical context was based on the accounts of the European travellers to Mughal India and their descriptions and identifications of Surat and its buildings, although there are also references to places such as Diu, Daman, Cambay, etc. in their writings. We tried to pursue this problem but a bureaucrat from Gujarat wanted it to develop in his own way, and the whole thing got bogged down in a bureaucratic quagmire. Besides, our attempts to get a major research grant were not successful.

FIELD-WORK OUTSIDE THE GANGA PLAIN, 1999-2008

THE ROUTES FROM THE GANGA PLAIN TO THE DECCAN, 1999-2002

Considering that the routes which linked the Deccan, i.e., Andhra and Maharashtra, with the Ganga plain are among the arterial routes of ancient India, I decided to undertake field-work to understand the configuration of the relevant routes. It emerged that the route network had the following basic nodes.

The Rajagriha, Pataliputra and Varanasi Nodes

In the east, the Rajagriha-Pataliputra segment was the terminal point of this route network. The first target here was to reach the Kaimurs or the eastern Vindhyas beyond Sasaram and Bhabua. From Rajagriha one can approach Sasaram and Bhabua through Kurkihar on the Hisua-Gaya road or through the Barabar hills. The route to Sasaram-Bhabua from Pataliputra followed the Son valley. Sasaram possesses an Asokan MRE and Bhabua a hoard of punch-marked coins. The route from Bhabua to Chakia passed through the Kaimur hills, which have in this section the early historic city-site of Nindaur and the newly discovered MRE site of Basaha. The Chakia area can also be reached from Sasaram by following the course of the Son through Rohtasgarh. Further, there was possibly a difficult but negotiable path through the hills straight to the Vijayagarh fort area in the Sonbhadra plateau in order to reach the Agori crossing of the Son.

Between Bhabua and Chakia, the Karamnasa was crossed at Mongraur, and beyond it lies Latif Shah, from where there is a route to the upper stretch of the Karamnasa in the Sonbhadra plateau. After Chakia is reached, there is a route from Chakia to Benares via Sherawan and Bhuili. Ahraura is the main point after Chakia. The Bhuili-Benares route joins the Ahraura-Benares road at Bhuili, from where the road crosses the Ganga at Ramnagar for Benares. From Ahraura, which has a MRE on the road coming from Benares, one route climbs the Vindhyan scarp at Likhania and goes in the direction of the Pachmari hill at Robertsganj to reach the Agori crossing of the Son. The road coming from Chakia to Ahraura goes straight to Mirzapur where it is joined by a route coming from Benares along the alignment of the modern Grand Trunk Road on the east bank of the Ganga and by another route which comes all the way from Sravasti and beyond by Jaunpur. The Ahraura-Mirzapur road passes by Chunar, from the vicinity of which, there are trails to Shilpi Ghat where, like the Agori crossing, the Son is crossed.

On the other bank of the Son, the aim was to reach the Sarguja plain, either along the Rihand valley which leads straight to the heart of the Sarguja plain or by the 8th-century Brahmanical caves of Mara, from where there is a road to the Bisrampur segment of the Sarguja plain through an area which is now deeply forested and covered by a wild life sanctuary. In the Sarguja plain, the fixed point was the Ramgarh hill, famous for its second-third century BC inscription of Sutanuka. The Chhattisgarh plain is cut off at this point by a high range, and this range was crossed by following the Hasdo river till the modern Bilaspur area was reached. The Bilaspur area has a number of early historic finds in its vicinity, suggesting movements of early historic people through it. The most important site of this area is Malhar, a massive fortified early historic city site which certainly was the centre of the South Kosala janapada. From Malhar, one had to cross the Mahanadi, which could be done at its traditional crossing point at Seorinarayan. This crossing led to the modern Raipur segment of Chhattisgarh, which like its Bilaspur segment, has a number of early historic finds. The temple and monastery site of Sirpur, which came into primary focus in c.8th century AD, lies not far from Raipur.

From the Raipur area, the Sambalpur-Bolangir-Kalahandi zone of Orissa and the Orissan coast including Kalinga of the Orissa-Andhra borderland can be easily approached. For Kalinga, there is also a straight route via Jaypore and Kalahandi to the area of modern Vizianagram of Andhra, from where one has to move east to reach the ancient Dantapuranagara (modern Dantavaktrunikota in the Srikakulam district), the capital of Kalinga. Incidentally, if the Mauryan army had followed the route which was followed much later by the Gupta army, also arriving from Pataliputra, the battle for Kalinga was likely to have taken place between modern Vizianagram and Dantavaktrunikota. There is, in fact, a place called Ranasthalam between these two points. Just as the battles for Delhi used to be fought at Panipat, some miles ahead of Delhi on the Lahore-Delhi road, the battle for the capital city of Kalinga was likely to have been fought at Ranasthalam, as the Mauryan army marching from the Raipur area reached the Andhra coast near Vizianagram and turned towards the capital of Kalinga in Srikakulam. The Ranasthalam section would have lain on the Mauryan army's approach road to Dantavruktrunikota, the capital of Kalinga.

However, the route coming through the Sarguja plain and Chhattisgarh need not have turned towards Orissa and Andhra from the Raipur area. It could continue through the area of modern Durg to the Bhandara and Nagpur segment of Vidarbha. There are early historic finds in this zone but, more importantly, as we shall see later, a major route coming through the Balaghat gap north of Bhandara, moved downward to the Wainganga valley. The major Wainganga crossing was at Pauni, which was a fortified early historic city-site with a stupa of the period in its outskirts. The interesting point about the Pauni stupa is that it had four phases, the last of which belonged to the Sunga period or the second century BC. There can be no doubt that the first phase of this stupa was well before the Asokan period. During this phase, the stupa used mud-bricks/mud and had a diameter of 38.2 m. No circumambulatory path was traced in this phase, which is also associated with the NBP. This phase of the Pauni stupa is reminiscent of the first phase of the Amaravati stupa, which was made of mud and associated with the NBP. In its core area in the central Ganga plain, the date of the NBP is now pushed back to c.800 BC, and considering the detailed network of routes that linked the Gangetic plain with the Deccan there is no reason why the NBP could not have spread along this route network quite early in the history of its existence. In fact, there is now no reason to date the NBP found in central India, the Deccan and even south India later than its date in the Ganga plain. The fact that the first phase of the stupas of Amaravati and Pauni was found associated with the NBP can only mean that these stupas were built soon after the death of the Buddha in the 5th century BC. On the whole, there is substantial reason to put the Amaravati and Pauni stupas on the same chronological footing as the excavated first stupas at Kapilavastu, Vaisali and Rajagriha. Interestingly, the first phase of the fortifications at the city-site of Pauni is pre-NBP and should thus figure somewhat securely in the context of the 8th to the 6th centuries BC. The excavators' date for it is 6th-4th centuries BC, a date with which it is possible to disagree. Interestingly, the date of the earliest rampart with moat at Adam, the second major city-site of the area, is also pre-NBP, and may belong to the 8th-6th centuries BC bracket.

The basic importance of the Pauni-Adam area is the route that goes to the Chandrapura segment of Vidarbha and through it, to the Karimnagar section of Andhra. Sites like

Kotilingala and Dhulikottah lie in this belt and through it passes the route to the coastal Andhra. The road coming from Chhattisgarh continues to move towards the west and passes through Bhokardan and Ajanta till it reaches Paithan on the Godavari.

The Mirzapur, Prayag and Kausambi Nodes

From each of these three places, the road first led to Rewa. Mirzapur received the routes coming from Benares and Sravasti, and from Mirzapur one could proceed to Rewa via Hanumana near which the Vindhyan scarp was climbed at Manigarha. For Prayag and Kausambi, Shankargarh on the west bank of the Yamuna was the major starting point for the journey to Rewa. Shankargarh lies on the opposite bank of the Yamuna from Mau, which is a little downstream of Kausambi, whereas Shankargarh could be directly approached from Prayag through Bhita. From Prayag one could also travel straight to Sohagi Ghat crossing the Tons river on the way. From Shankargarh the route went first to Teonthar from where the Vindhyan scarp could be climbed either at Sohagi Ghat or at Baldaha Ghat. Of the two, the Sohagi Ghat access was more important because the major stupa site of Deur Kothar is located at the point where the Sohagi slope touches the top of the Vindhyan scarp. The Deur Kothar stupa and monastic complex with a number of painted rock-shelters in its vicinity enjoys a special significance of its own (cf. Chakrabarti 2005, pp. 74-75). On one level, it shows that the so-called dichotomy between the Mauryan and Sunga period stupa constructions and their characters is not valid, and on another, it demonstrates that an inscribed and monolithic pillar of the Mauryan period need not necessarily be a royally erected pillar. The Deur Kother inscribed pillar was put up by a Buddhist monk. In any case, the road to Rewa from Deur

Kothar led through Keoti, and in the vicinity of modern Rewa there is a major NBP-bearing site, Itaha with a rampart dating from the first phase of occupation there. Itaha was the ancient counterpart of modern Rewa.

Beyond Rewa

Two alignments were important beyond Rewa: Rewa-Amrapatan-Bharhut and Rewa-Amarpatan-Bandhogarh. The importance of the stupa of Bharhut is well-known, and here it may be noted that Bharhut could be approached more directly from Kausambi through Pabhosa, Chitrakut and/or Kalinjar and Satna. From Bharhut, the route led through Rupnath/Kakrehta and the Sagar/Damoh areas to Eran and Vidisa. Tripuri lay on the bank of the Narmada beyond Rupnath/Kakrehta, and from Tripuri there were at least two major alignments, the first one to Pauni through the Balaghat gap and the second one to the area south of Bhopal. The first route linked Tripuri with Vidarbha and Andhra whereas the route to the Bhopal area was connected with the city-sites of Nandner (Nadner) and Ninnore (on the bank of the Narmada) and the Buddhist monastic complex of Panguraria. Crossing the Narmada at Ninnaur, the second route led to Burhanpur to cross the Tapti and reach Bhokardan and Paithan. The Vidisa route was connected with the Nandner-Panguraria-Ninnore zone and could also lead to Ujjain via Beora.

The Kanpur-Etawah-Agra Node

Vidisa was a major target of the alignments emanating from the Kanpur-Etawah-Agra node. From Kanpur which received the route coming from the direction of Lucknow, with the Ganga being crossed at the large mound site of Jajmau, the Yamuna was crossed at the city-site of Musanagar, which has two Bharhut-type unexcavated stupas in its vicinity. Across the Yamuna here lies its junction with the Betwa, and the Betwa valley was followed till one reached the city-sites of Ehrich, Tumain and Vidisa. From Etawah, the road led to the city-site of Ekachakra across the Yamuna and from Ekachakra the route was open to the MRE site of Gujarra, and the city-sites of Ehrich, Tumain and Vidisa. From the area of Ekachakra, the route could also go to the Bhind/Gwalior sector and from there the Malwa plain and the areas of Vidisa and Ujjain could be easily accessed. Similarly, from Bateshwar in the Agra area, one could follow the Chambal valley from the junction of the Chambal with the Yamuna and easily reach the Malwa plain in the direction to Vidisa and Ujjain.

The Ujjain node

The importance of Ujjain is highlighted more if we think of an alignment moving from the direction of Delhi and Mathura towards the Malwa plain, especially Mandasore from where Ujjain is only but a step. Mandasore is easily accessed from the Mewar plain. From Ujjain there is a straight route through Nagda to Gujarat, but from Ujjain one can also cross the Narmada at Maheswar and follow the Kasargad-Burhanpur (Tapti crossing)-Ajanta-Bhokardan-Paithan alignment. From Ujjain one can also move towards Dhar and then go up to Barwani where also the Narmada can be crossed. From Barwani, the alignment beyond the Narmada is Dhulia-Chalisgaon-Pitalkhora-Ellora-Bhokardan (?)–Paithan. From Dhulia one can also go to Nasik, Kalyan or Sopara, the last two on the Konkan coast. From Nasik one can even go to Junnar and reach the Konkan coast through Malsejghat and Nanaghat.

My book *The Archaeology of the Deccan Routes, the Routes which Linked the Ganga Plain with the Deccan* was published in 2005, incorporating the relevant literary and archaeological data and some Mughal period and later travel writings which show that the pattern of movements along the old routes to the Deccan still survived in many ways.

The work on the Deccan routes was done in collaboration with R.N. Singh of Banaras Hindu University and Rakesh Tewari of the U.P. State Department of Archaeology. The funding of the work came from the Society for South Asian Studies where Michael Willis of the British Museum was then important, the MacDonald Institute for Archaeological Research, Cambridge University, and the Cambridge University Travelling Expenses Fund.

The Archaeology of European Expansion in India, Gujarat, c. 16th-18th Centuries

There are remains of European trading settlements almost all along the coast, and although there are voluminous European records on each of them, they have not yet been looked at archaeologically. In collaboration with Chris Scarre and Judith Scarre, I decided to study the British early seventeenth century landing place of Swally near Surat and the relevant building remains and tombs in Surat itself. This was followed by a similar study in Ahmedabad, Cambay and Diu. In Surat, Mr. M. Meghani was very helpful to us and Mr. Y.M. Chitalwala of the Gujarat State Department of Archaeology was also a source of great support. The early British tombs of Surat were published by Professor Scarre whereas I published a monograph giving the background historical details of the European contact in Gujarat between the 16th and 18th centuries. It was intended that we would excavate at Swally but unfortunately a bureaucratic muddle came to stand in our way, which was also seriously obstructed by the rejection of our grant application twice. I believe that the archaeological imprints of the British rule and early European presence in India on Indian landscape are worthwhile subjects of studies in their own right.

The Ancient Routes of the Deccan and the Southern Peninsula, 2004-2006

The three-year funding for this project came from the MacDonald Institute for Archaeological Research and the Cambridge University Travelling Expenses Fund. The project clearly grew out of my work on the Gangetic valley to the Deccan routes and aimed at determining the major alignments within Maharashtra, Andhra and the southern regions up to Cape Comorin and Kerala. A major focus of this study was also the coastline from Daman on the Konkan coast to Srikakulam in the Vamsadhara estuary of Andhra, which was home to almost innumerable preindustrial ports, some of which played a major role in the ancient context too.

In 2004, we studied the geographical features of the Konkan coast, the distribution of its port sites and the links of communication between these ports and their Maharashtra and Karnataka hinterlands through a large number of passes in the Western Ghats. We divided the entire Konkan stretch into a number of sectors: from the south of Daman to Elephanta, from the south of Mumbai to Ratnagiri, Goa, and North and South Kanara. Sopara, Elephanta, Sanjan, Kalyan and Thana were important ancient ports in the Daman to Elephanta sector, which has also a chain of small ports mentioned mostly in the Portuguese records: Umbergaon, Dheri, Gholbad, Dahanu, Savta, Navapur, Satpatti, Kelve-Mahim, Sassu Navghar, Ghodbandar, Bhiwndi, Versova, Bandra and Panvel. Of these, Dahanu is likely to be an ancient port. However, the small ports which possibly were nothing more than berthing places of small boats provide some depth to the local trading picture including not merely the trade beyond the seas but also coastal and regional trade. Links were maintained with the hinterland in this sector through the Thal, Nana and Bor passes. The hinterland places which were important were mainly Nasik, Junnar and Pune. The Sopara-Thana-Kalyan area was the focal point in the ancient context, leading to Nasik in the north and Junnar in the south. There was another focal point, although somewhat less significant, in the area of Dahanu and Sanjan, which was linked to Nasik. Between Mumbai and Ratnagiri, Chaul was the most important ancient port but there are several reported smaller ports: Nagothna, Roha, Mandad, Murud, Mhasla, Janjira, Danda-Rajpur and Mahad. The Western Ghats passes in this sector are oriented principally towards Mahabaleshwar, Satara and Pune, all of which played a role in mediating the movements between the coast and the hinterland. The Pir pass near Chaul was considered a kind of highway of traffic towards Chaul across the Ghats. From Chaul one could easily reach Junnar and Pune. The Ratnagiri sector also has its share of important and minor ports. Among its major ports, mention should be made of Bankot, Dabhol, Chiplun, Rajapur, Kharepatan and Vijaydurg. The following minor ports figure in the records: Mahapral, Kelshi, Ade, Anjarla, Harnai, Dapoli, Khed, Anjanvel, Ghagar, Boria or Adur, Jaygad, Sangameshwar, Ratnagiri, Jaytapur, Achra, Malvan and Vengurla. The Ratnagiri coast was connected with the hinterland by almost a maze of passes. Further, it is to be understood that Satara, Solapur, Kolhapur, Belgaum and Dharwar were important hinterland places in the Ratnagiri sector. As I wrote in my report on this fieldwork *The Ancient Routes of the Deccan and the Southern Peninsula* in 2010:

> ... on the eastern side of the Western Ghats, the north-south alignment of Satara, Kolhapur and Belgaum plays a crucial role in mediating the routes which linked the different sections of the Konkan coast to a vast region covering large sections of inner Maharashtra, the Gulbarga-Bijapur-Badamy-Bellary section of Karnataka,

> and through them Andhra, and at a further remove, Tamil Nadu. One can also add to this network Solapur in the east and Dharwar in the south. Viewed in the context of such wider links, the narrow coastal plain of Konkan and the associated openings of varying importance in the Western Ghats cease to be a closed world and become an integral part of the vast network of routes covering the Deccan and the southern peninsula (Chakrabarti 2010, pp. 184-185).

The same sort of picture is available for Goa, which was linked by way of trade with the Bijapur belt and with Belgaum in the north and Dharwar in the south. Between Karwar and Mangalore, North and South Kanara have a number of significant pre-modern ports: Karwar, Bhatkal, Kumta, Honavar, Malpe, Hangarkatta, Kundapur, Baindur, Barkur, Basrur, Udayavara, Udupi and Mangalore. In the case of North Kanara, the Dharwar region possibly played an important role in maintaining links between the coast and the Karnataka hinterland. Banavasi is the major reported early historic city-site of the region. The details of the linkages of South Kanara with its hinterland are not particularly clear but we took the help of F. Scott's treatment of the British military routes of this area in 1853. The Bangalore-Honavar route lay through Shimoga and the Gersoppa falls, and the route from Bangalore to Harihar lay through Tumkur and Chitaldurg. From Mangalore one went to Shimoga by the Agumber pass. From Hassan to Mangalore, one could travel by the Manjarabad Ghat.

From Daman to Ratnagiri, one of the most visible traces of links between the two sides of the Western Ghats is the presence of Buddhist rock-cut caves in and around the mouths of these routes. In the case of the Konkan coast, the basic geographical evidence of the passes across the Western Ghats, the location of the ports and the forts of different periods guarding access to them, the main hinterland places and the arterial routes spreading out from different hinterland places, and the locations of Buddhist remains have all been sharply defined and discussed.

In the case of Tamil Nadu and Kerala, the situation is different and has been so mainly because of their different geographical characters. First, because of the presence of the Palghat gap, Tamil Nadu and Kerala have been closely linked historically. There are also some less prominent but nonetheless important openings to the south of the Palghat opening. Apart from the Palghat gap, all the passes linked to the Kerala coast led either to the Mysore plateau or to the southern section of Tamil Nadu. In Tamil Nadu there are clear entry points in the north, which are linked to the Mysore plateau and the Rayalseema tract of Andhra. These entry points are important to judge the flow of events in Tamil Nadu history. There are also uplands in the interior of Tamil Nadu. The configuration of these uplands and the Palghat gap have greatly influenced its internal lines of movements. There is a chain of ancient and generally preindustrial ports all along the Kerala and Tamil Nadu coasts. They were naturally linked to their hinterlands with which they had no barrier of communications. Historical forces must have conditioned the lines of movements between these ports and their hinterlands. In the case of Tamil Nadu, we have argued for a continuity of the Tamil Nadu route network from the early historic period to the later contexts up to c.AD 1300.

> Two communication lines have always been important: the Coimbature-Salem-Dharmapuri axis, with its own approach to the Kerala coast, and the axis from Kanchipuram-Madras sector to the areas down south up to Madurai and Tinnevelly. Their relative importance might have varied from period to period, depending on the political exigencies and the needs of the coastal and inland trade (Chakrabarti 2010, p. 193).

Our study also involved substantial excursions in the Tamil Nadu political history and argued that the beginning of early history in Tamil Nadu dated from c.500 BC and that the early Pandya kingdom was possibly the first kingdom to rise in this belt.

The major internal barrier in Andhra lies in the Rayalseema sector. The Kurnool district has been cut up by the Nallamalais in the east and the Erramalas in the west, with the Nandiyal valley occupying its central section. This section has two passes: Nandikanama pass and Mantralamma pass, both across the Nallamalais. There are also two passes in the Erramalas: the Tammarazupalle and the Rampur passes. These passes kept the line of communication between the Raichur Doab and Bellary sections of Karnataka and the Andhra coast between the mouth of the Krishna and Nellore open. One also hears of a few small passes in Anantapur but more important is the opening of Tirupati, a camping ground of pilgrims from the north to Tirupati and further south. Thus, Tirupati maintains an important position in the route system passing through the Rayalseema section of Andhra.

Andhra's position in the route network has been summarized by us:

> ... this was easily linked to the historical developments of a very large part of India: the Kanchipuram sector of Tamil Nadu, the Bellary-Gulbarga-Bidar-Bijapur section of Karnataka, and through it, that section of Maharashtra which lies immediately to the east of the Western Ghats, the Aurangabad-Daulatabad area of Maharashtra through Nanded, the eastern or the Vidarbha part of Maharashtra through Karimnagar and Adilabad, the southwestern Orissa and Chhattisgarh from Vizianagram, and finally, the whole of the coastal sweep of eastern India up to the Bhagirathi from Srikakulam. The political forces emanating from all these regions affected the course of

> Andhra history at one time or another. Economically, the Andhra coast was the terminal point of some trade routes, especially the ones coming from the direction of Paithan in the upper Godavari and from the direction of the Ganga plain through Vidarbha and South Kosala... It is doubtful if outside the Northwest Frontier, including the mountain valleys to the northeast of Peshawar, the Buddhist establishments were as dense in any other part of the subcontinent as they were in Andhra. All these factors and the fact that Andhra has a long coastline with its chain of pre-modern and in many cases, ancient ports, endow the ancient history of Andhra with an eclectic character of its own (Chakrabarti 2010, p. 126).

Haryana and Indian Panjab

The major alluvial strip which abuts the Ganga plain is the plain between the Yamuna on the east and the Ravi on the west, i.e., the plains of Haryana and Indian Panjab. In recent years, this area has become noted for its sites of the Harappan tradition, but this has some major early historic sites as well. As an extension of my Ganga plain studies, I thought that this would be a very interesting area to study for my own understanding of the archaeological problems and geographical foci of the related sites. The field-work was undertaken in 2007 and 2008 in collaboration with Sukhdev Saini of the Department of Ancient Indian History, Culture and Archaeology of Kurukshetra University. It was published as *The Problem of the Sarasvati River and Notes on the Archaeological Geography of Haryana and Indian Panjab* in 2009 (Chakrabarti and Saini 2009).

West of the Yamuna, the drainage is dominated by the currently moribund or only seasonally active Sarasvati system and the system of its major tributary Drishadvati. This is especially true of Haryana. In Panjab, two of the 'Panjab rivers', the Beas and the Ravi, gain importance but even in Panjab the problem of its drainage is touched by the problems of the Sarasvati system.

The existence of the Sarasvati system, a river system to the east of the Indus and running almost parallel to it, has been known since the late eighteenth century. It was identified with the Sarasvati river mentioned in the Rigveda by the French historical geographer V. St.-Martin in 1860. In recent years, in view of the fact that a large number of Harappan sites—in fact, more Harappan sites than found in the Indus system itself—have been found in this river system, the question of the association of the Rigveda with the Harappan civilization has emerged strongly. Further, the entire system from the Siwaliks to the Rann of Kutch has been subject to various satellite imagery studies and their interpretations in the context of the Sarasvati-Drishadvati system. Even before such recent studies, geologists and others studied this drainage system. According to C.F. Oldham in 1874, the Sutlej used to flow into the Sarasvati bed when it was fully alive and that it grew moribund or extinct after the Sutlej deserted it. The most exhaustive review of the mediaeval literary sources in this regard were undertaken by H.G. Raverty in 1892, showing that there were references to the flow of the Sarasvati till at least the 14th century when the Hakra or the Sarasvati continued to be a perennial stream.

Academically, the problem as viewed by scholars from James Rennell (1788) and James Tod (1832) onward is worth studying for its own sake. Such a study forms the background of our field-work in the area, beginning with Haryana which has emerged as one of the core areas of the origin of the Harappan civilization. Both at Bhirrana and Kunal in the Fatehabad section of the state, the Early Harappan level has been found preceded by the Hakra Ware level which may date from c.3800 BC or earlier. So, it is not a case of west to east movement of the Harappans in Haryana. It seems to be one of the Harappan core areas.

The British Indian gazetteers of the modern Haryana districts such as Karnal and Hissar throw light on the agricultural system of these areas in the 19th century. The Sarasvati passes through both of them. The Karnal gazetteer of 1884 clearly mentions that "throughout the northern portion of the district, in various directions, there are traces of ancient canal cuts from the Ghaggar and the Suruswati" and that much of the floodwater currently wasted could be utilized by opening these canal cuts. It mentions that in the area of a place called Sotha, there was so much water in the river for a few months in a year that a regular ferry system was necessary for this period. In the Fatehabad section of Hissar, grasses grew abundantly on the banks of the Ghaggar, and both here and further north, crops were grown on the tracts irrigated from one or the other branches of the Ghaggar. In the northern or the *Sotar* villages of the Fatehabad section of Hissar, two crops, the autumnal one being rice, could be grown in good years, and the river irrigation was supplemented by the digging of wells. The point is that as late as the end of the 19th century, there is a clear record of prosperous agricultural pockets in modern Haryana based on the floodwater of the Ghaggar-Sarasvati and the canal system built around it. The question which is being increasingly important is whether it is necessary to invoke a theory of climate change to explain the growth, development and decline of Harappan settlements in Haryana. I have come round to the belief that the Harappans in Haryana were tuned to a basically arid environment where they brought about agricultural prosperity by building a canal network based on the floodwater of the Sarasvati system.

That the Harappans were living in a basically arid context in Haryana is clear from the presence of sandy deposits before, during and after the Harappan occupations at some relevant sites. That it is a perfectly acceptable scenario in view of a tenth century text which we have cited in our book (Chakrabarti and Saini 2009, p. 51).

> The Yaudheya country (i.e. the Panjab-Haryana stretch) was like an ornament of the earth, and was replete with all requisites of good and happy life ... Its villages were full of cattle wealth, cows, buffaloes, goats, sheep, camels and horses. Abundance of irrigation works rendered them free from the vagaries of rains. Their well-watered fields of black soil... were green with harvests and gardens. They yielded such bouncing harvests that the farmers were unable to beat the grain and stack them properly.

The Haryana route network is based on two arterial routes: Delhi-Karnal-Ambala alignment to Ludhiana, Jalandhar, Ferozepur and beyond, and Delhi-Hansi-Hissar-Fatehabad-Sirsa alignment which leads to Fazilka and eventually the frontier with Afghanistan. The Powindah traders used to frequent the second route in winter.

We visualized the archaeological development of Haryana in the context of such irrigated agriculture and two arterial networks. Apart from the Harappan, protohistoric and historic sites studied directly by us, we depended on the large mass of data collected by various Ph.D. and M.Phil researchers of Kurukshetra University. Regarding the Harappan distribution in Haryana, our study led to the following main point:

> The pattern is that in a large tract of Haryana covering Panchkula, Ambala, Yamunanagar, Kurukshetra, Karnal and Panipat, no mature Harappan site has yet been reported. The broad trajectory of Harappan distribution in Haryana seems to be Sirsa, Fatehabad, Hissar, Hansi,

> Bhiwani, Rohtak and Jhajjar, with only one site--Balu--in the Jind-Kaithal stretch. This was the broad line of movement from Sirsa to the area of Delhi in the historical periods too ... (Chakrabarti and Saini 2009, p. 221)

The location of Harappa is on the second route coming from the Gomal valley and the Afghanistan frontier and going in the direction of the Delhi-Mathura heartland. This explains the basic geographical importance of the site.

As far as the distribution of early historic sites is concerned, Sugh was the most important early historic site of north Haryana and its importance has to be understood in relation to the approach across the Yamuna to the sub-Himalayan terrain extending up to Kalsi where an Asokan inscription is located. The fact that there was a Mauryan period Buddhist stupa site at Chanetti near Sugh is also important. Along the Delhi-Ludhiana alignment via Kurukshetra and Ambala, the most important early historical site is Amin, which has a stupa dating from c.1st century BC, if the surviving sculptured railing pillars of the site are any indication. Also interestingly, the site of Asandivat possesses a Dhamek-type stupa of about the Gupta period. The most important city-site in the Delhi-Mathura to Hissar, Abohar, Fazilka alignment is Rohtak, although little of it has been exposed horizontally.

The early agricultural situation of Indian Panjab is comparatively less clear. In the late 19th century, the fertility of the Jalandhar section was unmatched, but it is worth noting that in 1878, 33 percent of the district was irrigated from wells, 4 percent was flooded and the rest, i.e., 63 percent was dependent on rain for cultivation. There is a 5-km wide Ghaggar plain in Sangrur, but otherwise the agricultural picture of the different parts of Indian Panjab used to vary significantly in the late 19th century. However, this was no deterrent to the wide distribution of Harappan sites in this region. The sites of the Harappan tradition are distributed all over the State. The sites in the southern part of the State may partly be an extension of the sites in the Hissar-Fatehabad section of Haryana and may even be related to the branches of the route leading eventually to Multan near the Gomal valley. The distribution of Harappan sites in the Amritsar and Gurdaspur districts is important in its own right and suggests their occurrence in the Lahore-Gujranwala-Sialkot stretch across the border. The sites of the Ferozepur section also suggest their occurrence across the border. The sites in the interior districts of Patiala, Ludhiana, Moga, Faridkot and Jalandhar also suggest a spread along the Ambala-Ludhiana alignment and the Ludhiana-Moga-Firozepur alignment. There was possibly another alignment from Ludhiana to Jalandhar via Phagwara or via Phillaur and Nakodar. These Panjab alignments of the Harappan sites will need more work in future.

When one considers the sheer fact of Harappan distribution in a massive zone going across the riverine plain to the long Siwalik belt from Jammu to Hardwar, covering Panjab, Haryana and western Uttar Pradesh, it nullifies the idea of west-to-east migration of the Harappans.

> Just the sheer geographical expanse of their distribution makes one realize that such a close adaptation to this landscape can only imply a deep root and long developmental process (Chakrabarti and Saini 2009, p. 270).

The distribution pattern of historical sites in Panjab reflects to some extent the distribution of earlier protohistoric sites. The location of Sunet, the largest early historical site of Panjab, shows that the Ambala-Ludhiana alignment was rooted in early history. Along the Ludhiana-Moga-Firozepur alignment there is a chain of early historical sites. As we noted,

> from Sunet the ancient road was apparently going in the direction of Firozepur on the one hand and bifurcating towards the Tarn Taran-Amritsar area from Moga on the other. Firozepur, as we have noticed in the context of the Harappan distribution, was a marker in the line of movement towards Pakpattan, which in turn was oriented towards Multan. This is the dominant impression in the case of the early historic context as well. (Chakrabarti and Saini 2009, p. 270).

We consider the stretch from Dera Baba Nanak to Gurdaspur another significant one in this context.

Sialkot is linked to Dera Baba Nanak and Kalanour, and the Kalanour-Gurdaspur alignment would lead straight to Pathankot. We also believe that the Jalandhar-Pathankot alignment was a significant line in Panjab's early history. This is the line that connected Jalandhar with Kangra as parts of the Trigarta kingdom. The last major pocket of early historic occupation in Panjab is its southeastern part, comprising the whole zone from Sanghol to Rupar and from Rupar to Rahon. This zone falls conveniently at one of the major gateways to the Himalayan region. I am not sure if the importance of this zone has been properly appreciated in ancient Indian history and archaeology. This extends from Pathankot to Rupar. Pathankot gives access to Chamba and Kangra and is linked with Sialkot or ancient Sakala. The Rupar area serves as the access route of a major section of the Himalayas in Himachal Pradesh including the Kulu area and the famous mother-goddess cult spots of the Siwaliks—Jawalamukhi, Nayana Devi and Chintpurni. In Haryana, Sugh was likely to be the centre of a political unit in the Siwalik belt.

A number of ancient political units are relevant to Haryana and Indian Panjab: Kuru, Trigarta, Yaudheya, Audambara, Agacha janapada, Kuninda, Vemaka and Kadasa. The whole of the modern state of Haryana seems to belong to

Kuru which has its extensions beyond it. Trigarta is basically Jalandhar-Kangra. The Audambaras are put in the Pathankot area whereas the core of the Yaudheya area was Haryana (Naurangabad near Bhiwani) and Panjab (Sunet near Ludhiana). Agroha near Hissar was the centre of Agacha janapada. The Kunindas are limited to the Siwaliks between Jwalamukhi and Rupar. The Jwalamukhi area is also associated with the Vemakas. Kadasa janapada is associated with Sugh.

It is interesting to reflect that in 1980 I began my field-survey in Kangra, a part of the ancient Trigarta territory, approaching it from Pathankot. In 2008 I brought my field-programme covering the whole of the alluvial sweep from the Bhagirathi mouth to the Indian part of the Ravi to a close in the territory between Pathankot and Rupar, which lies at the approach to Kangra. For me at least, the process of reaching a close familiarity with the historical geography of this vast stretch of land was very exciting.

MY PUBLICATIONS 2005-2011

My second book on the Ganga plain survey, which dealt with the upper Ganga, was published in 2007. As noted earlier, the book on the lower and the middle Ganga sections of the survey was published in 2001. The survey of the alluvial strip which leads west of the Yamuna and continues up to the Indian Panjab border with Pakistan was published in 2009. Taken together, these three volumes offer admittedly broad but nonetheless accurate study of the distribution of sites and related urban centres, ancient territorial units and trade or communication routes of the entire alluvial corridor between Bengal and Panjab. In the opening chapter of the book on the middle and the lower Ganga, I located this work in the theoretical context of historical geography, archaeology and history. I also located it in the context of the survey work which had hitherto been done in the sub-continental archaeology. With a year's break in 2002, the Ganga plain archaeological fieldwork was done over 14 field-seasons between 1991 and 2005. The Haryana-Panjab work was undertaken in 2007 and 2008. Thus, it took me a total of 16 years to have a historical-geographical comprehension of this alluvial region between Bengal and Panjab. If I add to this, roughly two seasons of experience of sites in Bangladesh, the result of which has been published in my *Ancient Bangladesh,* I can state that I have spent 18 years in all to understand the historical-geographical pattern of archaeological sites between the Chattagram or Chittagong coast and the hills of Uttarakhand on the one hand and between the Yamuna and the Ravi on the other. I also tried to understand how the Ganga plain is connected with the Siwalik and Himalayan belts of Uttarakhand, and my understanding in this regard is incorporated in my book on the upper Ganga. The plain of Indian Panjab intrudes in one corner into the Kangra valley of Himachal Pradesh. This valley was surveyed by me in 1980 (Chakrabarti and Hasan 1984), and thus 19 seasons have been spent in the field to acquire some understanding of how sites are disposed over a large chunk of northern India.

The second segment of my fieldwork dealt only with routes. The detailed analysis of the routes, which led from the Ganga plain to the Deccan, was published as a book in 2005, incorporating my field-study for four seasons (1999-2002). In 2010 I published a book containing my study of the routes inside the Deccan and within the southern Peninsula. This study was undertaken for three seasons in 2004-2006. This book shows how the routes which arrived in the Deccan from the Ganga plain were connected with the routes leading to the south up to the furthest ends of Tamil Nadu and Kerala. This book also shows how links were maintained between the

Konkan coast and the mouth of the Godavari and a little beyond. Thus, the field study of 7 seasons was needed to work out the overall configuration of routes between the Ganga plain and the deep south.

However, my Cambridge-based books went beyond those based on field-studies. In two earlier sections I have dealt with such publications till 2003. It remains for me to discuss the relevant publications after that.

In 2006 I published my *The Oxford Companion to Indian Archaeology. The Archaeological Foundations of Ancient India, Stone Age to* AD *13th Century*. Most of the books in the 'Oxford Companion' series are edited volumes and not single-authored attempts like mine. The reason I was bold enough to undertake such a study and the previously published *India: An Archaeological History, The Palaeolithic to the Early Historic Foundations* (Chakrabarti 1999, 2nd edition in 2009) was that I had been discussing the archaeological complexities of the sub-continent as a teacher for many years on the basis of primary sources and a clear understanding of how the different branches of the concerned disciplines historically developed.

The first five chapters of the book deals with prehistory, beginning with a systematic review of how Stone Age research developed in India and how the basic structure of this research was laid down in the second half of the nineteenth century. The sections on Hominid fossils, earliest stone tools and the place of India in the current scheme of human evolution are followed by a summary of the Palaeolithic sequences and materials and the basic historical knowledge derived from them. The next section on the Mesolithic evidence includes sections on rock art and why this phase is important in the study of Indian culture and history. The problem of the beginning of food production in India and the beginning of villages from Baluchistan to western Uttar Pradesh and

Gujarat, which are discussed in the two chapters after the Mesolithic one, form the setting of a detailed discussion on the Indus civilization from the problem of its origin to that of its legacy in the following four chapters. The beginning of rice cultivation in the Ganga plain and other issues and the Neolithic-Chalcolithic cultures outside the Harappan orbits are discussed next and lead on to the problem of the beginning of iron and the base or the foundations of the early historic India. Early historic cities are discussed along with the material basis of the contemporary life, such as settlements, technology, agriculture, trade and trade routes. Art and architecture, inscriptions, coins and the archaeological aspects of religions of early historic India are all considered, at least in outline, and followed by an outline of the political and economic history between the 7th and 13th centuries AD. Settlements, irrigation, technology and trade of this period are specifically considered and so are its inscriptions, coins, temples, monasteries, sculptures and painting. Finally, there is an assessment of the exclusively archaeological perspective of the history of India. There are a few appendices, including one on the archaeology of the Andaman-Nicobar and Lakshadweep-Minicoy islands. There are notes on the history of archaeology and conservation and Aryan issue as well. The complexities and various possible implications of the data have been emphasized throughout the volume.

In 2008. two books were published, both dealing with the socio-politics of the ancient Indian past. One of these was *The Battle for Ancient India, an Essay in the Socio-politics of Indian Archaeology* (Chakrabarti 2008a) and the second one, a collection of essays, was titled *Globalization and Indian Archaeology and Other Essays* (Chakrabarti 2008b). An important part of the first volume was a detailed examination of the socio-politics of the study of the Indus civilization, especially with reference to the debate over its so-called Vedic/non-Vedic affiliation. In recent years, this has boiled down to a debate between the progressives (champions of the non-Vedic theory) and reactionaries (champions of Vedic affiliation). However, it has been shown with a great amount of detail that this debate is the product of recent history. The earlier scholars who were involved in this debate did not view the problem from the political angle at all. For example, both P.V. Kane, the great historian of the Indian *Dharmasastras*, and B.N. Dutta, one of the founders of the communist movement in India, wrote in favour of the Vedic affiliation of the Indus civilization. The volume also discusses other issues such as the chronology of the early historic stage of south India, especially Tamil Nadu and Kerala. In the context of the various disputes of the study of Tamil Nadu history, it was observed that the Brahmins preferred to link the advent of historical phase in Tamil Nadu to the influence of the so-called Aryans from the north and that some Brahmin scholars were still against the acceptance of the date of c.500 BC for the beginning of writing in Tamil Nadu, a date suggested both by some archaeological evidence and the presence of Tamil-Brahmi writing in Sri Lanka around that period.

'Globalization and Indian archaeology' underlines an increasingly important issue, and the basic point I made with reference to international participation in Indian archaeology is the following:

> The major point of my argument in the context of globalization and Indian archaeology is that it has to be viewed from various angles, primarily with long-term national interest in mind. The question—with whom do we collaborate and on which level of Western archaeology do we seek our collaborators—is as important as the question of globalization itself. Further, which types of

> field-problems deserve our priority, especially in regard to our collaborators? Here, detailed surveys conducted by young Ph.D. students from the Western universities can play an important and beneficial role for the subject in the country. Finally, far more careful attention should be given to the socio-politics of the individual archaeological writings than it has been the practice in Indian archaeology so far. Socio-politics of the past is an integral part of the teaching curriculum of archaeology in many Western universities today, and it has been so for a long time. A nation's sense of its past can be a mine-field, and here one should be watchful and tread cautiously (Chakrabarti 2008b, p. 13).

Another essay of this volume discusses 'the crisis of the study of India's ancient past' and points out that "what has suffered most among the current branches of Indian historical studies after Independence is the study of ancient India" (Chakrabarti 2008b, p. 19). It has become a marginalized subject.

In 2010, I published my *The Geopolitical Orbits of Ancient India* which bears the subtitle 'the geographical frames of the ancient Indian dynasties'. The work was written in the University of New England in Armidale, New South Wales, Australia, in April-June 2007, with support from a fellowship at the university's Asia Centre which was under the care of Professors Howard Brasted and Ian Metcalfe. This work is the result of my long-term interest in the geographical factors of India's political history. After critically reviewing some of the earlier geographical premises such as the idea of 'perennial nuclear regions', etc. I find them wanting in terms of historical accuracy. What I offer instead is expressed clearly in the following passage:

> In this volume, I have elaborated how the political history of ancient India has been enacted in various geographical

> orbits and how these orbits have kept on interacting throughout history and how, contrary to general impressions, there has not been any fixed boundary line or 'divide' (Chakrabarti 2010, preface).

Without trying to locate a set of relatively permanent lines of political boundaries, we thought that a much more historically fruitful exercise would be to mark out the various paths of dynastic movements throughout ancient India.

> In a sense, there was a geographically conditioned pattern of route network linking the various political components of ancient India. It is this network which makes possible a proper geographical understanding of the ancient Indian and later Indian dynastic framework. Which parts of this network were significant and became so in which period? Questions like this are likely to infuse an element of ground reality in the study of the political history of ancient India. (Chakrabarti 2010, p. 189).

My study of the historical geography of the Asokan edicts —*Royal Messages from the Wayside: Historical Geography of the Asokan Edicts* was published in 2011 (Chakrabarti 2011). To an extent this is an offshoot of my interest in early historic India, but more than that this an expression of interest in the distribution of Asokan edicts and how this distribution throws light on the geographical nuances of Mauryan India. The volume contains detailed notes on every place where the existence of an Asokan inscription or an uninscribed Asokan pillar has been claimed with or without any firm proof. It also comments on the identifications of various places and groups of people mentioned in the edicts. One of the conclusions we reached is the following:

> In retrospect, the historical-geographical world behind the Asokan edicts surprises us both by their vastness and complexity. Each and every section of the subcontinent

> seems to be very well-lit and reveals a route network with which we have been familiar in various ways right up to the modern period. ... There is nothing tentative about Mauryan India. This is an India which had long passed into the historical period... In the third century BC India, the subcontinent did not belong to diverse stages of socio-economic development. The fact that in some areas the megalithic burial customs were still prevalent does not mean that these areas were not well-rooted in early history; the megaliths simply reflected some local ways of disposing the dead (Chakrabarti 2011, p. 165).

SOME MAJOR HAPPENINGS INVOLVING INDIAN ARCHAEOLOGY SINCE 1990

Ayodhya, 1992 and the World Archaeological Congress, 1994

There were two incidents involving Indian archaeology in the early 1990s: the demolition in 1992 of a sixteenth century mosque which, according to the belief of a vast mass of Hindus, stood at the site of the birthplace of the Hindu god Rama in Ayodhya, and the open conflict between two political groups in the World Archaeological Congress in Delhi in 1994. Both these incidents have intensified the rift between the so-called 'progressives' and the so-called 'reactionaries' in Indian historical and archaeological circles, and I discussed in some detail the implications of the Ayodhya incident in my *Archaeology in the Third World: A History of Indian Archaeology since 1947* (Chakrabarti 2003, 201-204). Ayodhya is a major early historic archaeological site with a fortification wall still standing in places. There is also a major Asokan pillar capital lying more or less openly in a local temple. A Sunga period inscription lies in another temple in a different part of the site. The archaeological past of Ayodhya, which has long been neglected, did not even figure in the so-called academic debate between the two warring groups over the '*Babri Masjid*'. This debate was solely about whether or not a temple stood at the site of the demolished mosque. The judiciary has judged that a temple did in fact stand at this site before the mosque. Long before the judiciary made up its mind on the basis of the data obtained from the judiciary-controlled Archaeological Survey of India excavations at the spot, the find of a twelfth century AD inscription in the demolished ruins of the mosque made it clear that there was a temple of that period at the disputed site. The Ayodhya incident is a singularly unfortunate incident, and there is every possibility in future of such incidents happening at mercifully small number of sites which are claimed by contesting religious groups. However, this has not spelt the doom of the objective pursuit of archaeology in India nor are similar incidents in future likely to do so.

I was not present in the World Archaeological Congress in Delhi in 1994 and cannot thus pass any comment on the confusion and mayhem that took place there. From what I have heard about it from various participants, I can infer that the control of this 'congress' richly funded by the Government of India was an issue, and the 'progressive' historians were upset that those whom they considered 'reactionaries' were running the show on this occasion, and they left no chance to show the organizers in poor light. On the other side, the 'reactionaries' tried to derive some propaganda advantage out of it. Sensible behaviour was outside the consideration of any of the two groups. Meanwhile, the image of Indian archaeology seriously suffered in the eyes of the international participants, many of whom, if what I have heard is true, suffered shabbily in the hands of the organizers. For this, the international section of the organizers also deserves some blame. Basically, the international leadership of this Congress decided to collaborate with the Indian Archaeology Society and its adjunct organizations which do not have any organized leadership or a proper chain of control to organize a big international event. If the World Archaeological Congress leadership had roped in the Archaeological Survey of India or any such major organized body for this purpose, things would have been different.

Selection of a Professional Director General, 2010

The third major happening was that the leadership of the Archaeological Survey of India passed into the control of the Government of India's administrative cadre during this period. Since 1948, the Director-Generals have been invariably recruited from among the senior officers of the Survey. This chain got broken with the induction of M.S. Nagaraja Rao for about 3 years in the mid-1980s. However, Rao, the Director of Karnataka State Archaeology, was an archaeologist who had several publications to his credit, and at the end of his term, the person who took charge as the Director General was R.C. Tripathi, an Indian Administrative Service officer. After Tripathi, the then seniormost officer of the Survey, J.P. Joshi, took over as the Director General and was succeeded by M.C. Joshi who was then the seniormost Survey officer.

After M.C. Joshi's tenure ended in about 1993-94, the bureaucrats of the Indian Administrative Service began to be posted as the Director General of the Survey. Why and how the service rules for the post of the Director General of the Archaeological Survey of India were changed at that point are not known to me, but one hopes that in future somebody with access to the files of the Archaeological Survey of India will write this history of change. The Archaeological Survey of India has always been considered an academic body. If its leadership is handed over by the government to persons unfamiliar with the country's archaeology, the government owes it to people to give an explanation.

The handing over of the post of the Director General to the officers of the Indian Administrative Service caused a fair amount of discontent among the country's archaeologists, including the present author. Eventually, in 2010, the Director of Archaeology of the Government of West Bengal, Gautam Sengupta, was brought in as the Director General. Sengupta did not belong to the IAS cadre and is essentially an art historian. The only touch he has with archaeology is that his government department had conducted excavations under the leadership of the Superintendent of Archaeology of his department. He was also the director of a government-sponsored centre of archaeological research and training in Kolkata. As by and large he filled it up with Ph.Ds. from the Deccan College, he can even claim some indirect familiarity with the jargon of academic archaeology. My reference to the Deccan College in this connection is not fortuitous; a junior colleague of his once referred to his 'Centre' as a branch office of the Deccan College. Further, it is well-known that the Deccan College scholars (cf. Paddayya) were frequently invited to his 'Centre' in Kolkata to attend seminars, give lectures and receive miscellaneous academic honours.

It certainly went in favour of Sengupta that one expert of his 'selection committee' was from the Deccan College and had close earlier links with him, and another expert, Nagaraja Rao, is also a Deccan College Ph.D. I do not know if Nagaraja Rao had previously been to Sengupta's 'Centre' but I do know that Paddayya cited Rao's work, without the remotest justification, as something approximating 'New Archaeology'-type research in Indian archaeology. I perfectly understand the reason of the support that Sengupta received from Paddayya and Rao, but it is interesting that two people who are not known to have been involved in archaeology beyond a limited area of Karnataka should be asked to be members of a committee to select the Director General of the Archaeological Survey, which is supposed to research the archaeology of the entire country. It is interesting that in the name of handing over the Director Generalship of the Archaeological Survey of India to a 'technical person', the Government of India should manage to appoint somebody who cannot claim any direct familiarity with the subject.

When Sengupta was appointed the Director of Archaeology of West Bengal, there was some grumbling in the concerned quarters in Kolkata because he was not an archaeology person. *The Statesman,* a daily newspaper, published a note on it (August 12, 1989) and even cited the fact that he is a 'pass course' graduate ('failed English honours') who scored very poor marks (43.1%). I do not take the last point seriously, because his school-leaving and MA records are good. However, there is little doubt that not everything was above board in his selection as the Director of Archaeology, Government of West Bengal.

The same can be said about the way he has been appointed the Director General of the Archaeological Survey of India. I wrote a brief essay commenting on this selection and sent it to a daily newspaper in Delhi. A friend of mine got it published in a Delhi weekly called *Organizer* (28 February, 2010). I have quoted this essay below because this throws light on how the selection process was conducted and how casual did the Government of India feel about finding a suitable person to fill up the post of the Director General of Archaeology in India.

> The websites of the Ministry of Culture, Government of India, and one of its subordinate offices, the Archaeological Survey of India, cannot be accused of attaching any special significance to archaeological research. The 'mission statement' of the Ministry refers to only the "maintenance and conservation of heritage,

historic sites and ancient monuments", and following this, the Archaeological Survey announces that the "maintenance of ancient monuments and archaeological sites and remains of national importance" is its "primary concern".

From this official point of view, the Archaeological Survey of India is not a research or academic body. It is essentially a maintenance organisation on the model of the PWD. Whereas the PWD is concerned only with the construction and maintenance of modern structures, the Archaeological Survey of India's focus is on the maintenance and preservation of historic sites and monuments. We should soon get rid of the notion that the Archaeological Survey and its State level counterparts are supported by the Government to advance the academic cause of archaeology. After all, in very few countries of the modern world, the governments would take the direct responsibility of conducting archaeological research. That research has played only a minor part in the Archaeological Survey's post-Independence agenda is also clear from the sheer number of the unpublished explorations and excavations done by it.

Once we see things in this light, we shall realise that the head of the Archaeological Survey of India, i.e. its Director General, need not have much to do with archaeology as an academic discipline. He need not have the position of the chief archaeologist of the country. His basic qualification should be that of a conservator with expertise in one of the two aspects of conservation—structural and chemical.

If only this simple issue was kept in mind, the recent selection of the Director General of the Archaeological Survey would not have been as disgusting as it has been. First, this was preceded by some media interest. The Hindu of April 24, 2002 carried a news item on the "move to appoint archaeologist as the ASI Director General". The

ASI had, in fact, been without an archaeologist Director General since 1993. More than seven years later, on 25 October, 2009, the same newspaper reported that the Ministry of Culture had set in motion "the process of professionalising premier institutions of art, culture and literature under it" and that the first post to be advertised and filled up on "search-cum-selection" basis under this scheme was that of the ASI Director General.

Secondly, when the advertisement came out (F.No-4-36/2009/ASI), the only firm requirement was that the aspiring candidates had served three years on a specified senior salary-scale. Otherwise, the net thrown was very wide: a post-graduate qualification (subject unspecified and no emphasis on the academic track record) and 15 years' experience in the fields of any of the following subjects: Archaeology, Architecture, Conservation, History, and Anthropology. Further, there had to be five years experience (out of the specified fifteen years) in 'administration matters'. A bachelor's degree of Management was considered desirable. Apparently, the Ministry was not looking exclusively for a field-archaeologist of proven brilliance to run its Archaeological Survey which, incidentally, is possibly the largest organisation of its kind in the world.

In a sense, this lack of emphasis on research or even on Archaeology was not surprising. As noted earlier, the Ministry and the Survey both consider conservation to be their main task.

Thirdly, the selection of the three 'experts' was equally interesting. One of them, Dr. Lokesh Chandra, had never anything to do with archaeology in his working career. The second one, M.S. Nagaraja Rao, is not known to have published anything significant related to field-archaeology since 1974. The academic credibility of the third one, Prof K Paddayya, is beyond dispute, but let us note that, although a retired Director of a research institute and an archaeologist, he has not worked in any other part of India except two districts of Karnataka which happens to be the only professional field of the second 'expert' as well.

The selection process did not pass through the Union Public Service Commission. There are reasons to believe that this process was controlled basically by the Ministry, and the fact that the selected person, Dr. Gautam Sengupta, and the present Secretary to the Ministry, Shri Jawhar Sircar, have had their administrative experience in the same CPI(M)-controlled State government lends some credence to this belief. The 'experts' did not form a coherent group; the first one, in fact, did not reputedly turn up after the first day of meetings.

As I look at it from a distance, I realise that the whole hype about handing over the leadership of the Archaeological Survey of India to a professional archaeologist was nothing but a charade. Before the Selection Committee met, the Prime Minister gave a speech to the members of the Central Advisory Body of Archaeology, and one suspects that the people who contributed to this speech were simply not aware of the malaise which afflicts the subject in India. To add more spice to the proceedings, the serving officers of the Archaeological Survey of India decided to make a representation to the Government, outlining what they thought was their specialist work.

The Archaeological Survey of India has been the victim of mediocre leadership, both academically and otherwise, for a long time. It has not even been able to find a balance between archaeological research and the maintenance and preservation of protected sites and monuments as its objectives. One finds that the present state of affairs weighs heavily in favour of 'conservation' but has one looked closely at the state of structural and chemical conservation all over the country? The Government of

> India, if it were serious about the things it announces in the relevant websites, could try to improve things by appointing at least an efficient conservator at the helm of the ASI. If it were serious about pushing archaeological research in a new direction, it could have appointed somebody whose research track-record is impeccable. The fact that it threw all academic criteria to the winds while appointing the person it has appointed shows that whatever pious thought the PM may utter in the name of Archaeology, that is one of the last priorities the country has, if it can be considered a 'priority' at all.

Flouting of the Government of India Rules by Some Foreign Archaeologists and Their Indian Collaborators

Long before this new Director General of the Archaeological Survey of India took charge, there was indication that the Survey's excavation rules were flouted by some foreign archaeologists and their Indian colleagues. On 16 May 2005, there was a report in the *Deccan Herald* to this effect:

> Expressing concern over "uncontrolled excavations" at Indian archaeological sites, a group of archaeologists have alleged that rules and regulations regarding excavations are openly flouted by several Indian scholars and their foreign collaborators. The experts who have submitted their complaints to the Archaeological Survey of India (ASI), told *Deccan Herald* that a number of foreign collaborators had undertaken excavations in India without prior approval of the ASI and even some of them had worked here with a tourist visa.
>
> "The Indian national interest in archaeology will be gravely impaired if things are ignored. The significance or insignificance of the research being undertaken is not the point. The question is whether we as a nation can afford to ignore our sites and turn a blind eye to our archaeological regulations being openly flouted," they said.

> Citing the case of Earthwatch website, where an advertisement was put up offering an experience in excavation at Attirampakkam in Tamil Nadu for $1900, they said for the first time an Indian archaeological site had been thrown open to foreign commercial participation flouting government norms. Even in the case of Cambridge-Dharwar-Bellary project, they alleged that a number of foreign participants in the excavation did not have proper research visa and the ASI was not aware of the fact that foreign scholars and students were involved in the excavations.
>
> Describing the project on the Neolithic sites in Karnataka as a blatant violation of archaeological norms and ethics, the experts said, "what is amazing here is that somebody can go around the country re-excavating sites excavated by others and collecting biological samples from them without the knowledge of the government".

No comment is necessary on the complete indifference to archaeological ethics shown by the involved foreign researchers and organizations. They would not have dared attempt this in the context of, say, Greece. As it is India where they do not lack puppet native collaborators, they showed no inclination to think of the rules and regulations in these matters.

Comments on the Developments in Indian Archaeology, 1990-2011

General Features till 2000

Much of this chapter has been concerned with the role of Cambridge in ancient Indian historical and archaeological studies, including notes on my field-programme and publications. However, in no way can my studies be separated from the basic strands of Indian archaeology during this period. The developments in the 1990s were discussed by me earlier (2003, pp. 124-148). Here, I shall briefly outline the major trends between 1990 and 2000 and focus in some detail on the trends observable in the last decade.

The ethnographic approach to prehistory was strongly visible throughout the 1990s, along with a greater preoccupation with the study of the technological attributes of the stone tool industries. There was also a specific focus on the geomorphology of the Stone Age sites and areas, although in many cases how our knowledge of prehistory was affected by the information derived from geomorphology was not always clear. There were more dates from the prehistoric profiles, and although these dates have not always been borne out by further dates, the fact that the different techniques like ESR were applied to Indian prehistoric sites is a hopeful point. Some attention was also given to proper sampling strategies of surveys, micro-wear studies, etc. The study of rock art developed into a sub-discipline of prehistoric studies in the 1990s (for the details of prehistoric studies during this period, Chakrabarti 2003, pp. 126-134).

The scope of archaeological science increased manifold but remained focussed mainly on mining, metallurgy and archaeo-botanical and archaeo-zoological studies. The technical studies of ancient pottery were on a limited scale and the same may be said about underwater archaeology, remote-sensing studies, etc. Progress continued to be made in skeletal and population studies, the latter occasionally helped by DNA analysis (for the details of this paragraph, Chakrabarti 2003, pp. 134-143).

The basic excavations and discoveries continued to be made in different parts of the country, and if any area has to be specifically named, the middle Ganga valley with its published reports on Narhan and associated sites, and Raja Nal

Ka Tila, Malhar and Dadupur deserves consideration. Dholavira was the most important Harappan site to be excavated whereas among the generally protohistoric sites mention may be made of Golbai Sasan in Orissa, Balathal in Rajasthan, and Kodumanal in Tamil Nadu. Different kinds of historical analysis based on archaeological data are also a feature of this period (for the details, Chakrabarti 2003, 143-148).

Trends of Indian Archaeological Research, 2000-2010

The most significant development in the Indian Palaeolithic studies in the first decade the of the twenty-first century is the dating of the earliest level of the Acheulian at Attirampakkam around 1.5 million years ago. What gives this dating confidence which is missing from the somewhat similar dates from Bori and Isampur is that this was obtained by using two dating methods: palaeomagnetic mesurements of the excavated profile and the direct 26AL/10Be burial of the stone artifacts. This level is now found to be no younger than 1.07 million years ago, with a 'pooled average' of 1.51+/— 0.07 million years ago. This date is comparable to the date of the Acheulian in Africa and at the site of Ubeidiya in Israel (Pappu *et al.* 2011).

There was a cumulative body of evidence regarding the occurrence of a pre-Acheulian stone tool industry in the Siwaliks (for a review, Chakrabarti 2006, pp. 16-17). In Peninsular India, indisputable evidence was wanting (for a review of Bori and Isampur evidence, *Ibid.*, pp. 17-18). In recent years, the debate about whether there was an early Pleistocene Acheulian industry or not in Peninsular India intensified (Gaillard *et al.* 2010, with a rejoinder by Chauhan and a counter-rejoinder by Gaillard *et al.*, all with extensive references). In this context, the new Attirampakkam dating is a very important step forward.

The find of a few *in situ* Palaeolithic artefacts in a generally fresh condition and a highly weathered fossil herbivore tooth from a thin rubble horizon at the bottom of the Dhansi Formation in the Narmada valley is interesting because the Dhansi Formation is dated in the late Pliocene and early Pleistocene (Chauhan and Patnaik 2008). The bed from which the Hathnora fossil find was recorded has been subjected to re-analysis, leading to the inference that many of the present conclusions about this hominin find are tentative (Patnaik *et al.* 2009). Mulagapalli, Patnaik and Verma (2007) offer a vegetational and climatic sequence of the quaternary sediments of the Hathnora locality. More fossil finds from Hathnora were published in 2005 (Sankhayan 2005) arguing that both the old and new finds represented a single individual, possibly a 25-35 year old female who was 135 cm tall and had a pigmy body frame characterised by a very robust body build.

A study of the Toba ash deposit in the Jureru valley, Karnataka, and the middle Son valley, Madhya Pradesh, tries to study the impact of the spread and deposition of this volcanic ash bed on the late Pleistocene Palaeolithic landscape of these parts of India and concludes that the impact varied from area to area but must have considerably affected the human and environmental scenarios.

> The results indicate that ash-fall deposits in both valleys underwent several phases of reworking that possibly lasted for several years, indicating that ash was mobile in the landscape for a considerable period of time prior to burial. This could have enhanced and lengthened the detrimental effects of the ash on vegetation and water sources, as well as animal and hominin populations. (Jones 2010)

The speculations about the arrival of the Anatomically Modern Humans from Africa between 70,000 and 50,000 years ago or later are tentative. The continuity of the Indian prehistoric sequence is so seamless that it is almost impossible to mark the distinct arrivals of new technology in it. The period II of Patne near Chalisgaon in Maharashtra, which has upper Palaeolithic tool-types and beads made of ostrich egg shells is a direct continuation of its Period I, which is called mainly middle Palaeolithic with some upper Palaeolithic elements like blades and burins. If Patne II is a continuation of Patne I, it cannot be taken to mark a phase of migration from across the sea. Further, the idea of a post-Miocene land-bridge across the Red Sea has been denied (Fernandes, Rohling and Siddell 2006). The postulated 'southern dispersal' would thus imply a maritime crossing in the late Pleistocene, an implication unlikely to be accepted by all.

There is a fair amount of scientific posturing in the recent Indian Stone Age studies (cf. Petraglia and Allchin 2007). What Ravi Korisettar (2007) calls the 'basin model' of Palaeolithic distribution with reference to its core and peripheral areas may not stand close scrutiny because, among other things, his idea of the rest of the subcontinent beyond Karnataka does not inspire confidence. For instance, his map does not seem to include the whole of the Chhotanagpur plateau within the Palaeolithic distribution area. To argue that there were extinct sources of water in the areas surveyed by him and his group will possibly need more convincing argument and proof, I wrote the following earlier in this context:

> The tradition of looking at the Indian Palaeolithic landscape primarily through geo-archaeology, which is being increasingly prominent among scholars who have never been trained in geology and who seldom carry their arguments beyond jargon, is slowly making the study of Palaeolithic India almost irrelevant from the point of view of the nation's history. The impasse can be overcome only by the induction of professionally competent Indian

> geologists and soil scientists in the domain of environmental archaeology. (Chakrabarti 2008, p. 34).

The settlement-subsistence approach to the study of the Indian Palaeolithic has not made any significant headway after Raju's study of 1988 (Raju 1988), although Paddayya (2010) has recently made a strong plea for it. It may be noted that without extensive chronological back-up this approach is unlikely to impart any historical depth to the prehistoric landscape but this will at least make us aware of the 'relevance of the understanding of modern land to the understanding of its prehistory and vice versa' (Chakrabarti 2003, p. 107).

In the area of the middle Palaeolithic, the evidence from Kalpi on the right bank of the Yamuna, which shows three 'events' (event-I: a sand deposit dated 76 Ka plus/minus 11 Ka-moderate to dry climate; event-II: 69 Ka plus/minus 13 Ka – mid-level 45 Ka plus/minus 9Ka –; event-III: 43 Ka plus/minus 7 Ka, humid in the lower part and dry in the upper part), with the interface of the events I and II showing flaked quartzite pebbles and worked bone industry, is a highly significant discovery in view of the location of the site.

An area of prehistoric study, which has been making quiet and steady progress in recent years, is the study of prehistoric Indian art in relation to the study of Palaeolithic 'cupules' (Kumar *et al.* 2005, Bednarik) in central India.

The antiquity of the Indian microlithic industry, which can be observed in a number of places in association with upper Palaeolithic tools, has been placed on a secure footing at Jwalapuram in the Kurnool sector of Andhra between 35000 years BP and 12000 years BP and it shows the association of four cranial fragments, an isolated tooth, stone beads and pieces of red ochre (cf. Clarkson *et al.* 2009). Far to the east, a fossil wood industry of upper Palaeolithic affinity shows close analogues with the upper Palaeolithic Anyathian industry near

Mandalay in Myanmar, thus suggesting a previously unknown extensive cultural development covering parts of Indian Tripura, eastern Bangladesh and the Mandalay area of Myanmar. A fossil wood prehistoric industry has also been noticed in Mizoram of eastern India (personal information from D.K. Medhi). The early radiocarbon dates from Lekhahia, Damdama and Mahadaha have put the early chronological status of the Mesolithic in the Ganga plain beyond doubt.

Significant advances have been made in assessing the problem of transition to food production in the subcontinent in recent years. The discoveries in the Kotumsar and Dandak caves of Bastar (Yadava *et al.* 2007) highlight the tradition of early plant collection in the subcontinent. Traces of fire were located on their floors considerably away from the cave-mouths and dated in the calibrated radiocarbon date-range of 4990-2080 BC. The plant remains comprise three types of grasses and two types of millets. The grasses include a variety locally called *Chenchrus*, which are still cultivated in this area as animal fodder, and another variety called *Sirwari* whose leaves and tender shoots are still used as food. The identified millets—foxtail millet and another millet of the *Setaria* group—are still collected in the area as edible foods. A similar tradition of collecting wild grains as a prelude to full-fledged agriculture has also been testified by the phytoliths of wild rice around the site of Lohuradeva in the central Ganga plain around 8250 BC.

The 8th-6th millennia BC evidence of rice cultivation in the Vindhyan region and central Ganga plain has been obtained from a number of sites but the most significant of them is Lohuradeva near Gorakhpur (Tewari *et al.* 2008). Studies of geomorphology, pollen records, phytoliths, diatom and micro-charcoal were undertaken along with the excavations at the site. The presence of micro-charcoal in the 2.8-m thick succession of sediments in the marshy depression, on the bank of which the site is situated, suggests slash-and-burn cultivation around 10000 BP. This is supported by the evidence of cerealia pollen and micro-charcoal in the sediments of Sanai Tal in the adjacent Lucknow area since 15000 BP. The related evidence from Dadupur (near Lucknow) and Bateswar (near Agra) attests 'human activity' in a larger area of the Ganga plain during the late Pleistocene and early Holocene. The domesticated rice found in the lowest archaeological deposit of Lohuradeva has been dated 6309 BCE. The phytoliths and cerealia pollens in the lake sediments indicate well-developed agriculture in the area in the 7th-6th millennia BCE. Pottery of the earliest phase comprises handmade and ill-fired plain red and black-and-red types, whose clay is mixed with rice-husk, which is also used in the mud plaster of the wattle-and-daub houses. There are circular mud-floors, post-holes and hearths in association with microliths, the latter somewhat sparse because of the unavailability of stone as raw material in the plain.

The domesticated rice in the lowest level of Lohuradeva occurs in association with both wild rice (*Oryza rupifogon*) and foxtail millet (*Setaria* sp.). They occur intermittently in several layers in association with other wild seeds and fruits. Barley appears at the site around 2700 BCE and wheat a little after that. Rice was present throughout.

Lohuradeva is no longer an isolated site. The crop-remains of the Neolithic level of Jhusi, dated in the 8th-6th millennia BC (Pokharia, Pal and Srivastava 2009), include domesticated rice, hulled barley, bread wheat, dwarf wheat, lentil, green gram, grass-pea, field-pea, horse-gram, sesame, linseed, grape, common vetch, job's tear and a common Indian fruit, *Anwalaa* (*Emblica officinalis*). Such an early date of wheat and barley in the Ganga plain has problems regarding its contact with the supposed epicentre of wheat-barley agriculture in Baluchistan, to which there is no archaeological answer at present. Rice and wheat also occur in the Neolithic level of Tokwa in the Mirzapur part of the Vindhyas. There is a sixth millennium BC date from this level of this site.

I have discussed the claim of the Aravalli system as an early and independent centre of agricultural origin in a number of places. The mesolithic level of Bagor (6th millennium BC) with the domesticated remains of cattle, sheep and goat is likely to contain the seeds of food production, and the same is likely to be true of the first 'mesolithic' phase of the similar site of Ganeshwar which contains a profusion of copper tools in its period 3 dated in the 4th millennium BC, being preceded by a few copper tools in its period 2 itself. The point is that Ganeshwar, period 1, from where there is a straight transition to metal-smelting in its period 2, is likely to possess, like Bagor I, an agricultural component and date similarly from the 6th millennium BCE. This date is highlighted also by the mid-6th millennium BCE date for a 60-cm thick Mesolithic deposit on the eastern face of Gilund-2 (Bhilwara district where Bagor also is located). What is further noteworthy is that the beginning of the chalcolithic occupation at Balathal in the same region has been found to be about 3700 BC, suggesting a considerably earlier beginning of agriculture in the region (Chakrabarti 2006: 225-234).

It now appears that the subcontinent had developed early pockets of agriculture based on different types of cereals. The date of the beginning of agriculture in the southern peninsula cannot still be pushed beyond c.3000 BC but it may be noted that cerealia pollens occur in the early Holocene pollen profiles in the Nilgiri hills. Such pollens were also reported in the similar contexts of the salt lakes of western Rajasthan (Chakrabarti 2006: 105-106).

The recent research on the Indus civilization is characterized both by major discoveries and changes in theoretical orientations. The discoveries have taken place all over Gujarat, Haryana and western U.P., some of the major sites in this regard being Bagasra, Kanmer, Shikarpur, Khirasara and Juni Karan in Gujarat, Bhirrana, Farmana and possibly Karsola in Haryana and Sinauli and Alamgirpur in western Uttar Pradesh. The sites in Gujarat have basically added to the details of the civilization, but the sequence at Bhirrana, which begins with the Hakra ware, seems to put the Hissar-Fatehabad area of Haryana in the core zone of the Indus civilization. The burial grounds of Farmana and Sinoli are still undated but provide rare examples of the profiles of Harappan burial grounds, with Sinoli providing proof of the link-up between the Harappans and the upper Ganga plain 'copper hoards'. Similarly, the discoveries at Mandi, which include plenty of gold, silver and semi-precious stones suggest that there was no clearly perceived sense of decay at the so-called late Harappan sites of western Uttar Pradesh. The recent excavations at Alamgirpur show that there was no break between the Harappans and the Painted Grey Ware at the site and that the beginning of the Harappan occupation here may date from as early as c.2500 BC. The distribution of Harappan sites all along the foot of the Siwaliks from Jammu to Rupar and from Rupar to Haridwar confronts us with a vast distribution area spread from the Rajasthan and Cholistan deserts to the shadow of the Siwaliks. This distribution area is something which cannot be explained by referring to the idea of a west-to-east migration of the Harappans. Till now there is no reason to believe that the Harappans of western UP or large sections of Haryana were significantly later than their counterparts further west. Equally interestingly, the Sinauli evidence that the 'copper hoards' of the upper Gangetic valley fell within the Harappan domain in the sense that they were contemporaries at this site has the implication of incorporating, however indirectly or faintly, the upper Gangetic plain within the Harappan tradition. Another point which has clearly emerged in recent years is that the Indus civilization was not in the direct arrow line of development beginning with Mehrgarh in Baluchistan. The agricultural diversity of this civilization clearly shows that there was considerable agricultural contribution to it from the eastern regions as well.

Whatever may be the scientific judgement on the change in the quantum of water flow in the Ghaggar-Hakra or the Sarasvati river and its date, there is yet no reason to doubt H.G. Raverty's analysis of some mediaeval texts and the report of a late eighteenth century survey, which showed that there was a perennial flow in this river system until the 15th-16th century. A tenth century AD inscription from Haryana mentions *Prachi Sarasvati* or 'eastern Sarasvati'. There is also enough evidence from the nineteenth century to show that during the monsoon months at least there was no lack of water in this drainage system. One also notes a distinct tendency towards environmental determinism in some recent attempts to view the growth and decline of the Indus civilization in terms of the fluctuations of the monsoon.

There are many bits and pieces of new information from all over India in the context of protohistory outside the orbit of the Indus civilization. The emergence of Orissa as a centre of chalcolithic black-and-red ware is an important point in this regard along with the identification of Golabai Sasan as a late third-early second millennium BC Neolithic-Chalcolithic settlement. More radiocarbon dates are available for the chalcolithic of West Bengal, with the increasing probability of its dating from before 2000 BC. Excavations at Adichanallur on the bank of the Tamraparni river in the Tirunelveli district have revealed three phases of burials and a separate habitational area by the side of the burial ground. The burial area was used for mining of copper and iron ores before the beginning of burials at the site, probably in the second millennium BC. Iron at Dadupur near Lucknow has been dated around 1700 BC and at Malhar near Banaras around 1800 BC, if not a little earlier. The find of an iron ploughshare at Malhar in association with the first iron at the site indicates that there was beginning of iron in the Gangetic valley agriculture by the beginning of the second millennium BC.

Our perspective of the beginning of the early historic period has changed with the earlier dating of the NBP at c.800 BC and possibly earlier. Further, it has been realized that there is no reason to think that the date of the NBP outside the Ganga plain has to be significantly later than its beginning in the Ganga plain. This will have its impact on the dating of the early historic period in the southern regions where the early historic period is supposed to be considerably later than that in the Gangetic areas. The publication of the full excavation report on Nagarjunakonda under the editorship of K.V. Soundara Rajan is a major event in the study of Indian historical archaeology and ranks equally with the significance of the report on Taxila. Further, with a better understanding of the route network which extends from the south of the Ganga plain to the furthest tip of the southern peninsula has imparted a better sense of perspective to the link between the locations of urban sites and routes in this vast region.

A substantial amount of progress has been obtained in the field of the material analysis of excavated artefacts, especially in the case of the metallic objects (Singh 2007). Progress in other areas has been noticeably slow. There has been no major breakthrough in the dating of the old preindustrial mines of the country. A notable study is that of the old deposits of mining ores suitable for wootz-smelting in the northern areas of Adilabad, Nizamabad, etc. in the northern section of Andhra. The study has been undertaken by S. Jaikishen in his *Iron and Wootz Steel Industry in Northern Telangana (A Historical Perspective)* in 2009. In Tamil Nadu, the two-volume *Catalogue of Archaeological Sites in Tamil Nadu* and the maps to go with the catalogue by K. Rajan, V.P. Yathees Kumar and S. Selvakumar (2009) are outstanding events, putting Tamil Nadu archaeology in a singularly wide context. Of similar importance is K. Rajan's *Ancient Irrigation Technology, Sluice Technology in Tamil Nadu* (2008), an equally outstanding publication.

Not much attention is paid to the archaeology of later periods, but one hopes that the importance of archaeology in studying the Indian mediaeval and later periods will soon gain an increasing focus.

5

Epilogue

The present volume may be judged on two levels. On the first level, it deals with the beginning and the current status of archaeology in the Indian university system, focussing primarily on the author's own experience as a long-standing teacher of the subject. In this context, it also outlines the author's personal background and early academic roots, hoping to give an idea of the types of students who were drawn to archaeology in India in its early phase. There are also notes on his professional experience in the various universities he has been associated with. It should be possible to assess on the basis of these notes the general state of affairs in the historical studies section of the Indian universities.

On the second level, this book offers a detailed review of the development of various ideas, research themes and field-projects in Indian archaeology over the last fifty years with special reference to the author's own work. Indian archaeological writings have seldom been concerned with the historiography of ideas and research themes, and from this point of view the present book may be considered a reasonably elaborate examination of how archaeology has developed as an academic discipline in the Indian university framework. History of Indian archaeology has been a distinct focus of study in recent years, and the present author himself wrote two books and a number of papers on this topic. This does not necessarily mean that the historiography of different ideas in Indian archaeology and the basic frame of its theoretical development in various fields is quite clear to us. For instance, detailed archival studies have recently been made of Bruce Foote's life and career (Pappu 2008) without making explicit the fact that he was only one of the geologists who laid the basic stratigraphical and typological framework of Indian prehistory by the end of the nineteenth century. Foote's ideas fitted closely with the general ideas of prehistory of the time.

SOME BASIC ISSUES AND DEVELOPMENTS

In a series of essays in 1986, later published as *Theoretical Issues of Indian* Archaeology (1988), I tried to examine some of the core issues of Indian archaeology including prehistory, the transition from food-collection to food-production, both Indus and early historic urbanisations, trade, metallurgy, and the pernicious frame of race-culture-language correlation. The archaeological discoveries since then have brought forward a clearer understanding of the broad picture but the pace of progress has been by and large rather slow and uneven. In prehistoric studies, a clear admission of the early Pleistocene antiquity of stone tools in India seems to have been just made with a firm two-fold dating of Attirampakkam tools at 1.8 mya. The indications of such an early antiquity have been with us since the dating of the artefacts at Riwat and Pabbi hills in the northwest, which were preceded by the opinions of some Indian geologists who were not hesitant to put some of the tools they found in Jammu, Ladakh, Himachal Pradesh and elsewhere in the northwest in the early Pleistocene or even earlier. The discovery of stone tools in the Pinjore bed of certain localities in the Rawalpindi area of Pakistan should have been an eye-opener in this regard but curiously the significance of these discoveries has gone unnoticed in the current professional Indian literature on prehistory. The Pinjore bed is a well-recognized and dated bed of Indian geology and there does not seem to be any confusion about its date in 2 mya. Its boundary with the overlying Boulder Conglomerate bed, although with an uneven chronological line, need not blind us to the overall significance of the occurrence of stone tools in the Pinjore bed. The only reason I can think of for the absence of this Pakistani discovery in Indian professional literature on prehistory is that its discoverer, a Pakistani archaeologist, does not belong to the small professional group of Indian prehistorians and their Western colleagues. A number of discoveries in India, such as those at Nadai near Chandigarh and Odai in Tamil Nadu, are also ignored in this literature precisely for this reason. In fact, the discussion between Claire Gaillard and her associates on the one hand and P. Chauhan on the other in *Quaternary International* on the issue of the lower Pleistocene antiquity of Indian stone tools is noted not merely for its singularly vituperative tone on the part of Chauhan but also for its atmosphere of a club-level debate where the opinions of 'outsiders' like the geologists of the Geological Survey of India or the Pakistani discoverer of stone tools in the Pinjore bed were ignored by both sides. In fact, Chauhan's refusal to consider anything—any discovery or opinion—unless it is internationally published and assessed is an example of the kind of attitude which is being increasingly common among modern exclusively science-oriented archaeologists.

It is not that the impact of science on many known archaeological profiles is not devastating, if not highly confusing. The recent assessment of the Hathnora profile by Patnaik and others (including Chauhan), which basically argues that the entire sequence is not merely mixed up but also chronologically late, is an example of this development. On the other hand, Sheila Mishra's and others' opinion that the Acheulian of the Pinjore Formation is 'Large Flake Acheulian' which is found in the comparable Java deposits as well, suggesting the migration of *Homo erectus* to Java through India is an intriguing hypothesis which has long appealed to people who believe that the early Pleistocene stone tools of the northwestern part of the subcontinent were likely to have been fashioned by *Homo erectus*. Sheila Mishra's hypothesis also puts in shade the belief that the chopper-chopping element was the earliest component of the Indian Palaeolithic.

It appears that the Toba ash deposit is a fairly widespread deposit in various parts of India including Karnataka, Maharashtra, Madhya Pradesh, Orissa and West Bengal. As I understand it, geochemically this deposit has been found to be coeval with the Younger Toba Deposit of c.74000 years B.P. The intriguing point is that that the date of this deposit, as suggested by the dates or possible dates from sites like Bori and Morgaon, are not the dates of the Younger Toba Ash Deposit. This again is another slippery patch in the study of Indian prehistory.

Equally slippery is the focus on the evidence of the Anatomically Modern Humans in the Indian context. The Indian Palaeolithic sequence, as far as one can judge, is uninterrupted and continuous and to infer that the occurrence of crossed designs on ostrich shell beads of places like Patne heralded the arrival of the anatomically modern humans in India does not make sense. If the excavator's report is to be believed, Patne reveals a seamless sequence from the middle Palaeolithic upwards.

The chronological situation of the Indian lower Palaeolithic has no doubt improved but still there is no worth-mentioning picture of the accompanying cultural details beyond tool technology. Even assertions like that the Indian Acheulian was essentially a large flake technology has to be worked out in detail and not put forward as a proven thing. To offer some depth to what seems to be a hopelessly muddled picture of typo-technology, the settlement-subsistence approach to the study of Indian prehistory was no doubt useful but it is important to acknowledge at the same time that this approach hardly goes beyond suggesting probable ways in which a particular landscape could have been put to use by prehistoric hunter-gatherers. The reason why site after site of Indian Palaeolithic materials failed to yield worth-mentioning biological and cultural remains may be due to the fact that their tool-manufacturing sites were not the camping sites where they lived for some length of time. Besides, in a hot climate as ours, there was also not much necessity of erecting semi-permanent shelters, which would survive the first torrents of the next monsoon. In *Oxford Companion to Indian Archaeology*, I referred to the ethnographic work on the Chenchus and Irulas to drive home this point. However, the fact remains that except rare flashes of facts like transportation of raw materials from some distance, the presence of a cognitive sense behind the fashioning of stone and bone tools according to a design, and artificially made cupules on the rock-surface, the picture of Palaeolithic India, especially that of the lower and the middle Palaeolithic, has not advanced much beyond what Mortimer Wheeler once expressed as 'stone tools' and 'more stone tools'. The use of geomorphological and/or geological jargon by non-specialist students of this scene is unlikely to make this long phase of human existence particularly relevant to the study of ancient India.

The hunting-gathering tradition became more intense and diversified with the Mesolithic, the earliest beginning of which is still problematic. As the work at Jwalapuram conclusively shows, its beginning goes back to what otherwise would be considered an upper Palaeolithic phase. This is not surprising because microliths as a tool-type are found to occur in many upper Palaeolithic profiles. A sharper problem is to estimate when the mesolithic as a distinct cultural phase as apart from the upper Palaeolithic began. The Mesolithic evidence which has been excavated in the Ganga plain around Allahabad, Pratapgarh and Banaras and in its Vindhyan fringe as at Chopani Mando in the Belan valley points toward permanent settlements with a diversified hunting-gathering economy with evidence of domesticated rice at Damdama in Pratapgarh. The evidence of domesticated cattle, sheep and goat occurs at Bagor in southeast Rajasthan and Adamgarh in central India and possibly other places as well. It appears that the cultural level characterized by microlithic industries was associated in a significant way with the beginning of cultivation and animal domestication in India. Also, the hunting-gathering tradition of this phase continued till a much later period with the pieces of such evidence coming from a large number of the so-called Neolithic-Chalcolithic sites of various parts of the country. At Dihar in West Bengal, bottle-glass microliths are found to occur possibly in the early historic context. Occasionally, microliths continued to be used as late as the early mediaeval period.

The most striking fact about the transition to food-production in India seems to be its diverse pattern. After the excavations at Lohuradeva, the claim of the central Ganga plain as a centre of early rice cultivation has been securely established, and this has a lot to do with the different pieces of evidence collected from the study of archaeological and soil profiles not merely of the site and its excavated trenches but also of some other soil sections of the neighbouring region. The idea that the rice excavated at Lohuradeva did not belong to the domesticated variety immediately falls through when one remembers that rice husk was found mixed with mud-plaster of the earliest Lohuradeva mud walls, suggesting a close familiarity with the potential of rice husks. The discovery in the Kanger National Park of Bastar of the edible variety of some grass and millets in a context of the fifth millennium BC suggests that slow steps towards food-production were being taken in different parts of India, and but for discoveries of this kind we would not know about them. I have long believed that there was an early food-producing area in the Aravallis of Rajasthan mainly based on the fact that if there was an element of animal-domestication in the 6th millennium BC microlithic level of Bagor, there is no reason why there could not be such an element in the first period of occupation at Ganeshwar. I find it inconceivable that the extensive copper metallurgy of Ganeshwar, period II, which dates from the late fourth millennium BC, could spring from a mere hunting-gathering stage, which Ganeshwar, period I, on the basis of the present evidence, is. That there was an early fourth millennium tradition of food-production in Rajasthan is proved by the dates from Balathal in southeast Rajasthan. Even at the site of Gilund, a so-called Mesolithic occupation has been dated in the 6th millennium BC, and there is as yet no reason to believe that this level did not have any element of food-production and/or animal domestication.

What is likely to emerge in the near future is the picture of an uneven development of food-production in various parts of the subcontinent, some as early as 7000 BC or earlier and some possibly not earlier than c.3000 BC. In south India, there is as yet no evidence of the beginning of agriculture before c.3000 BC. From the northeastern part of the country, there is virtually no dated evidence.

Here I would like to mention a word of caution about postulating, on the basis of the wide occurrence of microliths in different contexts and parts of India, a hunting-gathering tradition which ran parallel to its food-producing economy. Foraging for food has no doubt been an integral part of the Indian life till today, but that is due to the fact that a large number of people do not have access to the resources of the land on the same level that many settled farmers have. They can survive mainly by foraging in the countryside, which assumes many forms even in the modern Indian countryside.

If one is allowed to pass on to a consideration of the Indus civilization at this point, we have to point out that this civilization did not lie on a straight arrow-line of time beginning with the wheat-barley cultivation at Mehrgarh in Baluchistan. In view of the early cultivation of rice in the central Ganga plain and the presence of rice at several early Harappan and mature Harappan sites, it has to be admitted that the agricultural base of the Indus civilization was more broad-based than a narrowly focussed wheat-barley one. This simple fact should lead to a perceptible change regarding the spread of this civilization. It does not have to represent a dispersal from the earlier western settlements to the later eastern ones. The mid-third millennium BC date of the lowest level of Alamgirpur is a proof in favour of this assumption, and I am sure that as more and more excavations take place in the east and are dated, the Indus civilization belt from Haryana and Indian Panjab to western Uttar Pradesh will assume a separate focus of its own, apart from the focus of the settlements further west. After the excavations at Kunal and Bhirrana, the Fatehabad section of Haryana seems to lie in a primary area of Harappan origin. How this idea takes shape will depend on the future discoveries, but at this stage I feel that the possibility of its coming true is strong.

Regarding the beginning of wheat-barley agriculture in the subcontinent, an important perplexing event is the identification of wheat and barley in the 7000 BC Neolithic levels of Jhusi and Tokwa. The implication of the discoveries has not yet sunk in but the idea that there could be such a rapid dissemination of the cultivation of particular crops from Baluchistan to the heart of the Ganga plain is startling, to say the least. Here also, one would rather wait for the further discoveries.

As far as the major Harappan settlements are concerned, important categories of evidence are now emerging from Gujarat where the excavations at Bagasra, Juni Karn, Kanmer and Khirsara have to some extent elaborated the picture obtained earlier. In the whole of Gujarat, the problem of Harappan site locations is still not clearly understood in all cases, and from this point of view even the location of Dholavira is not as clear as it should be. In the case of Harappa, it is now clear that the site lies on a route which traverses from the Delhi area to Mooltan and the Dera Ismail Khan-Dera Ghazi Khan zone, meaning that this site was an integral part of a vast chain of sites which linked the western section of these sites with the sites well in the east.

The problems regarding the Harappan civilization are legion, and here I can mention only a few of the ones which interest me. The discovery in the burial ground of Sinoli near Baghpat in western Uttar Pradesh clearly showed the incorporation of the Gangetic copper hoard tradition in the Indus tradition of the region. The antennae-hilted swords of the Gangetic valley tradition have been found in the Harappan graves. Again, the implication of this discovery has not yet sunk in but it may no longer be considered that the Indus civilization was not something disassociated from the cultural traditions which were developing in the upper Gangetic region. Although the Harappan site distribution in werstern Uttar Pradesh has long been its proof, the Sinoli evidence shows how closely dovetailed was the Indus tradition with the upper Gangetic valley copper hoard tradition. The possible late Harappan association of the upper Gangetic valley copper hoards was pointed out in a book on 'copper and its alloys in ancient India', which was authored by me jointly with N. Lahiri in 1996. The idea has been vindicated at Sinoli.

The discovery of the Mandi hoard in Muzaffarnagar of western Uttar Pradesh may be said to have done away with the notion that the term 'late Harappan' denoted something decaying. With its rich hoard of silver and gold jewellery and a large cache of beads, this discovery from a site which would otherwise be termed 'late Harappan' has shown that the use of precious items and extensive trade were as common in the late Harappan of this region as in the mature Harappan of better known sites elsewhere.

No recent discussion on the Indus civilization can ignore the problem of the Sarasvati river system which constituted a river system parallel to that of the Indus to its east. The fact that the river is mentioned glowingly in the Rigveda and the fact that the majority of the Harappan sites may be considered to belong to this system have lent an air of piquancy to the whole problem. I have summarized my ideas and basic sources regarding this in my book (co-authored with S.K. Saini), *The Problem of the Sarasvati River and Notes on the Archaeological Geography of Haryana and Indian Panjab* (2009). In addition to the studies of the modern satellite imageries of the concerned region, which have in fact been able to outline a whole network of drainage lines between the Haryana and Panjab Siwaliks and the Rann of Kutch, the most important historical study is that by H.G. Raverty who based himself on some Muslim texts of the 9th-10th centuries and later. The river was a living entity then and it was so even later. The evidence is unequivocal and borne out by a 10th century AD inscription from Pehowa, which refers to the 'eastern Sarasvati' and thus shows that there was an eastern branch of the Sarasvati river in the 10th century. Raverty also used the results of an unpublished survey of the river system of the whole region, which was apparently undertaken in the late 18th century. In view of Raverty's unequivocal evidence and some other relevant literary sources, there is no need to claim that the Sarasvati river system has long been a dead river system along which the water stopped flowing significantly long before the Indus civilization had come to flourish. The current scientific research seems to argue that this river was not a glacially fed river but was basically dependent on the monsoon rains. Whatever might have been the case, the late nineteenth century district gazetteers of modern Haryana write of the presence of considerable water-bodies along its bed during the monsoon and of the prosperity of agriculture based on it. The problem is simple: whether or not the Indus civilization could flourish in the Sarasvati river system even if the river carried no significant flow of water during that period. The answer is that even under the conditions described by the Haryana district gazetteers of the late nineteenth century, there could be prosperous settlements based on irrigation networks in this region. In fact, a time has possibly come when we have to ask ourselves if the Indus civilization could not have flourished under the conditions which one could observe in its distribution area in the nineteenth century, i.e., before the natural drainages of this area were seriously disturbed by human activities.

In an American Geophysical Union meeting on "climates, past landscapes and civilizations", 21-25 March 2011, Santa Fe (reported in *Science* vol.332, 1 April, 2011), the following was reported:

> To determine when the Ghaggar-Hakra last was an active river, researchers looked for the youngest sediments deposited by flowing water. Each of the three groups dated sediments primarily with optically stimulated luminescence, a technique that uses the light energy stored in quartz grains to estimate when the grains were last exposed to light. Gupta's team drilled several 40 metre cores near the Indus city of Kalibangan, in today's India, and found that river sediment deposits ceased after approximately 14000 BCE, long before the Indus culture. Gupta said in his talk that the river may have jumped into the bed of the Sutlej river to the west at this time. Hideaki Maemoku of Hiroshima University led a Japanese team that found that sand dunes surrounding the Ghaggar are older than 10000 years, another indication any river present had long since dried up by that point.

It is worth pointing out that in *Puratattva*, 2010, I wrote that a time had come when one had possibly to visualize the growth of the Indus civilization in the context of an environmental setting which can be deduced from the descriptions in the nineteenth century gazetteers of Haryana.

B.B. Lal has in his recent book *The Sarasvati Flows On* draws attention to the similarity between a terracotta object reported from Mohenjodaro and the wooden tablets carried by school children of ordinary vernacular medium schools all over northern India. They practice their writing on these tablets by first giving them a coat of mud. The similarity between these tablets and the Mohenjodaro terracotta specimen is striking and opens up the possibility of a wide writing and even a schooling system in the context of Mohenjodaro and the Indus civilization. Such systems were current in the Mesopotamian civilization and thus not beyond the range of possibilities even in the case of the Harappan civilization. The fact that many of the surviving Harappan signs have been very sparingly used suggests that there was possibly a system of writing on perishable materials, as indeed was the case in historical India.

M. Danino has categorically shown how the system of linear measurement in the Harappan civilization has been carried over into the later, historical India. Danino has argued that Dholavira was planned following the linear measurement systems of *Dhanus* (190.1 cm) and *Angula* (1.76 cm), the former 108 times the latter. This is a major step forward in our understanding of the Harappan linear measurement units and the fact that this linear measurement scheme persisted even in the *Arthasastra* of Kautilya highlights once more the idea that the Harappan civilization foreshadowed much that we find developed in historic India, although the exact way in which these ideas continued into the later periods still remains somewhat of a mystery just as we cannot trace the steps of continuity between the terracotta representation of a wooden writing tablet from Mohenjodaro and the ubiquitous wooden tablets that we find even now in poor people's schools.

Such fine threads of a large tapestry of links between the Indus civilization and historical India underline, along with the more visible signs of intellectual and spiritual continuity such as the evidence of *Yoga*, *Siva*-worship, miscellaneous other forms of religion and the way of modelling stone sculptures, leave no doubt that this civilization stands at the apex of a long chain of Indian High Tradition. One may assume with confidence that more and more evidence of the continuities of this type will keep on being discovered, as research proceeds.

Personally, I am familiar with the distribution of Harappan sites in Indian Panjab and Haryana, and I have no doubt that these sites extended from the Ghaggar course in Rajasthan, i.e., from the Kalibangan area near Hanumangarh in Rajasthan to the Siwalik belt between Jammu and the Haridwar-Nainital foothills. One is also likely to find Harappan sites in the Siwalik belt of Pakistan. Interestingly, a part of this zone (cf. the Fatehabad section of Haryana), if the radiocarbon dates from Bhirrana and Kunal are any indication, seems to fall within the primary zone of development of this civilization. Moreover, the recent Alamgirpur evidence suggests that its bottommost level, which is 'mature Harappan', goes back at least to c.2500 BC. Even without knowing anything of geomorphology or the environmental archaeology of these sites, one may point out that many of them are located on sand dunes and in cases where a section through the site is observable, one notices that the site came up on a sand dune. The point is that these settlements seem to have flourished in a generally arid environment, something which is the characteristic of this region today. Previously, I have argued that the time has come when we have to postulate that the Indus settlements developed in this belt in an environmental setting which is not significantly different from what currently persists in the same area. Agriculture was apparently dependent on an irrigation network based on a network of major and minor drainage lines representing the ancient Sarasvati river system. A further definition of this general premise will, of course, need further research but its general validity seems to be acceptable even now.

Another point which has similarly suggested itself is that there was an initial agricultural base over the whole region and that this base was initially influenced by the diversity, if any, of its agricultural growth. If our idea that the Aravallis marked an independent growth of agriculture and metallurgy is true, we may not find this region's agricultural base overwhelmingly uniform. There will be regional variations of the 'early Harappan' in this whole sector, variations which are also likely to have continued in its mature phase. This may be the reason why the so-called 'early Harappan' pottery designs and shapes continue to occur even in what has here been called 'late Harappan'. The picture which emerges only in a shadowy outline is that instead of being a vast and uniform phenomenon, the Indus civilization, in its essentials, was an idea which expressed itself in a number of distinct ways but had in its background a locally diverse agricultural and other types of economic base. In future, this diversity may be as true of the Indus civilization as the idea of its uniformity.

Even my elementary study of the distribution of Indus sites between the Siwaliks and the Ravi has told me again and again that some aspects of the Harappan landscape have not changed much over the years. From the Delhi side, there is a chain of historical mounds through Rohtak, Hansi, Sirsa, Abohar, Pak Pattan, and Harappa to Multan and other places on the frontier. The entire alignment is also strewn with Harappan sites. The Delhi-Sirsa-Multan/Dehra Ghazi Khan/Dehra Ismail Khan alignment is apparently one of the abiding lines of communication in Indian history, with its antecedence firmly going back to the Harappan times.

Another aspect which is as exciting as any other major feature of this civilization is the fact that resources were on the move across vast areas. The fact that the economic scaffolding of the civilization was secure enough to permit various metal ores and stones to be carried from one end of the civilization to another is worth pondering over. The crafts which survive in the subcontinent's villages were known, possibly both in its technical and commercial manifestations, all over the concerned land. The fact that it could depend for its tin on the rich deposits of tin at Tosam is indirectly shown by the general density of sites in the region, although no direct evidence of preindustrial mining and smelting tin ores is yet available in this area. By and large, the Indus civilization was a fairly self-contained civilization as far as its needs for different raw materials are concerned. It was not that it did not interact with central and west Asia, and I believe that the location of Ras-al Junayej as a place of landfall for the boats coming from Gujarat and also as a place where the Mesopotamian crafts sailing to the area of the Red Sea and Egypt broke their journey suggests that the Indus traders were familiar with the Arabian coast up to the Red Sea, if not directly Egypt. On the whole, the Harappan traders acted within an orbit which was the orbit of the Indian traders through the ages. The character of the Harappan trade itself may be visualized more within the frame of this traditional trade than within any arbitrarily imposed theoretical frame. The links with the traditional trading frame of the subcontinent are there for all to see. The trade coming through the Bolan pass debouched in the area of Shikarpur in the nineteenth century, and quite unsurprisingly, Mohenjodaro is located exactly in this area, thus reminding us that Mohenjodaro, like Shikarpur, received the Bolan trade before the Indus boats possibly took up its riverine circulation. Mohenjodaro could be the ancient counterpart of modern Shikarpur.

It is not often realized that it is the Indus traders who significantly opened the Hindukush passes to central Asia. One of the implications of the location of Shortugai at the lower end of the Oxus valley is surely this. In their own ways, the Indus traders were very much on the move. They were familiar with both the northern and southern routes across the plateau of Iran, entering Mesopotamia both in the north and the south. In central Asia, they were visible as far as Turkestan. The pattern of the Indus external trade covering the Gulf,

Afghanistan, Iran, Mesoptamia and central Asia is remarkably reminiscent of the Indian early historic and later trade all over the region, showing once again that in certain matters the Indus landscape is still with us, or was with us till recently.

One is also intrigued by the long span of Indus chronology, from about 2700 BC (the two types of mature Harappan beads in the Royal Graves of Ur, dated c. 2600 BC; 100 years added as the gestation period of the civilization) to about 1200 BC (Indus seals in the Kassite context of Nippur), 1500 years in all, with a long formative stage in the background. This phase is not less long than what follows in Indian history after the Indus civilization was over. There is no reason to disagree that this civilization was one of the major cornerstones of the growth of Indian High Tradition. This is something we must understand, without looking back at all the signs of its contact with west and central Asia and the Gulf every time an Indus artefact is discovered in one of those areas. These areas have all been traditionally linked and the signs of these contacts, although archaeologically significant by themselves, may be seen within this traditional frame.

Among the areas which call for detailed investigations in the context of the last phase of the Harappan civilization, emphasis may be placed on the upper section of the Ganga-Yamuna plain. The reason is the evidence of its interaction with the Copper Hoard tradition of this region. The two traditions were no doubt interacting, but unless we know more about the cultural contents of the Copper Hoard tradition, we are unlikely to develop insight into how the ramifications of the interactions between the late Harappan and the Copper Hoard traditions were affecting the Ganga-Yamuna plain as a whole. This is likely to emerge as a crucial area of Indian archaeological investigations in future.

The details of the archaeological situation beyond the Harappan orbit are available from all corners except northeastern India, where there is virtually no dependable, published and dated context. Even in the areas where the dated contexts are clear, let us not ignore the uncertainties. The most important uncertainty relates to how the agricultural developments of the respective regions developed phase by phase. The cultural sequence of the different areas is known, but within each culture or even within the main one, such as the black-and-red ware culture of eastern India, can we break the story down to the sequence of major developments, say, over a 500 year period?

Again, there are variations in the extent of knowledge of this kind. If the situation is more or less under manageable grip in a large section of India, up, to Maharashtra and upper Karnataka, the situation further south can be confusing, although not totally dark. The importance of the phase generally addressed as "Neolithic-Chalcolithic beyond the Harappan orbit" lies in the fact that the shape of village India that we know became clearly visible over a very large part of India during this phase. This is something which has been emphasized by me again and again but this is always worth drawing attention to.

The position of the Iron Age including the problem of its beginning is far more secure than what it was in 1976 and earlier when I first argued that even on the basis of the data available then, India could be argued to be an independent and multi-centred area of iron technology. Now that Malhar and Dadupur have convincingly demonstrated the development and spread of this technology in the first half of the second millennium BC, possibly more attention should be given to how the technology spread in the Ganga plain itself and what were its major centres. One suspects that there was a lot of trade in metals by this period all over the country. Not much is known of this trade yet.

The same may be said about the process of early historic urban growth which I currently place between c.800 and c.500 BC. However, the regional pictures are frequently uncertain, although there is not much doubt regarding the number and identity of urban centres throughout the country. That different trade routes have had an impact on their locations is much clearer now than when I wrote my Ph.D. thesis on the early urban centres in India. To some extent, this has been achieved by my concern with trade routes in the alluvium between the Bay of Bengal and the border of Indian Panjab with Pakistan, in the stretch between the Ganga plain and the Deccan, and finally, in the Deccan and southern Peninsula. The routes of other areas also have to be looked at, but the pan-Indian network of a vast part of the country is now reasonably clear and along with it, the distribution of its urban sites.

To argue that we have reached a stage of archaeological research in India which can give us a cause of satisfaction would be completely wrong, but compared with what we began with in 1960, the archaeological knowledge of the country has expanded manifold. I would say that much of it has been due to the fact that willy-nilly archaeology is now an academic discipline in the portals of at least some Indian universities. Its inclusion in the university system, however patchy it may seem from the objective point of view, has inculcated a critical sense towards it, and in the growth of any subject as an academic discipline the importance of this critical sense cannot be minimised.

POSSIBLE AREAS OF DISCONTENT

Religious Susceptibilities

I do not imagine the path of Indian archaeology to be smoother in future. A number of possible areas of friction are likely to loom large. One is the growth of religious susceptibilities regarding monuments, the base of which has already been laid down by what happened at Ayodhya. It was a completely unnecessary thing to happen, but now that it has happened, religious groups will, in the case of any dispute regarding a monument, be aware of their rights to it. To some extent, this development is rooted in what was happening at major places like Sanchi and Bodhgaya at the turn of the century when they emerged as essentially Buddhist sites under Buddhist control (for details, Lahiri 1999, 2004)

Increasing Presence of Foreign Archaeologists

The second area of friction is the increasing presence of 'foreign archaeology' in India. There can be nothing wrong in this presence except when this takes the form of academic arrogance and denial of the Indian archaeological tradition. I have myself written that the First World archaeology, as it exists in India at present, is racist and neo-colonial. I would add that this has nothing to do with the First World society as such. That society is as fair and decent as human societies are all over the world. The problem lies with the First World archaeologists themselves, especially of the modern generation. There was a time when the difference between the First World and Third World archaeologies was not much. For one thing, a good part of the Third World archaeology used to be done by the First World scholars based in the Third World colonies. There was a good deal of interaction and a general lack of 'science' in both situations. The situation has been changing fast over the years. Most of the First World archaeology is ruthlessly 'science-based', and that is something which Third World archaeology in places like India will take years to develop. In fact, the only credible way in which a First World archaeological group in India can claim superiority over the native groups is the extent of their access to the different types of scientific back-up. This has also made the various First World archaeological groups working in India very arrogant. The extent of this arrogance will be clear from the way they do not hesitate to flout the basic archaeological rules and regulations of the country. In Chapter 4, I have already drawn attention to an Indian newspaper report to this effect.

What is disturbing is also the way the First World scholars align themselves vis-à-vis Third World scholars. Whether it is "Ancient India and Iran Trust" or "European Association of South Asian Archaeologists", such groups are basically exclusive clubs which the Third World scholars can enter only as receivers of hand-outs. Eventually, this is a question of retaining power over how the Third World thinks of its own past. Contempt for the Third World scholarship is one of the ways in which this power game is played. For the uninitiated, let me explain that there are two ways in which the First World scholars do not hesitate to make explicit their feelings of superiority towards Third World scholars in a subject like archaeology: anonymous reviews of grant proposals and manuscript submissions. I have not come across many First World archaeologists who will pass up a chance of feeling superior to a Third World archaeologist at the slightest opportunity.

From the Third World point of view, let me also add that as far as India is concerned, the academic opinions of most of the current First World archaeologists are simply not worth listening to for the simple reason that their knowledge of ancient Indian history and archaeology is almost invariably fragmented and shallow. They also do not have any sense of commitment to India's past, nor do they have any respect for the country's cultural heritage, academic traditions and its scholars. To them, it is essentially a matter of making one's archaeological career within their own academic traditions.

Unless the First World archaeology learns to have a quiet and civilized attitude of tolerance to the academic traditions of the Third World archaeology, there is no reason why its path should be smooth in the Third World. In the current scenario its path is smoothened by offering free airfare and hospitality to the pliant Third World collaborators in the form of seminars, conferences and short-term fellowships. In fact, organizing seminars in Indian institutions in association of their western clients/ patrons seems to have become the speciality of some Indian university teachers. Self-respect does not seem to loom large in the mental make-up of some Indian university teachers of archaeology and ancient history.

In India unsupervised foreign participation has also led to the emergence of some regional interest groups in Indian archaeology. Vijayanagar/Hampi where sundry foreign archaeologists and/or heritage experts have been around for a long time, especially under the protection of the Karnataka State Department of Archaeology since the days of M.S.N.Rao, is usually projected as an area where they have been doing much original and innovative work. The truth of the matter is that the basic ground-work in the history and archaeology of this area has been done by the Archaeological Survey of India and many Indian historians and epigraphers who can handle the primary sources relevant to the period. How Hampi has emerged as 'new Goa' and why it has received so much attention from the West may call for a detailed study on its own. Another of these regional interest groups is focussed on the prehistory of Karnataka where the writings have ranged from the scholarly to the bizarre and haughty, with even young foreign participants advising the Indians in the pages of *Man and Environment* on how to conduct surveys. One such lady (American) accuses the Archaeological Survey of India being a political organization:

> The Archaeological Survey of India (ASI) has always played a key role in understanding the "political" in Indian history. This is because the agency is the direct connection between the government and the establishment of history. The ASI has not let go of the colonial legacy of bureaucratically based, state-sponsored research. Every permit granted (or not, as the case may be) for research for non-Indian scholars has created a pattern of blatant political overtones. With such a formidable wall of permits to climb, most researchers who may be interested in working on the history of Ayodhya are clearly dissuaded, and in fact, continue to be victims of veiled threats of being blackballed. Some would argue that the issue of Ayodhya is an extremely volatile subject matter leading to communal violence, and is a domestic issue—and therefore, not one that should become an international platform upon which activism should congregate. I, in contrast, would argue that the (ab)use of archaeology as science in the political realm is not acceptable; especially when there is open manipulation of data in order to further national political rhetoric.

(Uzma S. Rizvi, '(Ab)uses of Archaeology, the politics of Ayodhya and the Archaeological Survey of India', in *SAMAR, South Asian Magazine for Action and Reflection*, issue number 18 (available in the web, undated).

The point is that here the writer basically accuses the Archaeological Survey of India of "open manipulation of data in order to further national political rhetoric", something which I thought could never be laid at the door of the Archaeological Survey of India, whatever might be its demerits.

The basic responsibility in such matters lies entirely with the Indian archaeologists and historians who seem to be completely immune to the notion of the socio-politics of the past. They are taking too long to realize that archaeological knowledge is political and that there is no utopian world of pure knowledge, not at least in the world of humanities and social sciences. Richard Witmore, apparently a young archaeologist, expresses this graphically with reference to the ideas of M. Shanks and C. Tilley.

> For Shanks and Tilley this production of the past is impacted by contemporary political agendas – there are no 'disinterested' pursuits of the material past; there are no value-free explanations. This production of the past is set within particular enabling structures – a heterogeneous scaffolding – termed 'discourse'. It is precisely here, in archaeological discourses, that we find specific webs of relations with power effects. To Shanks and Tilley's understanding of discourse, power is not a catchall over dramatized term. Underneath power we find an academic 'police' minding their cordons. We find petty gate-keepers and citation friends, all linked in arms within exclusive groups who, by virtue of title, institution, and secure position, may determine grant winners and grant losers, 'who gets read and who gets ignored,' and, ultimately, who gets a job. (Witmore's article,' A politics of the past present: four quandaries of archaeology' is available in the net, to be published in J Dixon ed. *'Fragmenting Archaeology or Taking a Leaf out of Shanks and Tilley's Book* (Oxford, Archaeopress)

The West has developed over a long period of colonial and post-colonial domination a well-entrenched structure of ancient Indian studies where the theories and dates in circulation have all received the sanctions of the Western (read 'white') academics. This structure has been passed from one generation of academics to another, not merely among the Western enthusiasts of India themselves but also among those Indians who are tied to their apron strings. There is nothing inherently sacrosanct with this structure and in fact the time has come to question its every bit. It is very unlikely that the

West will accept any such questioning, and their scholars will not mind stooping to any level to counter it. For instance, my idea of the beginning of iron in India has been cited by G.Possehl with the rider that according to me the knowledge of iron-smelting spread from India to other areas (in his review of my *The Battle for Ancient India* in *Journal of the American Oriental Society*, 2009). This is a lie because I never wrote such a thing, and the whole purpose of spreading such a canard in print is that the idea of an independent beginning of iron in India has to be discredited by associating it with an apparently ultra-nationalistic notion. Possehl also writes that I use past writings to castigate the present generation of Western archaeologists in India. This is not the case. My attitude is based on the fact that many Western archaeologists in India still carry on the attitude that has been ingrained in the study of India for a long time in the West.

The most significant area where the impact of the First World archaeology can be very beneficial for the Third World is, in fact, the area where archaeology is pursued on the local level outside the main university teaching and research frames. The 'archaeology units' of various universities operate locally very much on their own, submitting their bids for local archaeological works which are paid for, among others, by different construction agencies. Taking advantage of the regulation that before any major construction work takes place, the area has to be archaeologically surveyed and explored in depth, such units have organized themselves like any other commercial unit, bidding for tenders for particular pieces of work and executing them provided their tenders are sanctioned. The units are largely self-contained, with a wide body of archaeological and scientific expertise, and by and large they move fast, generating a great deal of archaeological data and publications. This is a model which Third World countries like India may seriously try to emulate, and cooperation with the First World 'archaeology units' of this kind will in the long run be very effective. Co-operations with organizations like English Heritage will be beneficial. It is not really a question of pushing First World archaeology away. It is really a question of seeking those aspects of First World archaeology which will help the Third World countries to expand and reorient their archaeology programmes.

Current Archaeological and Museum Set-up

The third major source of friction regarding the future of archaeology in India is the current archaeological and museum set-up in India. The following analysis of this set-up may be disappointing but it reflects reality in good measure.

One may begin with the preservation of monuments. The ASI has had the responsibility of preserving monuments since the early years of the 20th century. In 1915, the then Director General, John Marshall, published a book, *Conservation Manual*, which remained for many years the bible of the ASI officers. In 1953, in the ASI publication *Ancient India*, vol. 9, there is a section on structural conservation, and one notes that the basic principles as laid down by Marshall were still in place. Somewhere along the line the attitude began to change. I cannot pinpoint its precise time but I noticed it first in the mid-1980s when the dome of Subz Burj in the Mathura road traffic circle near Nizamuddin was found wearing a mantle of new tiles. Apparently, the ASI conservators decided to make this dome look like a new one! This propensity to give old monuments or portions of old monuments new looks has gained momentum in recent years.

The principle is that where preservation of the decaying parts demands that they have to be completely renovated, the renovated portion should be clearly marked so that people can distinguish between the original section and the renovated ones. Further, while undertaking renovation, original material and technique should be used as far as practicable.

I received a great shock when I visited the Bagh caves in Madhya Pradesh. I found a good number of the caves blandly reconstructed, giving a modern look to this old place. The same approach was on display in the conservation of the lesser stupas around Sanchi. I remember the Satdhara example rather clearly. Perhaps the most atrocious reconstruction of this type is on display at the stupa site of Deor Kothar near Rewa.

As far as I can judge, this is a problem area of the ASI's style of functioning in the field of preservation. The reason is fairly simple. To preserve monuments in the old way needs a lot of patience and care, both of which are in short supply now.

Secondly, not always attention is given to the local conditions affecting monuments. A very serious example of this kind was observed at Lauriya Nandangarh, which has the only completely preserved standing Asokan pillar in the subcontinent. When I visited the place as a young man, there was no problem of water-logging there. However, a few years back I found the base of the pillar under water. I even published a photograph of the pillar standing in water in my *Oxford Companion to Indian Archaeology*. Unless the problem of water-logging is taken care of, the pillar will one day fall down.

Thirdly, it may be noted that occasionally paintings on the walls are an intrinsic part of the monument. Preservation of ancient paintings is a disaster area of the ASI. Near Pudukottai in Tamil Nadu, there is a cave-site known as Sittanavasal. There, in the early 1960s, I found the ceiling of its 'mandapa' covered by magnificent paintings of the Pallava period. One of the issues of *Lalitkala* has a detailed article on it, constituting a major record. In 2005, I could not see even a faint trace of paintings on this ceiling. The ASI apparently committed some serious mistake in preserving these paintings, all of which are gone now.

The preservation of Ajanta paintings is a serious issue of this kind. It may be remembered that our classical paintings convey their sense of modelling through charged colours, the vibrancy of which could shine even in half-dark caves. When as a young student I visited Ajanta in the early 1960s, I was amazed by the glowing colours of the Ajanta paintings. This glow of the Ajanta colours is gone now. The paintings are now covered by a darkish patina, which has robbed them of its primary quality. I have written about it in my *Oxford Companion to Indian Archaeology*, but without any effect. Apparently, the chemicals that were applied over the Ajanta paintings for their preservation were no good.

Fourthly, there has been a remarkable laxity in the preservation of old objects kept in monuments under religious care. The Bodh Gaya temple is a glaring example. Under the Bodhi tree in this compound, there is the famous stone throne donated by Asoka in the third century BC. This throne has superb sculptural panels on its sides. The original quality of these rare Mauryan/Asokan sculptures has been destroyed by a thick coat of gold applied over by them by the Buddhist monastic order in control of the Bodh Gaya temple which, as far as I know, is a 'protected' monument.

Fifthly, the examples of administrative laxity are common. The 'monument attendants' who are supposed to see that no physical harm comes to the protected monuments are seldom at the site at their appointed hours. This has been usually my experience in the case of sites in the interior. The occupation of monuments by vagrants can be prevented if the monument attendants are present at these sites in their duty hours.

The ASI is supposed to protect sites which may be considered nationally significant. I am not sure if objective criteria exist in print, but if no such criteria are there, they should be in place.

For instance, I do not know if the magnificent Pala period brick temples of Boram near Jhalda in West Bengal are now under the ASI protection, but when I saw them, they were not centrally protected. They ought to have been taken over by the ASI long back. These temples fell into the hands of mendicants and are in a bad condition. Thus, there should be transparency in declaring monuments to be of 'national significance' and thus worthy of ASI protection.

When a monument is identified as worthy of protection, the normal procedure is to document them thoroughly with plans, sections, etc. Where is the documentation of our 'protected' sites? How do we know that they have been truly recorded in detail? These documentations should be suitably published so that the ASI work of preservation acquires proper credentials.

The setting up of site museums is important in the case of the major excavated sites and may serve as the focus of display of antiquities found at the site and in the general region. The problem is that the published catalogues of antiquities displayed (or kept in the store) in these museums are few and far between. I can think of a few old catalogues but cannot think of any new one. The site museum staff may also be deployed to undertake archaeological explorations locally. I do not know if somebody has taken any initiative in this regard. Secondly, in many cases, the setting up of site museums has taken ages and this has meant insecurity and physical degradation of the objects at the concerned sites. I can think of two examples. Malhar near Bilaspur in Chhattisgarh has a shed in which hundreds of pieces of sculpture found at this site have been kept. There is no scholarly access to the material, which also has lain unpublished all these years. The most ignoble example that I can cite relates to the site of Kanganahalli near Sannati in Karnataka. Kanganahalli is a stupa site where excavated materials are identical in many ways with those found at the famous site of Amaravati in Andhra. I visited the site in 2004 and was horrified to see that the sculptures which should be the pride of the nation have been lying in the open in mud since excavations were completed at the site several years back. Thus, if site museums have to be set up, the process should be expedited.

The excavation licenses are issued by the Standing Committee of the Advisory board of the Archaeological Survey of India. Basically, it depends on the links an individual excavator has with the members of this committee or with the DGA. There is no transparency, as far as I know. The criteria for a successful application must be discussed threadbare in the Advisory board and no member of the Standing Committee can be accused of being guilty of the violation of any of these criteria himself/herself. One of the general principles is that if the report of the earlier excavation is pending, application for a new site will not be encouraged. If one applies this principle seriously, ninety per cent of the people who are granted licenses will not be eligible, and this will include the officers of the Archaeological Survey. The Advisory board and the Standing committee are full of people who will not be able to name two archaeology textbooks published in the last twenty years!

The issue of granting licenses to foreign excavators is also important. There have been cases when foreign excavators and their Indian collaborators have operated without license. While issuing license to this group of people, the Standing Committee should insist on all the proper clearances (especially of Home and External Affairs) for the foreign excavators.

A basic purpose of the implementation of Ancient Monument and Archaeological Sites and Remains Act, 1958 and Antiquities and Art Treasures Act, 1972 is to prevent smuggling of antiquities from the country. If one goes around the major international markets of art, one can easily see superb objects of Indian origin on display in the local antiquity dealers' galleries. Most of these objects have been smuggled out of the country in recent years. If the acts cannot prevent smuggling, the Government should at least try to monitor the presence of these objects in the international circuit of art dealers and document them as far as practicable.

It may also be noted that smuggling will be virtually impossible to control unless the people who actually find archaeological objects in their lands can be given compensation. This system of compensation prevails in Britain and thus the finds of British antiquities are always scrupulously reported.

In my book *Archaeology in the Third World: A History of Indian Archaeology since 1947* (2003), I have given lists of the excavated sites on which proper reports have been published/unpublished. According to my estimate, only 15 per cent of the excavations done after 1947 have been published in detail. It may please be noted that excavations without proper publications on what one has done at the site and what has been found there in different contexts are acts of destruction. Any archaeology book will tell us that. From this point of view most of the Indian archaeologists, including the big names of the Survey and the universities, have been destroyers of sites.

There is more to this than this statement. Every year, many excavations take place all over the country and in an Archaeological Survey of India publication called *Indian*

Archaeology - A Review, which is supposed to be published annually, there should be brief reports on all these excavations. The aim is to draw peoples' attention to what has been done all over the country pending the publications of detailed reports on these sites. We may as well forget the detailed reports; even the publication of *Indian Archaeology - A Review* is in arrears for several years. Thus, if I want to know what happened in Indian archaeology, say, in 2008-2009, I have absolutely no way of knowing about it.

The officers of the Archaeological Survey have many excuses of not publishing their excavated materials. One of the valid ones is that they get transferred in routine matter irrespective of whether an excavation report is pending or not. If you have excavated in Gujarat in 2005-2006 and get transferred to Bihar in 2007, you are unlikely to have ready access to your field-notes and material. Secondly, while considering the officers' promotion, etc., their record of publication/non-publication of excavations they have done does not count at all. So, they are not bothered. Thirdly, a recent tendency is to employ retired officers on daily wages to work on the reports of the excavations they did while in service but did not publish. The Survey has made the non-publication of reports a profitable business. Fourthly, like modern criminal investigations, archaeological excavations need a lot of input from the forensic sciences. After all these years, there is no national institute of archaeological sciences for different varieties of dating and material analysis.

What is singularly distressing is that nowadays I hear that a number of Archaeological Survey officers have begun to claim that the brief paragraphs on their excavations in *Indian Archaeology - A Review* should serve as proper reports. Nothing is more shameful for an archaeologist than this. The general condition of the preserved sites is mostly all right, although in many cases the public access and information are either absent or very perfunctory. Unless there is a local awareness of the significance of the site, the local school and university students are unlikely to visit it. The Survey or the staff of its site museums do not do any outreach work.

I gather from young friends in the Survey that money is not a problem but there is an inordinate amount of skulduggery in spending it. I am not sure if the conservators are given proper in-house training.

The role of the different agencies in conservation work must be properly published and clarified. For instance, how do the roles of the Survey and INTACH overlap? I do not know, and in my book *Archaeology in the Third World*, I could not properly discuss the roles of INTACH and other bodies simply because of the lack of the published details.

I cannot comment professionally on the Indian museum set-up because I am not a museum person, but it will be useful to be aware of the following issues.

If the archaeologists do not publish their excavations or whatever they do, our museum people do not publish the catalogues of the objects they are in charge of. This is plain unadulterated truth. The National Museum has no published catalogue of its sculptures, archaeological materials, etc. It is not the availability of manpower or anything like that. It is just pure and simple laziness to sit at tables and get on with the business. I am told that museums like Indian Museum, Kolkata, employ academics of various kinds for the identification of museum objects. This may be taken as a joke because what have the museum staff been doing so long?

A number of universities currently offer MA/M.Sc. courses in Museology and possibly one institution offers an 'integrated course' in the subject covering both the undergraduate and postgraduate levels. Most of the universities, of course, do not think of setting up their own museums.

Regarding the issues of safety, display, etc. of these museums, let me give the example of the government museum in Chennai, which is a repository of the Amaravati sculptures, a priceless part of the Indian heritage. In 2005, I found these sculptures disfigured by visitors' attempts to write their names on them. There is no lack of gallery watchmen who obviously cannot care much for the safety of the objects in their galleries. What do the senior officers do? In Western terms, the disfigurement of the Amaravati sculptures will be comparable to the disfigurement of the paintings of the Great Masters in Western museums. This is something unthinkable but unthinkable things keep on happening in the dusty lacklustre collections of objects which we call museums run at enormous government expense.

Our major museums have conservation laboratories attached to them. We do not know what they do but the scope of their activities may be enlarged to undertake scientific examination of various materials in their care. There used to be a tradition of research in this regard, but this tradition seems to have withered in recent years. The same is true of the scientific wing or the science branch of the Archaeological Survey. I have only a sketchy idea of what they do. Some good work was done in old times but it seems to have lost its identity in recent years. This branch could be converted into a major centre of scientific research in Indian antiquities.

The fourth major cause for concern regarding the future of archaeology in India is the paucity of scientific facilities for dating, environmental studies and material analysis. Most of these facilities are available on the national level. What is problematic is there is no framework to relate them to archaeological research. First, there is no national laboratory or centre to offer a scientific umbrella to the investigations of the country's past. Secondly, the education system is built in such a way that an individual scientist will hesitate to get involved in a general 'arts subject' like archaeology. This boundary is crossed only rarely. For instance, in the case of Lohuradeva investigations, Professor I.B. Singh of Lucknow University played an important role organizing scientific studies of phytoliths, pollens, soil profiles, and AMS dating in the background. In the case of Lohuradeva, Professor K.S. Saraswat of the Birbal Sahni Institute of Palaeobotany, Lucknow, was also a pillar of support as far as the identifications and studies of ancient grains are concerned. The same is true of the investigations at Kalpi. This tradition of collaboration built up by Rakesh Tewari, K.S. Saraswat and I.B. Singh in these cases is exemplary in the context of India, but unless this is taken up on a large scale and with proper acknowledgement from the scientific and archaeological establishments of the country, archaeology in India will steadily lag behind international developments.

In addition to such direct involvements of scientists from outside archaeology, a time has possibly come when there should be training facilities for archaeology students in various scientific analyses, preferably in the teaching departments themselves. Some universities like Deccan College, Baroda, Allahabad and Banaras possess some of these facilities on severely restricted scales. This should be far more broad-based. Some science undergraduates these days opt for MA/M.SC courses in Archaeology or ancient history. The departments should organize proper laboratory facilities for such students so that they can investigate archaeological materials on their own. This is something which can be achieved with some effort on the university level. As far as I can judge, no archaeology/ancient history department in the universities is quite willing to put in this effort.

CONCLUDING REMARKS

Mr. Ajay Shankar, a former Director General of the Archaeological Survey of India and a member of the Indian Administrative Service, once gave a lecture in the Cambridge University department of archaeology. He was a good speaker and a suave and bright person, and conveyed a nice and rounded picture of Indian archaeology. A colleague asked me later if I agreed with what he said. My answer was that foot soldiers looked at things differently. Whereas the Director General would look only at the smooth functioning of his archaeological apparatus, a foot soldier of the subject would be acutely aware of its general complacency, slow pace and misuse of the available resources.

Whatever picture of the development of Indian archaeology over the last fifty years this book has conveyed, there should not be any doubt on one score: but for the introduction of archaeology at the university level, Indian archaeology was unlikely to have advanced a lot beyond the academic level of *Ancient India 9*, a volume with which we student entrants began our archaeological studies in 1960. That archaeology has not yet been integrated wholly and widely in the Indian university set-up is a testimony to how poorly the new Indian elite view their country's ancient past.

References

Agrawal, D.P. 1964. New evidence for a shorter Harappan chronology. *Science* 143: 950.

——. 1966. Harappan chronology: A re-examination of the evidence. In, *Studies in Prehistory: Robert Bruce Foote Memorial Volume* (D. Sen and A.K. Ghosh, eds.), Calcutta: Firma K.L. Mukhopadhyay, pp. 139-148.

——. 1969-70. The metal technology of the Indian protohistoric cultures: Its archaeological implications. *Puratattva* 3: 15-22.

——. 1972. *Copper-Bronze Age in India.* Delhi: Munshiram Manoharlal.

Agrawal, D.P. and Sheela Kusumgar. 1974. *Prehistoric Chronology and Radiocarbon Dating in India.* Delhi: Munshiram Manoharlal.

Allchin, B., A. Goudie and K.T.M. Hegde. 1978. *The Prehistory and Palaeogeography of the Indian Desert.* London: Academic Press.

Allchin, F.R. *et al.* 1986. *Lewan and the Bannu Basin.* British Archaeological Reports.

Allchin, F.R. and J.P. Joshi. 1995. *Excavations at Malvan.* Archaeological Survey of India.

Armand, J. 1983. *Archaeological Remains in Durkadi Nala: An Early Palaeolithic Pebble-tool Workshop in Central India.* Delhi: Munshiram Manoharlal.

Badam, G.L. 1979. *Pleistocene Fauna of India with Special Reference to the Siwaliks.* Pune: Deccan College.

Baskaran, M. *et al.* 1986. Geochronology of palaeolithic cultures in Hiran valley, Saurashtra, India. *Journal of Archaeological Science* 13: 505-514.

Bendall, Cecil. 1882. On European collections of Sanskrit manuscripts from Nepal: Their antiquity and bearing on chronology, history and literature. Paper, Orientalist Congress, Berlin, 1881. Berlin: A. Asher and Co.

Bharadwaj, H.C. 1979. *Aspects of Ancient Indian Technology*. Delhi: Motilal Banarsidass.

Chakrabarti, Dilip K. 1968. The Aryan hypothesis in Indian archaeology. *Indian Studies: Past and Present*. 9: 343-358.

——. 1972-73. Concept of the Urban Revolution and the Indian context. *Puratattva* 6: 27-32.

——. 1974a. Some theoretical aspects of early historic urban growth. *Puratattva* 7: 73-74.

——. 1974b. Beginning of iron in India: Problem reconsidered. In, A.K. Ghosh ed., *Perspectives in Palaeoanthropology*. Calcutta: Firma K.L. Mukhopadhyay.

——. 1974c. Comments on C.C. Lamberg-Karlovsky's paper on 'Trade mechanisms in Indus-Mesopotamia interrelations'. *Puratattva* 7: 74-75.

——. 1976. The beginning of Iron in India. *Antiquity* 50: 114-124.

——. 1977. India and West Asia—An alternative approach. *Man and Environment* 1: 25-38.

——. 1977b. Distribution of iron ores and the archaeological evidence of early iron in India. *Journal of the Economic and Social History of the Orient* 20, pp. 166-184.

——. 1977c. Research on early Indian iron, 1795-1950. *Indian Historical Review* 4: 96-105.

——. 1978a. The Nippur Indus seal and Indus chronology. *Man and Environment* 2: 90-91.

——. 1978b. Reserved slip ware in the Harappan context. *Puratattva*, 8: 158-164.

——. 1978c. Seals as an evidence of Indus-West Asia interrelations. In, D.P. Chattopadhyay ed., *History and Society, Essays in Honour of Professor Niharranjan Ray*. Calcutta: K.P. Bagchi, pp. 93-116.

——. 1979a. Iron in early Indian literature. *Journal of the Royal Asiatic Society*, pp. 22-30.

——. 1979b. Ideas and discoveries in Indian archaeology till the middle of the nineteenth century. *Indian Historical Review* 5: 94-118.

——. 1979c. Robert Bruce Foote and Indian prehistory. *East and West* 29: 11-26.

——. 1979d. The problem of tin in early India – a preliminary survey. *Man and Environment* 3: 61-74.

——. 1979e. Early Iron Age in the Indian northwest. In, D.P. Agrawal and D.K. Chakrabarti eds. *Essays in Indian Protohistory*. Delhi: B.R. Publishing, pp. 347-364.

——. 1981. Indian archaeology: The first phase, 1784-1861. In, G. Daniel ed. *Towards a History of Archaeology*. London: Thames and Hudson, pp. 169-185.

——. 1984a. Preindustrial Indian iron. *Indian Horizons* 33: 5-20.

——. 1984b. The study of the Indian Iron Age. *Puratattva* 13: 81-85.

——. 1985a. The issues of the Indian Iron Age. In, S. Deo and K. Paddayya eds. *Recent Advances in Indian Archaeology*. Pune: Deccan College, pp. 74-77.

——. 1985b. Iron and urbanization: An examination of the Indian context. *Puratattva* 13-14.

——. 1990. *The External Trade of the Indus Civilization*. Delhi: Munshiram Manoharlal.

——. 1993. *Archaeology of Eastern India: Chhotanagpur Plateau and West Bengal*. Delhi: Munshiram Manoharlal.

——. 1999. *India: An Archaeological History*. Delhi: Oxford University Press.

——. 2001. *Archaeological Geography of the Ganga Plain: The Lower and the Middle Ganga*. Delhi: Permanent Black.

——. 2001. The Archaeology of Hinduism. In, T. Insoll ed. *Archaeology and World Religion*. London: Routledge, pp. 33-60.

——. 2003. *Archaeology in the Third World: A History of Indian Archaeology since 1947*. Delhi: D.K. Printworld.

——. 2006. *The Oxford Companion to Indian Archaeology*. Delhi: Oxford University Press.

——. 2007. *Archaeological Geography of the Ganga Plain: The Upper Ganga (Oudh, Rohilkhand and the Doab)*. Delhi: Munshiram Manoharlal.

——. 2008. *Globalization and Indian Archaeology and Other Essays*. Varanasi: Banaras Hindu University.

——. 2008a. *The Battle for Ancient India*. Delhi: Aryan.

——. 2010. *The Ancient Routes of the Deccan and the Southern Peninsula.* Delhi: Aryan.

——. 2010. *The Geopolitical Orbits of Ancient India.* Delhi: Oxford University Press.

——. 2011. *Royal Messages by the Wayside: Historical Geography of the Asokan Edicts.* Delhi: Aryan.

Chakrabarti, Dilip K. and Parveen Moghadam. 1977. Some unpublished Indus beads from Iran. *Iran* 15: 166-168.

Chakrabarti, Dilip K. and Sukhdev Saini. 2009. *The Problem of the Sarasvati River and Notes on the Archaeological Geography of Haryana and Indian Panjab.* Delhi: Aryan.

Chauhan, P. 2010. Comment on 'lower and middle Pleistocene Acheulian in the Indian sub-continent' by Gaillard *et al.* *Quaternary International* 223-224, 248-259.

Chauhan, P. and R. Patnaik. 2008. The Narmada valley palaeonthropology project in central India. *Antiquity* 82, September, Project Gallery.

Clarkson, C. *et al.* 2009. The oldest and longest microlithic sequence in India: 35000 years of human occupation and changes at the Jwalapuram Locality 9 rock-shelter. *Antiquity* 83: 326-348.

Corvinus, G. 1981. *A Survey of the Pravara River System in Western Maharashtra, India, Vol. I.* Tubingen: Verlag Archaeologica Venatoria.

——. 1983. *A Survey of the Pravara River System in Western Maharashtra,* Vol. II, Tubingen: Verlag Archaeologica Venatoria.

Cowell, E.B. 1867. *An Inaugural Lecture Delivered, October 23, 1867.* Cambridge: Macmillan and Co. (This volume is accompanied by "an address to the members of the Electoral roll of the university of Cambridge by E.B. Cowell, MA candidate for the Sanskrit professorship with an appendix of testimonials".)

Craddock, P. *et al.* 1985. Early zinc production in India. *Mining Magazine (January issue)*, pp. 45-52.

Craddock, P. 1987. The early history of zinc. *Endeavour (New Series)* 11: 183-191.

Dange, S.A. 1949. *India from Primitive Communism to Slavery.* Bombay: People's Publishing House (4th edition 1972).

Deotare, B.C. 1983. Determination of the extent of settlement area by phosphate analysis. *Bulletin of the Deccan College Post-Graduate and Research Institute.* 42: 40-48.

Dhavalikar, M.K. 1988. *The First Farmers of the Deccan*. Pune: Ravish.

Dhavalikar, M.K., H.D. Sankalia and Z.D. Ansari. 1988. *Excavations at Inamgaon*. Vol. I, Parts I and II. Pune: Deccan College.

During-Caspers, E.C.L. 1972. Etched cornelian beads. *Bulletin of the Institute of Archaeology*. 10: 83-98.

Gaillard, C., V.N. Misra and M.L.K. Murty. 1989. Comparative Study of Three Series of Handaxes–One from Rajasthan and Two from Andhra Pradesh. *Bulletin of the Deccan College Research Institute* 49: 137-144.

Gaillard, C. *et al.* 2010. Lower and middle Pleistocene Acheulian in the Indian sub-continent. *Quaternary International*. Vol. 223-224 (Sept. 2010): 234-241.

Gaur, R.C. 1983. *Excavations at Atranjikhera*. Motilal Banarsidass.

Ghosh, A.K. 1970. The Palaeolithic cultures of Singhbhum. *Transactions of the American Philosophical Society* 60(1): 1-68.

Guzder, S. 1980. *Quaternary Environment and Stone Age Cultures of the Konkan, Coastal Maharashtra, India*. Pune: Deccan College.

Hammond, N. 1973. *South Asian Archaeology 1971*. London: Duckworth.

Hammond, N. and F.R. Allchin. 1978. *The Archaeology of Afghanistan*. Academic Press.

Hegde, K.T.M. 1985. Scientific studies in Indian archaeology. In, S.B. Deo and K. Paddayya eds. *Recent Advances in Indian Archaeology*. Pune: Deccan College, pp. 100-109.

Hockings, P. 1976. Paikara: An Iron Age burial in south India. *Asian Perspectives* 18: 26-50.

Jacobson, J. 1980. Investigations of Late Stone Age cultural adaptations in the central Vindhyas. *Man and Environment* 4: 65-82.

Jayasawal, V. 1982. *Chopper-Chopping Component of Palaeolithic in India*. Delhi: Agam.

Jones, S. 2010. Palaeoenvironmental response to the ~74 Ka Toba ash fall in the Jureru and middle Son valleys in Southern Central India. *Quaternary Research* 73: 336-350.

Joshi, R.V. and Anupama Kshirsagar. 1986. *Chemical Analysis of Archaeological Bones from India: Fluorine and Fossilization Process*. Pune: Deccan College.

Kennedy, K.A.R. 1975. *The Physical Anthropology of the Megalith-Builders of South India and Sri Lanka*. Canberra: Australian National University.

Kennedy, K.A.R., N.C. Lovell and C.B. Burrow. 1986. *Mesolithic Human Remains from the Gangetic Plain: Sarai Nahar Rai*. Ithaca: Cornell University.

Korisettar, R. 2007. Toward developing a basin model for Paleolithic settlement of the Indian subcontinent: Geodynamics, monsoon dynamics, habitat diversity and dispersal routes. In, M. Petraglia and B. Allchin eds. *The Evolution and History of Human Populations in South Asia*. London: Springer, pp. 69-96.

Kshirsagar, A. 1983. Nitrogen contwents of the sediments from chalcolithic Inamgaon. *Bulletin of the Deccan College Post-Graduate and Research Institutte*. 42: 99-101.

Kumar, Giriraj. *et al*. 2005. The EIP project in 2005: A progress report. *Purakala*. 14-15: 13-68.

Lahiri, Nayanjot. 1999. Bodhgaya: An ancient shrine and its modern history (1891-1904). In, T. Insoll ed., *Case Studies in Archaeology and Religion*. Oxford: Archaeopress, pp. 33-44.

——. 2004. *From ruin to restoration: The modern history of Sanchi*. In, *The Proceedings of the 2002 Manchester Conference on Archaeology and Religion*. Oxford: Archaeopress, pp. 99-114.

Lukacs, J.R. and S.R. Walimbe. 1986. *Excavations at Inamgaon*. Vol. II. Pune: Deccan College.

Marathe, A.R. 1981. *Geoarchaeology of the Hiran Valley, Saurashtra, India*. Pune: Deccan College.

Mathpal, Y. 1984. *Prehistoric Rock Paintings of Bhimbetka, Central India*. Delhi: Abhinav Publications.

Mehta, R.N. 1984. Valabhi—A station of Harappan cattle-breeders. In, B.B. Lal and S.P. Gupta eds. *Frontiers of the Indus Civilization*. Delhi: Books and Books, pp. 227-230.

Misra, V.N. 1970. Cultural significance of three copper arrowheads from Rajasthan, India. *Journal of Near Eastern Studies* 29(4): 221-232.

——. 1973. Bagor, a Mesolithic settlement in northwest India. *World Archaeology* 5(1): 92-110.

——. 1989. Stone Age India: An Ecological Perspective, *Man and Environment* XIV (1): 17-64.

——. 2010. Frank Raymond Allchin. *Man and Environment* 35(1): 128-130.

Misra, V.N., S.N. Rajaguru and H. Raghavan. 1988. Late Pleistocene environment and Acheulian culture around Didwana, Rajasthan. *Proceedings of the Indian National Science Academy* 54A, pp. 425-438.

Misra, V.N. and Y. Mathpal. 1979. Rock art of Bhimbetka region, central India. *Man and Environment* 3: 27-33.

Misra, V.N. and M.S. Mate. 1965. *Indian Prehistory: 1964*. Pune: Deccan College.

Momin, K.N. 1984. Village Harappans in Kheda district of Gujarat. In, B.B. Lal and S.P. Gupta eds. *Frontiers of the Indus Civilization*. Delhi: Books and Books, pp. 231-234.

Mughal, R. 1970. *The Early Harappan Period in the Greater Indus Valley and North Baluchistan (ca 3000-2400 BC)*. Ann Arbor: University Microfilms.

Mulagapalli, R.R., R. Patnaik and Poonam Verma. 2007. Vegetation and climatic change of hominin bearing Quaternary sediments of central Narmada valley, India. 17th INQUA congress paper.

Murty, M.L.K. 1968. Blade and burin industries near Renigunta on the southeast coast of India. *Proceedings of the Prehistoric Society*, 34: 83-101.

——. 1974. A Late Pleistocene cave site in southern India. *Proceedings of the American Philosophical Society* 118(2): 196-230.

——. 1981. Hunter-gatherer ecosystems and archaeological patterns of subsistence behaviour on the southeast coast of India: An ethnographic model. *World Archaeology* 13: 47-58.

——. 1985. Ethnoarchaeology of the Kurnool cave areas. *World Archaeology* 17: 192-205.

Nanda, Rajni and Dilip K. Chakrabarti. 1985. Lead in Early India: A Study of the Geological, Archaeological and Literary data. *Indian Historical Review* 7: 1-18.

——. 1989. Silver in Early India. *Calcutta Review.*

Neumayer, E. 1993. *Lines on Stone*. Delhi: Manohar.

Paddayya, K. 1973. *Investigations into the Neolithic Culture of the Shorapur Doab*. Leiden: Brille.

——. 1982. *The Acheulian Culture of the Hunsgi Valley (Peninsular India), a Settlement System Perspective*. Pune.

——. 2009. Revisiting Lewis R. Binford: Fresh frameworks for pursuing hunter-gatherer studies. *Man and Environment* 34(2): 91-97.

Pal, J.N. 1985. Some new light on the Mesolithic burial practices of the Ganga valley: Evidence from Mahadaha, Pratapgarh. *Man and Environment* 9: 28-37.

Pappu, Shanti *et al.* 2011. Early Pleistocene presence of Acheulian hominins in south India. *Science (25 March, 2011)* 331(6024): 1596-1599.

Pappu, Shanti. 2008. Prehistoric antiquities and personal lives: The untold story of Robert Bruce Foote, *Man and Environment*, XXXIII(1): 30-50.

Patnaik, R. *et al.* 2009. New geochronological, palaeoclimatological and archaeological data from the Narmada valley hominin locality, central India. *Journal of Human Evolution* 56(2): 114-133.

Petraglia, M. and B. Allchin, eds. 2007. The evolution and history of human populations in south Asia. London: Springer.

Philips, C.H., ed. 1961. *Historians of India, Pakistan and Ceylon*. Oxford: Oxford University Press.

Raghavan, H., S.N. Rajaguru and V.N. Misra. 1989. Radiometric dating of a Quaternary dune section, Didwana, Rajasthan. *Man and Environment* 13: 19-22.

Raju, D.R. 1988. *Stone Age Hunter-Gatherers, an Ethnoarchaeology of Cuddapah Region*. Pune: Ravish.

Rao, M.S.N. 1965. Survival of certain Neolithic elements among the Boyas of Tekkalakota. *Anthropos* 60: 480-486.

——. 1971. *Protohistoric Cultures of Tungabhadra Valley (a report on Hallur excavations)*. Dharwar: MSN Rao.

Sahi, M.D.N. 1979. Iron at Ahar. In *Essays in Indian Protohistory* (D.P. Agrawal and Dilip K. Chakrabarti, eds.), Delhi: B.R. Publishing, pp. 365-368.

Sankhayan, A.R. 2005. New fossils of early stone age from central Narmada valley. *Current Science* 88 (5): 704-707.

Semans, Cheryl A. 1981. Analysis of an Acheulian collection from Peera Nullah, Narmada valley. *Man and Environment* 5: 13-31.

Sharma, G.R. 1973. Mesolithic lake cultures in the Ganga valley. *Proceedings of the Prehistoric Society* 39: 129-146.

Sharma, R.S. 2003 (new edition). *Advent of the Aryans in India*. Delhi: Manohar.

Singh, Gurdeep. 1971. The Indus valley culture: Seen in the context of post-Glacial climatic and ecological studies in northwest

India. *Archaeology and Physical Anthropology in Oceania* 6(2): 177-189.

Singh, R.N. 1989. *Ancient Indian Glass: Archaeology and Technology.* Delhi: Parimal Publications.

——. 2007. *Archaeometallurgy in India: A Study of Copper & Iron Objects from North India,* Varanasi.

Singhvi, A.K., Y.P. Sharma and D.P. Agrawal. 1982. Thermoluminiscence dating of sand dunes in Rajasthan. *Nature.* 295: 313-315.

Tewari, R. *et al.* 2008. Early farming at Lohuradeva. *Pragdhara,* pp. 347-373.

Tewari, R., R. Srivastava and K.K. Singh. 2002. Middle Palaeolithic human activity and palaeoclimate at Kalpi in Yamuna valley. *Man and Environment* 27(2): 1-13.

Verma, B.C. and J.P. Srivastava. 1984. Early palaeolithic sites of the outer Siwalik belt in Sirmur district, Himachal Pradesh – Their age and stratigraphic position. *Man and Environment* 8: 13-19.

Wakankar, V.S. and R. Brooks. 1976. *Stone Age Paintings in India.* Mumbai: Taraporewala.

Yadava, M.G. *et al.* 2007. Evidences of early human occupation in the limestone caves of Bastar. *Current Science* 92(6): 820-823.

Yashpal. *et al.* 1980. Remote sensing of the "lost" Sarasvati river. *Proc. Indian Academy of Science.* Earth and Planetary Sciences 69: 317-331.

Index